DOSTOYEVSKY

Judith Gunn began her career working for BBC radio as a researcher, producer and writer. She has published biographies, a film novelisation, and co-writes and has written film education books for Auteur. A graduate of Bristol University, she taught Media and English for fourteen years and now writes full time.

DOSTOYEVSKY

A LIFE OF
CONTRADICTION

JUDITH GUNN

AMBERLEY

This book is dedicated to my husband Simon and to our children James and Isabelle

First published 2016

Amberley Publishing
The Hill, Stroud
Gloucestershire, GL5 4EP

www.amberley-books.com

Copyright © Judith Gunn, 2016

The right of Judith Gunn to be identified as the Author of this work has been asserted in accordance with the Copyrights, Designs and Patents Act 1988.

ISBN 978 1 4456 5847 6 (paperback)
ISBN 978 1 4456 5848 3 (ebook)

British Library Cataloguing in Publication Data. A catalogue record for this book is available from the British Library.

Origination by Amberley Publishing.
Printed in the UK.

CONTENTS

Do you know that I am absolutely aware that if I could have spent two or three years at that book – as Turgenev, Gontscharov and Tolstoy can – I could have produced a work of which men would still be talking in a hundred years from now!

Fyodor Dostoyevsky, 1870

FOREWORD

I first came across Fyodor Dostoyevsky and his work while at university in Bristol. I was reading Religion with Literature, a course tailor-made for all three of us, run between the English Department and the Theology Departments of the university. We studied a variety of texts but the module that covered Russian literature was, for me, the most compelling. I was fascinated by Dostoyevsky's account of prison in Siberia, *The House of the Dead*. I was enamoured by the conflicted anti-hero Raskolnikov of *Crime and Punishment,* and as an active member of the National Union of Students I was enthralled, if not a little alarmed, by the chaos of the political cell represented in *The Devils*.

After university I worked for the BBC and began to write a variety of books, and I found that Dostoyevsky was perceived a difficult author; too many long words! Whilst I must concede that his vocabulary is extensive and his books are long, there is much that is accessible, and a plethora of short stories, all displaying his own streak of humour, can act as an introduction to the man and his work. His life was fraught with ill health, rash decisions, prison, two marriages, gambling and some of the best books ever written.

Dostoyevsky was a tough man; he was rebel, revolutionary, prisoner and soldier, but always also a writer. He faced execution, loved and lost, and struggled with epilepsy. He had an eye for the real and a love of the magical. His insights into the psychology of human beings were searing. He claimed as his artistic territory the urban sprawl of the Russian cities, in particular St Petersburg.

The first edition of this biography was published in 1990 and was and still is intended to demonstrate just how accessible the novels and stories of Fyodor Dostoyevsky are. I do not speak Russian and I researched the book in the days before the Internet had become accessible. I still remember fondly my hours in the British Library Reading Room, then in the British Museum, searching through the journals and biographies of Dostoyevsky that were only available there.

Since that original publication I have had an awareness of the relevance of the themes he explored so effectively in his novels; while Tolstoy is repeated and Turgenev is a more specialist taste, Dostoyevsky's themes and characters have survived to be remodelled and reimagined by modern media, from the X-Files, through Martin Scorsese to Peter Falk and more. Dostoyevsky populated his literature with characters that have endured to haunt our modern media; their psychology, guilt and desires are as cogent today as they were then.

The purpose of this biography was and is to make accessible the writing of this complex man. In addition to the retelling of his experiences are studies of the main novels and stories. Themes are explored, characters revealed and the strong connection between his work and modern media is explored. Dostoyevsky's work has endured long beyond the hundred years that was his hope.

Judith Gunn

I

THE POORHOUSE

Moscow's Mariinsky Hospital for the Poor was a place of death for the poverty-stricken people of the city. Few of its patients left the premises cured. The diseases that afflicted its residents varied, but the most consistent killer of their time was tuberculosis. The rich could stave off such chronic illnesses with mountain air, sunlight, rich food and a personal physician, but the patients at the Mariinsky could not afford such facilities; they faced a difficult death. Tuberculosis was the scourge of the poor, and not for nothing was it named 'consumption', the bacteria responsible attaching to every organ in the body, slowly wasting away the health of its host and consuming them. Thus the afflicted depended on the ministrations of charitable men such as Dr Mikhail Andreyevich Dostoyevsky – father to one of the greatest novelists of all time, Fyodor Dostoyevsky.

The elder Mikhail Dostoyevsky had begun his medical career as a military doctor. His father and grandfather were priests in the Uniate Church, a denomination based in the Ukraine. The Uniates attempted to reconcile traditional Catholicism and Orthodoxy by using the practices and rituals of the Russian Orthodox Church while accepting the authority of the Pope. This religious syncretism informed the home that nurtured Mikhail Dostoyevsky, but it did not define his career or his future. Thus, despite this clerical background, Mikhail Dostoyevsky broke with the family tradition of entering the priesthood and, at the age of twenty, left home, without his father's blessing, in order to study medicine.

His Uniate upbringing, however, was not wasted or lost, for it provided him with the basis for his medical training. In order to be conversant with Roman Catholic liturgy he had learned Latin and so was able to grasp the Latin of medical instruction with ease. After training at the Imperial Medical Surgical Academy in Moscow, Mikhail went into the army. His skills were first tested at the Battle of Borodino. This battle would have been a traumatic place for a young doctor to hone his skills. The confrontation marked the last great conflict with the French, led by Napoleon. On that day, of the 120,000 Russian soldiers that fought, 45,000 were lost and many more injured. Borodino was a baptism of fire for the young Dr Dostoyevsky, a hellish encounter in which neither side won. Napoleon went on to enter an evacuated Moscow, drawn forward to an abandoned city by the General Kutuzov who played a waiting game. The Russians waited for the winter and a lack of supplies to do their work. Napoleon was forced back along his own scorched route, and the Russian Army, the Cossacks and 'General Winter' eventually defeated the invader. The Battle of Borodino and its consequences were later to be immortalised by Leo Tolstoy, whose rendition of it in *War and Peace* still resonates today. Tolstoy was to become both a contemporary of and a competitor to Mikhail's second son, Fyodor.

While Mikhail struggled to save just a few of the half-million or so lives lost in the campaign, his future wife, Maria Fyodorovna Nechayeva, was fleeing Moscow with her family. Those who escaped the city in 1812 had no time to organise their evacuation, and her father, a merchant, had to leave his business behind, losing almost everything. When the family returned to Moscow they faced a less affluent future, and it thus became essential that the daughters of the Nechayeva family should marry young. Maria's older sister married a successful merchant, one Alexander Kumamin. This was fortunate for, long after her death, the wealthy couple were to be an important influence on Maria's children, Fyodor Dostoyevsky included. Maria's marriage took longer, but by 1820 she had found a partner in the war-weary Dr Mikhail Dostoyevsky, and a marriage was secured. The nuptials were much more in the nature of an arranged marriage, for Maria had little say in the provision of her life partner. Mikhail could not offer Maria the riches of the Kumamins, but he had a career and an income and she would be safe and respectable. They married and she soon fell pregnant with their first child. Their first son, Mikhail, was born in November 1820, and consequently Dr Dostoyevsky applied for a transfer out of the military. He was given work in government service at the Mariinsky Hospital. It was there that their second son, Fyodor, was born in November 1821, just a year after the junior Mikhail.

The new family moved into a small apartment in a neighbouring building belonging to the hospital. The hospital itself had been built on the grounds of a cemetery for outcasts. Nearby was a transit station for prisoners being sent to Siberia; Muscovites dubbed the whole area the 'poorhouse'. This, however, was to be the place that the young Fyodor Dostoyevsky would call home. Throughout his childhood it would both educate and inform him, providing him with a vision of life that a vivid imagination had yet to realise on paper.

The grounds of the Mariinsky Hospital were not the playground that most parents would have wished for their children, and the terminally ill and the chronically poor did not make easygoing, energetic companions. What concerned Maria Fyodorovna Dostoyevsky was not the poverty that forced the patients to come to the Mariinsky Hospital, nor their character, nor even the way they looked, but rather the illnesses that afflicted them; to be placed in close proximity to diseases such as tuberculosis seemed a potent threat to young lives. Thus, as all cautious parents would, Maria and her husband told their children not to speak with the patients and to keep away from them. There was no cure for tuberculosis and it was a highly contagious disease. However, children do not always heed their parents' wishes, and Mikhail and Maria's second son Fyodor did not always abide by their rules. Despite warnings from his father and threats that he would one day end up in hospital himself, he and his older brother often led their younger brothers and sisters on illicit adventures in the hospital's grounds. The space to play was a temptation that outweighed fear of the hospital's occupants, and sometimes the curious children would stop and talk with the lonely figures that haunted the hospital and walked in the fresh air within the limited confines of its walled grounds.

Fyodor Dostoyevsky lived most of his childhood within reach of this suffering. It was in the Mariinsky that he first observed the consequences of poverty on human lives, and against this background that he came to understand the link between poverty and ill health. He saw that often those who could not pay could not get the treatment they needed. He came to realise that, for many, poverty meant death; not for the poor were the benefits of good medicine or a change of air. His early experience left him unafraid of the 'poor' as a much-maligned class of people, although justifiably afraid of poverty itself. It gave him an insight into the harsher side of life, which as an adult he was not afraid to portray. His first published novel, *Poor Folk*, featured characters that were like the ones whose faces filled his childhood. These characters were not caricatures of poverty, but they were ruled by it. The young Dostoyevsky very quickly understood the limitations of a lack of money.

In Russia at that time the law stated only the nobility could own land or property with serfs, the serfs serving as the slave labour of the Russian landscape. They were servants indentured to a property or a family by geography; if they lived on the land owned by a family then they had to work for that landlord. The landlord did not, strictly speaking, own them, but the landlord could deny them the right to move. Thus they were slaves in all but name. Serfs owned nothing themselves and had to serve the owners of the land they were allowed to inhabit.

The Dostoyevsky family had once been noble, but some of their Orthodox ancestors were stripped of their titles when they refused to convert to Catholicism. Thus, since the family was no longer titled, Dr Dostoyevsky had little to say in the choice of his family's accommodation or ownership of land, but like many of his stature he did employ servants. There were seven servants in the small apartment at the Mariinsky Hospital; the family income was enough to cover domestic help and offer them some sense of respectability and stature. Even so, the Dostoyevsky family could never compete with Aunt Kumamina, who occasionally visited the apartment in a carriage drawn by four horses and equipped with a footman and postilion. Fyodor, like his father, came to regard the Kumamin's show of wealth as vulgar and did not always welcome her arrival.

Home life for the Dostoyevsky children was regimented but not cruel. Silence had to be maintained between the hours of two and four in the afternoon when Dr Dostoyevsky took a siesta. Dr Dostoyevsky struggled with the hot weather and was plagued by severe headaches in the summer, which may have made him a little quick tempered; the atmosphere in the home could be tense. Hence in the summer the children were required to sit by their father while he rested – their job was to make sure that they kept the summer flies from disturbing his rest. In the evenings Dr Dostoyevsky would read aloud to the family. Both parents were keen to raise well-rounded, educated children, and so they instilled in them a love of stories, of art and literature. To this end, Dr Dostoyevsky would often take the family to the theatre. The young Fyodor was greatly affected by his first trip to the theatre, to see *The Robbers* by Schiller. The play explored the relationship between father and sons, discussed competition for inheritance, explored alternative lifestyles such as bohemianism and anarchy, and explored the problem of evil – all themes that were to preoccupy Fyodor Dostoyevsky's own writing in later life. Evenings out with the family were a great treat, but evenings in were also to be treasured. No doubt Fyodor was also grateful for the evenings when both parents went out and their mother instructed Alyona, their nurse, to let the children have some play time, or, if the children could not amuse themselves, Alyona Frolovna told the children stories of ancient Russia. She told them about Saint Sergey of Moscow, who subdued a bear by the power of his holiness. She told them of heroes and legends and folk tales that intertwined Christianity with Russian myth. Her stories were the stuff of nightmares; they were so vivid that sometimes she held the children transfixed, terrified such that some nights they went to bed too afraid to sleep.

Dr Dostoyevsky fundamentally believed in the value of education, be it an understanding of Christianity or the gentle night terrors of Russian folklore. He believed in the need to be conversant in the arts and aware of the sciences. Thus, in addition to his work at the hospital and his own private practice, he took the time to tutor his children, teaching them Latin and insisting that they learn French. He saw education as the key to their advancement in a world fraught with class differences, and he was not a lenient teacher. The boys had to stand to strict attention in Latin classes while repeating Latin declensions. Dr Dostoyevsky was quick to lose his temper if a mistake was made, which in Fyodor's case was often. Dr Dostoyevsky did not believe in corporal punishment, although it was then common to flog children and servants, and he never hit his children. He felt that the worst punishment he could inflict on the boys, when they failed to meet his standards, was to deny them education. He thus would walk out on them during a lesson; to deny them education was the ultimate punishment. This was quite progressive thinking for a man of his time, but what the Dostoyevsky boys did with the time is unknown!

Although Dr Dostoyevsky studied medicine and not theology, he did not desert his father's faith. The family ended each day with prayers said before the icon, and they employed a deacon to teach the children the Bible. This man was a gifted entertainer who retold Bible stories with fire and colour, bringing the familiar tales to life. Maria, too, was well acquainted with the traditions of Orthodoxy, for her grandfather had been a proofreader at the Ecclesiastical Press in Moscow. She taught Fyodor to read using a text of retold stories of the Old and New Testaments; of his early childhood Dostoyevsky said, 'We in our family have known the Gospel almost ever since earliest childhood.'[1]

Christianity did not reach Russia until AD 988, when Kiev became the first Russian Christian city. In successive centuries, Moscow survived both the attacks of Genghis Khan and his Mongol

Empire and the more persistent threat from Islam and the Turkish Ottoman Empire. Allied with the East against Rome after failed negotiations and theological disputes, Moscow became the only independent representative of Orthodoxy (most other Orthodox nations were ruled by the Turkish Empire). As a result, Russian Orthodoxy flourished in Muscovite Russia, and the Russian people prided themselves on their ability to absorb Christianity, to adapt it and observe it without the horrors of the Spanish Inquisition or persistent persecution. While religious tolerance in Russia might have had its limitations, Russian pedagogy was not afraid to explore and discuss aspects of religious observance or doubt; religious conversation, agnosticism, doubt and faith were the currency of conversation in sophisticated society, and the young Fyodor grew up in a Moscow that was open to an influx of ideas, much of it coming from the liberal context of Europe and the West.

Russia's form of Christianity had entered the country from the Byzantine Empire and remained rooted in the Eastern and Greek traditions of spectacular churches, gorgeous icons and an unchanging liturgy. The beauty of Orthodox buildings and the magnificence of their icons owed much to their wish to capture something of heaven on earth. In their churches the artists tried to portray what God's holy kingdom would be like, and only the most perfect images, the most precious and pure materials were appropriate for such representations. In their icons they tried to present the saints in their heavenly form. However, icons were not intended to be idols. They were not to be worshipped, but were rather to help the worshipper visualise the perfect state and so meditate upon it and realise heaven through a state of mind. Thus the Church's promise of a heavenly future was perpetuated by increasing riches on earth – and as a consequence Russian icons can be very valuable today, and there remains a healthy tradition of icon art.

The Dostoyevsky family were not untypical in their observance of their religious duties, and once a year they visited the Trinity Monastery of St Sergey, the patron saint of Moscow, to pray and fast and retreat from the hospital. The monastery, sixty miles from Moscow, was considered to be the centre of the Russian Church: its spires and design, built in 1345, became the blueprint for Russian religious architecture, and its domes and towers are reputed to have inspired the cathedral of the Kremlin in Moscow. It has long been a place of pilgrimage and remains so even to the present day; in the time of the Dostoyevsky family it was considered a centre for healing, and its ornate and gilded reliquary made an appropriate destination for pilgrims.

At least once a year the young Fyodor could gaze upon the luxury of a church built in the Orthodox tradition of Byzantium. He could take part, from the earliest age, in the rituals of the Eucharist, for the Orthodox Church allows much more participation by children in the rituals of church life than do most Protestant and Roman Catholic denominations. He could repeat a liturgy that had remained almost unchanged for nearly two thousand years. He could watch the long-haired, bearded priests lead the congregation in worship amid a wonderland of gold, colour and candles. He could observe first hand the opulence that is orthodoxy in Russia.

The monastery was a stark contrast to the 'poorhouse' district in which the Dostoyevsky family lived. The golden domes of the monastery, which flashed in the sunlight, were very different from the cold stone of the hospital. The richly costumed priests were quite distinct from the drab and ragged patients in the hospital grounds. It is not surprising, then, that the adult Dostoyevsky was to concern himself with the paradox of human suffering permitted by a loving and awe-inspiring God, a God who tolerated the cruelty of poverty and disease and left humankind to deal with problems of existence, survival and evil. Even as a child he was greatly moved and fascinated by the biblical story of Job, a man who lost everything he had because God gave the Devil permission to test him to the limit. The paradox of the story informed Fyodor's faith and his doubt, and his life of contradiction probably began at the feet of the priests who directed their rituals to a God who looked down both on them and on the Mariinsky hospital.

Despite his occasionally serious preoccupations with stories such as Job and his stern home life, Fyodor was still a small boy and his main concerns were not theology or the nature of heaven. His father tried to keep him devout but with limited success, and his attempt to make the young Fyodor read an introduction to Orthodoxy by Metropolitan Filaret of Moscow, a contemporary theologian, was not well received. Analytical theology, understandably, did not appeal to Fyodor.

Fyodor shared one room with his older brother Mikhail, while there were two more brothers and three sisters who survived infancy to share their home. The family was generally content: their mother was more tolerant than their military father, and Fyodor forged a relationship with his brother, Mikhail, that meant he and Mikhail remained close throughout their lives. Together, the boys had a childhood friend from outside of the family, a girl, but her life was to end too soon, and tragically. Only nine years old, she was found dying in the hospital grounds after being raped. The manner of her death was to have a profound effect on the growing Fyodor; it was for him the first indication of the real evil of humankind. In his later novels Dostoyevsky was uncompromising in his portrayal of similar crimes and their effect on victim and perpetrator. Her death haunted his literature and his characters for the entirety of his literary career.

In 1828, when Fyodor was seven, the noble status of the Dostoyevsky family was restored and Dr Mikhail Dostoyevsky received a promotion. Yet, although the family fortunes were improving, this change did not catapult them into the ranks of the aristocracy. There existed a vast difference between nobles in service and the more exalted noble class, but they did receive certain privileges and could now own land, land that would include serfs. Three years later, anxious about the hospital as a place for children to grow up, Dr Dostoyevsky bought a small acreage with 'seventy-six souls' included. 'Souls' were defined as the male serfs who worked the land. The term did not include their families.

The land and smallholding were in a place called Darovoye, approximately a hundred miles from Moscow. The house and land were technically a dacha, a summer home for the wealthy of Moscow to retreat to when the city got too hot in the summer months, just as the British retreated to Simla in India and New Yorkers, even now, head to the Hamptons. Stalin spent the last twenty years of his life at his dacha; it is a Russian tradition that has informed Russian culture and life for centuries. However, financially the dacha was not a wise purchase: seventy-six souls and their families, buildings and land were a large responsibility, not a means to make money. The Dostoyevskys knew nothing about farming or landowning, the soil was poor and the house itself was little more than a rundown cottage. In addition, Dr Dostoyevsky's remaining finances were crippled by a second purchase he made to ward off an unfriendly neighbour. None of this, of course, bothered Fyodor and Mikhail. Their parents were right to think it would do the children good to get away from the oppressive buildings of the Moscow hospital, and the boys revelled in Darovoye.

Thus it was that the children spent their summers playing Robinson Crusoe and Cowboys and Indians. Despite being the younger of the two, Fyodor was the leader in the games and chose for himself what he saw as the best roles; something of his determination was beginning to show. On the whole, he preferred to play the role of Robinson and the Cowboys. The children had space and sun and a whole new way of life to explore, their pranks were energetic and usually harmless, although on one occasion they stole the icon from the local chapel and paraded it round a field in an imitation church procession. All adults concerned considered this to be going too far, and punishment was swift and severe.

Darovoye was the first time that the family came into prolonged contact with rural peasants and rural poverty. Serfdom was no easy way to live, but it looked better to the young Fyodor. The direct relationship between hard physical labour and the provisions they received, plus the strength in the peasants and the lack of obvious sickness, meant that Dostoyevsky tended to romanticise life for the serfs, seeing it as an extension of his own childhood revelling in the house at Darovoye; there was still poverty but less obvious sickness.

Even so, all new places hold their terrors for children, and the vast spaces of the open countryside and flourishing forests were no exception. One day Fyodor had been playing quietly in the woods, woods that he inhabited so much that they had been nicknamed Fedka's (the informal name for Fyodor) Wood. On this day he was probably looking for a suitable stick to hit frogs with when, as he recalled many years later,[2] he heard someone shout, 'Wolf! Wolf!' Wolves had not been seen in that area for several years, but the shout was so clear and so urgent that Fyodor wasted no time in running to the open fields. There he found a peasant, Marey, working with a plough. Marey, somewhat bemused by the little boy's terror, had heard nothing, but he calmed the boy down and assured him that there were no wolves. He told Fyodor that he must have been dreaming, and instructed him to cross himself for protection. Only partly convinced, Fyodor dusted himself down, crossed himself and began to walk back to the house. The peasant promised that he would watch until the boy was safe. When Fyodor looked back, the peasant was still watching him.

Whether the wolf and the warning cry ever existed can never be proved, but it is clear that on that day in Darovoye Dostoyevsky heard a voice. It may have been the product of an over-active imagination, or an indication of the epilepsy he was later to develop. Such incidents in his life have been attributed to aural hallucination. In his novels, Dostoyevsky would portray various kinds of hallucinatory experiences, using illusion as well as ordinary dreams as literary devices.

Initially the summers at Darovoye were everything the family could have hoped, but Dr Dostoyevsky had to remain in Moscow for long periods while he worked at the hospital. He struggled with being apart from his family and his wife. The headaches plagued him and he was haunted by an anxiety that his wife Maria was being unfaithful to him; so convinced was he of her infidelity that when she became pregnant with their seventh child he doubted that he was the father. Throughout this Maria remained tolerant and faithful. Their twenty-year marriage was a testament to her patience, if not to her love, particularly since her marriage to

Dr Mikhail had been much more one of convenience than of love. She wrote to him in reply to his accusations that his doubt is 'deadly for the both of us', and later she asserted her innocence: 'Natural gaiety of character is turned in sorrowful melancholy, and that's my fate, that's the reward for my chaste, passionate love; and if I were not strengthened by the purity of my conscience and my hope in Providence the end of my days would be pitiful indeed.'³

Maria was not just a good wife, she was a compassionate and capable manager, and in their first summer at Darovoye she managed to improve the access to water for the serfs and their livestock. She also provided them with seed in the spring if they had none. This was considered bad practice, but her kindness became legendary and is still referred to today. However, poor harvests and rundown facilities made running the estate a struggle – and then Darovoye suffered another, more serious blow.

Early in 1833 the estate was destroyed by fire. Now all Maria's attempts to put the business on a successful footing lay in ashes. The family was devastated. They had had such high hopes of their rural home, but even the serfs in their care were now homeless and without food. The outlook was so bleak that the Dostoyevsky's nurse, Alyona, offered the family all her savings to help pay their debts. The family did not accept her offer, but years later Fyodor would remember the generosity of a poor woman who offered all that she had to her employers. He was also to recall the devastation not just for them as a family, but for the serfs, whose lives were so utterly destroyed by the incident. He was also too aware that even though they were not the landed gentry that his father so longed for them to be, they were, to some extent, cushioned by their education and professions from the very worst that poverty can inflict.

The summers at Darovoye came to an end. The fire and the birth of her last and seventh surviving child had weakened Maria considerably, and for some years she herself had been fighting tuberculosis. On 27 February 1837 she called her family into her bedroom, blessed them all, prayed once more before the icon and died. Fyodor, now fifteen, mourned her deeply. She had been a consistent and devoted mother, and where Fyodor's feelings for his father were tinged with conflict and uncertainty, due to the unpredictability of his father's moods, his mother had managed her role as parent with strength and patience. Her loss to all her children was deeply felt.

However, hers was not the only death to grieve the young Dostoyevsky that year. Maria had passed to Fyodor her great love of literature and had introduced him to the power of the pen, and he had come to adore in particular the poetry of Aleksander Sergeyevich Pushkin. Unfortunately Pushkin burned brightly and died young, killed in a duel. Duelling was an important, if futile, tradition in Russia at the time, and features in much of its literature, not least the duel between Bezukhov and Dolokov, immortalised by Tolstoy in *War and Peace*. However, being dishonoured by another man, particularly if the culprit happened to be flirting with the challenger's wife, demanded a challenge to a duel. Thus, aged just thirty-seven, Pushkin headed to the Black River area of St Petersburg to get himself shot in the gut by a French cavalry officer who he deemed to have been flirting with his wife. He died a few days later. Fyodor Dostoyevsky was devastated, according to his younger brother Andrei. When Dostoyevsky received the news of Pushkin's death, he would have asked – if they had not already been in mourning for their mother – for permission to go into mourning for Pushkin.

From this moment on, literature became Fyodor's first love. It was to become his destiny, but his father did not agree: he did not regard literature as a safe career. While their mother was alive, Mikhail and Fyodor had both planned for a university place and a life with literature, but now they were smartly informed by their father that this was not to be: they were to apply for entrance to the Military Academy for Engineers and to embark upon tenured careers with a salary. Fyodor Dostoyevsky believed their future was doomed.

2

THE CYCLE OF VIOLENCE

With the cry of 'now', the mare tugged with all her might,
but far from galloping could scarcely move forward;
she struggled with her legs, gasping and shrinking from
the blows of the three whips which were showered
upon her like hail. The laughter in the cart and in the
crowd was redoubled, but Mikolka flew into a rage
and furiously thrashed the mare, as though he supposed
she really could gallop.[1]

Dostoyevsky, *Crime and Punishment*

Dostoyevsky told the story of the cruel death of the mare in the first of his most famous novels, *Crime and Punishment*, but it was almost thirty years earlier that he had witnessed the scene that would influence his work so directly in the years ahead.

Mikhail, Fyodor and their father were on their way to St Petersburg. It was the spring of 1837, both Dostoyevsky's mother, Maria, and hero, Pushkin, were dead, and the boys were at the mercy of their well-meaning but inflexible father. There had been no persuading him that a military career would not suit them, that they were destined for culture and not for war. Dr Dostoyevsky had made up his mind, and he was not without justification. After his wife's death he had grown increasingly anxious about his children's future. He was not a rich man, nor could he call upon the advantages of an 'old boy network' or aristocratic privileges to find them places in the civil service or to finance their university education. He and Maria might have instilled a love of literature in their two sons, but literature would not provide them with a living. In a world where only status could unlock the doors to wealth and success, a military career would allow them to rise through the ranks and achieve respect and job security.

The two teenaged brothers viewed their future with apprehension. They had not anticipated a career in the army. They had never dreamed that they would study mathematics and engineering, and they did not look forward to parade-ground drill, military exercises or the possibility of military action. Even so, they could not resist the excitement of leaving home. The promise of independence and the thought of St Petersburg set them dreaming optimistically of adventures and kept their minds off the impending prospect of hard military discipline.

The journey to St Petersburg took a week. En route they met fellow travellers, observed something of Russian peasant life and counted the days before their arrival in St Petersburg, when they could exchange their uncomfortable carriage for solid ground and a soft bed. Among their fellow travellers on the road were businessmen and merchants, other journeying families, the occasional soldier and government messengers.

One evening the Dostoyevsky party stopped at an inn for something to eat. From their table they could see a postal station where couriers exchanged their exhausted horses for fresh and speedy ones. While they watched, a government courier dashed into the station, probably looking for a glass of vodka and some hasty sustenance. Satisfied, he returned to his new horse and cart to continue his journey. Hardly had the man settled in his seat when he began punching his driver in the neck with all his power and shouting at him to get a move on. Again and again his fist crashed down on the driver's neck, and in the same rhythm and with the same persistence the driver's crashed down on the horse's back.

Dostoyevsky was horrified, not so much by the display of unprovoked cruelty as by the way in which it was perpetuated from the courier to the driver and from the driver to the horse. Years later, in his journal, *Diary of a Writer*, he recalled the scene and the effect it had on him: 'This little scene appeared to me, so to speak, as an emblem, as something which very graphically demonstrated the link between cause and effect. Here every blow dealt at the criminal leaped out of each blow at the man.'[2] Dostoyevsky became preoccupied with the suffering he saw inflicted so easily. He imagined the driver's shame and the mockery that he would receive at home because of his bruised neck. He imagined his rage at being so publicly punished, and he perceived that the cycle of violence might not have stopped there but may have extended to the man's wife and children in an attempt to expiate the violence perpetrated on him. In a Russia where for a few power over another human being was easy to come by, this may have seemed an ordinary event, but for Dostoyevsky it was a graphic, unforgettable, illustration of the injustices of serfdom.

Soon, however, his brooding was interrupted by their arrival in St Petersburg – Russia's 'window on Europe'. In St Petersburg the monied classes lived with grace and ease, influenced by liberal European trends. There was a growing feeling among many of Russia's wealthy that Western Europe was to be courted and imitated. Those who had the time and the money indulged themselves in what Europe had to offer – its art, fashions and scientific knowledge. Not that it was safe to espouse every Western idea: Tsar Nicholas I employed strict censors to make sure that no ideas that could threaten his political position were permitted to spread either in public discourse or in print. Those who lived in St Petersburg had to be particularly careful as they lived within sight of the tsar, something that Dostoyevsky was going to learn to his cost.

The tsar's reactionary policies may have had something to do with the unsteady beginnings of his reign. In December 1825 he hesitated before accepting the throne after his brother's death, for he had not prepared himself to be the tsar. While he was making up his mind, a small group of officers, known as the 'Decembrists', rebelled and raised a mutiny against him within sight of the palace.

He then felt obliged to take the throne for the sake of stability. The officers refused to stand down, and there was some bloodshed before the revolt was routed and the Decembrists punished by execution, prison or exile. Nicholas, then, was haunted by the brief but potent spectre of revolution outside his own palace, and the people of St Petersburg took care not to offend him. This was the climate the Dostoyevsky brothers first encountered in the city. The apparent liberality of the literary circles was, to some extent, an illusion, and the fate of the Decembrists was a more realistic measure – and reminder – of the type of freedom the Dostoyevsky could expect.

All this was of little relevance, however, to the young Dostoyevsky, who would grow to love St Petersburg, with its picturesque streets and canals and its apparent, if illusory, atmosphere of free discussion. Moreover, he and Mikhail were to be together, or so they thought, free from their father's stern regime. This at least would compensate for having to join the army cadets.

Their first destination in the city was not the military academy in which their father hoped to enrol them but a preparatory school for the necessary entrance exams. Throughout the summer the brothers studied hard, so that by the autumn they were ready for the examinations. When they arrived to take the exams, however, they discovered that entrance was gained by bribing the officials rather than by academic merit. Mikhail failed to gain entry on the grounds of ill health, and Fyodor was refused a scholarship. The boys had not realised that they should offer bribes to the examiners and, even if they had been warned, they did not have the money with which to make such offers.

Dostoyevsky felt the injustice of this keenly. He wrote to his father:

I heard recently that after the Examinations, the general used his influence for the acceptance of four of the new entrants at government expense, as well as for the candidate from Kostomarov's who robbed me of my vacancy – What meanness! I was thunderstruck! We, who have to struggle for every rouble, have to pay, while others, rich men's sons, are taken free, damn them![3]

It looked for a while as if Dr Dostoyevsky's plan to enter his sons in one of the best military schools in Russia would fail, but Aunt Kumamina came to the rescue and paid Fyodor's fees. She and her husband were childless and throughout their lives took a keen, if patronising, interest in Maria Dostoyevsky's children. Fyodor himself was never really grateful for their generosity, and he tended to resent them more for what they did not give than be thankful for what they did. Moreover, as a consequence of all this, the brothers were separated: Fyodor entered the St Petersburg school and Mikhail was sent to a less fashionable academy at Reval, five hundred miles away. Thus their childhood fraternity and friendship was severed, at least physically if not emotionally, and the boys had to greet manhood without each other's support. Dostoyevsky's immediate future was sealed, and for the next six years Fyodor was to study engineering in a building that had once served as a palace – something of a contrast to the Mariinsky Hospital in Moscow. He had done well to gain any kind of place at the academy, but his time there proved to be a mixed blessing and from the beginning he felt at a social disadvantage. Most of the officers in training came from a higher and richer class of nobleman than he did, and he felt pressured to imitate their lavish lifestyle. He wrote frequent letters to his father requesting money, which he spent enthusiastically in order to keep up appearances. He needed new galoshes, he pleaded, and a new cap for the parade so that the tsar would not notice him in the old one. It is difficult to see quite how the tsar could have noticed one cap in a sea of thousands of men on parade, but Dostoyevsky felt that it was essential to maintain his standing in the academy, and no doubt Dr Dostoyevsky, who longed for his sons to climb higher on the ladder of society, concurred. In addition, he was developing his lifelong addiction to tea and needed money for its supply, to keep him warm after exercises: 'When one has to sleep in a canvas tent during damp and rain, or when, in such weather, one returns weary and chilled from practice, one may easily fall ill for want of tea, as I have frequently experienced in former years at these times.'⁴ Dr Dostoyevsky always struggled to find the money Fyodor requested, but he was determined that his son should have the best start in life that he could provide.

His father's regime may have been strict but it played its part in preparing the young Dostoyevsky for taps and reveille and strictly disciplined lessons. The work at the academy that most suited him was the training to be a draughtsman, though his designs were sometimes more inventive than practical. He once designed a fortress that had no doors, presumably because that seemed to him the most logical way of ensuring that it would be impenetrable, or perhaps as satire. His design did not amuse his superiors, including the tsar. He never lost his interest in architecture: his later notebooks contain sketches that are evidence of his talent.

Fyodor did not get on well with some of his instructors and, when he was failed in one year's exams and forced to repeat that year, he claimed that he had been victimised by his tutors. Dostoyevsky's letters to his brother at this time are full of self-righteous indignation and protestations that his marks were clearly good enough to allow him to progress on to the next year. He conveniently forgot to mention his less good results.

His contemporaries at the academy remembered him as a pale and withdrawn youth, always reading, in a uniform that never seemed to fit. When he was officer of the watch he took a book with him and studied at night, a habit he never lost. He pored over the works of Victor Hugo, Walter Scott, Pushkin and George Sand. Maths was not his strength, but he showed an active interest in theology lectures, often staying behind to talk to the tutor, a priest; for his faithful observance of Orthodox practices he earned himself the nickname 'Monk Photius'. Perhaps his religious studies and observances helped him keep his sense of identity as a spiritual being, an artist in a military world with which he did not identify, full of uniformity, engineering and mathematics.

He was often seen reading the Bible and the works of a German-Swiss writer and novelist, Zschokke, who believed that the ideal of Christian love should have a practical application resulting in social justice. In his own position Dostoyevsky was not slow to defend the newer and younger arrivals against the usual cruelty and bullying endemic to boys' schools. As a consequence, his friendships within the academy were limited and, although not friendless, he remained something of an outsider.

One friend, however, made Dostoyevsky's time at the academy more bearable and introduced him more intimately to the world of literature and art. Ivan Nikolaevich Shidlovsky did not live in the academy, but worked in the finance department of the huge Russian civil service. The two men shared a love of literature and, perhaps, the fact that neither of them was doing what they really wanted to do with their lives. Although only five years older than Dostoyevsky, Shidlovsky's experience was enough to guide Fyodor through his first two years in St Petersburg and to provide him with a mentor. Together they studied literature, and Shidlovsky encouraged Dostoyevsky to write.

Shidlovsky was an exciting influence on his friend, but he was hardly a stable character. His moods shifted from ecstatic faith in God to overwhelming doubt and despair. He exhibited symptoms of what would now probably be defined as manic depression. And yet he introduced Fyodor to adult life and to a far wider appreciation of literature, particularly Schiller and Shakespeare. Shidlovsky embodied much of what Dostoyevsky would explore in his work: he was torn between the ideas of transcendental Romantic thought, and the sense of fatalism and doom that modern Russian thinking introduced through its encounter with science and Western ideas. Shidlovsky was truly a divided self, and the main character in one of Dostoyevsky's earliest novels, *The Double*, probably draws on Shidlovsky's wild swings between faith and despair, romance and determinism.

During those early years Shidlovsky was Dostoyevsky's most favoured companion. In some ways Fyodor had transferred his affection from his brother to Shidlovsky as geography had separated the family. Dostoyevsky was never to lose his relationship with his brother, but he spoke warmly of his new mentor:

Knowing Shidlovsky has given me many hours of a higher life, but that was not the reason. You perhaps criticised me, and will criticise me again, for not writing to you; my stupid military circumstances were the reason for that. But I must tell you the truth, my dear: I was never indifferent to you, I loved you for your poems, the poetry of your life, and your unhappiness – and that was all.[5]

The friendship was not to last a lifetime, however, for although Dostoyevsky always retained an affection for his friend, Shidlovsky went into a steady decline and they lost touch. He was reputed to have a great talent as an orator, but a brief spell in a monastery ended in disgrace when it was discovered that Shidlovsky had caused some other monks to turn to alcohol. It was drink that contributed to his death in 1872.

In June 1839 the message came that Dr Mikhail Dostoyevsky was dead. After Maria's death he had given up his job at the hospital and moved back to Darovoye, now decimated by fire and famine. The doctor did not recover easily from his grief. When he was not wandering the house in search of Maria he was either drinking himself into a stupor or taking comfort in the arms of a peasant girl on the estate. His treatment of his serfs was at best petulant, at worst cruel.

There were no witnesses to Dr Dostoyevsky's death. His son Andrei stated that he was murdered during an angry row with his serfs. Some said that he was ambushed, dragged from a carriage and suffocated with a cushion; others that in a fit of temper he provoked the peasants into an attack; others that he had drink poured down his throat and was then suffocated; yet others held that he was severely mutilated. Not everyone thought it was

3

THE GLIMMER OF HOPE

In 1841 Dostoyevsky passed his exams. In 1842 he was promoted to second lieutenant and in 1843 he moved outside the academy, assuring himself of more time to pursue his own interests, especially reading and writing. In the next few years he moved several times, always trying to get an apartment near a church. At the time St Petersburg was experiencing a serious housing crisis, its population was crammed into dingy flats, sometimes sharing rooms by sheltering behind partition screens. In 1846, just as Dostoyevsky was coming to prominence, he wrote a short story published in the *Notes of the Fatherland*, a St Petersburg magazine. The story, 'Mr Prokcharkin', was about an old man who slept on a mattress behind a screen. The old man is content to do this until the other space in the room is rented to some new – and louder – occupants. After this event the story takes a bitter and dark turn. It transpires that the old man is not as penniless as he looks, and the new neighbours pursue this to a dark conclusion. The story, like so many of Dostoyevsky's stories, was based on a true-crime news item; there would be several such events in the future that would inspire some of his greatest and most disturbing works. However, for the moment it was difficult enough for him to find accommodation, especially as he imposed on himself the additional condition of being near a church. Whether Dostoyevsky wanted to be near a church because he attended services regularly or found comfort in the nearby presence of the sublime, or whether he had a more pragmatic reason, such as the safety of the area, is unknown. His final apartment, now the Dostoyevsky Museum, overlooked the Vladimirskaya Church; it was there that he wrote his final novel, *The Brothers Karamazov*, often feted as the greatest Christian novel. Perhaps the churches were his inspiration, or perhaps this impulse was an attempt to keep in touch with the earthly evidence of his beliefs, for the young Dostoyevsky was in the first flush of independence in his early twenties, and faith and ideology were all interrogated and challenged both by his contemporaries and by his work.

His first move, near St Petersburg's Vladimir Cathedral, was to an apartment he shared with Adolph Totleben, a man from high society whose brother, Eduard, was to become a hero of the Crimean War. The Crimean War was the conflict in which Russian expansionism threatened Turkish dominance of the Crimea, at a time when Britain and France also feared a land-grabbing Russia. The powers challenged each other for the region, which remains controversial to this day, and for Great Britain this meant one of the most famous military failings in its history: the Charge of the Light Brigade, which spawned the famous poem of that name by Alfred Lord Tennyson and several films. The Crimean War itself presaged the trench battles and brutal losses of the Great War that was to come in 1914 and echoed the bitter battles of Austerlitz and Borodino during the Napoleonic Wars, immortalised by Leo Tolstoy in *War and Peace*. In the 1840s, though, ten years before the Crimean War, Dostoyevsky was pleased to have such an aristocratic flatmate. It delighted Fyodor's sense of society, especially when later in life he found he needed all the well-placed friends he could get to attest to his good character and stand by him through exile.

However, not many of his flatmates found him easy to live with, and he had a high turnover of companions. He had already begun the habit that was to hinder him throughout his life. He had begun to gamble, at first in a small way, usually losing at billiards, but this habit was to dog him throughout most of his life, such that it became a barely controllable addiction. He was not a careful guard of his money when he had it either. On at least one occasion his cash was stolen and, when it was not stolen, he was inclined to give it away. Dostoyevsky's older brother Mikhail was alarmed at Fyodor's capacity to lose money, and so arranged for a Dr Riesenkampf to share rooms with Fyodor, in the hope that the good doctor might have a stabilising influence on the errant younger brother. However, while Dr Riesenkampf may have been appropriate in character, he also ran a surgery for down-and-outs from the flat, and often Dostoyevsky would spend his last roubles, those not gambled that is, on the men who told him their tragic life stories. Later Riesenkampf was to reflect that he felt that these characters reappeared in Dostoyevsky's powerful depictions of poverty, drink and illness. Their wasted lives provided original material for the young writer.

When money ran out, Dostoyevsky borrowed from Riesenkampf or sent heart-rending letters to his brothers begging for money. He fought hard to get an advance on his inheritance, sending insistent and sometimes petulant letters to the Kumamins, who were trustees of the estate. They capitulated finally and sent him five hundred roubles despite the fact that this would create hardship for the rest of the family, who also struggled to make ends meet.

He lost it within twenty-four hours.

Perhaps not surprisingly, Dostoyevsky also struggled to sleep well. He frequently complained to Riesenkampf that he was prevented from sleeping by the sound of someone else in the room, snoring. He did not share his room with anyone, and this may have been another example of the kind of aural hallucination that Dostoyevsky experienced as a child when he heard the cry of 'wolf' in the forest. This could have been a precursor of the epilepsy that was later to develop in serious form from 1860 onwards. Whether connected to the onset of epilepsy or not, Dr Riesenkampf also noted Dostoyevsky's frequent mood swings. When he was with people, he was animated and jolly. In fact, he communicated his love of literature with such passionate speeches and such great enthusiasm that his friends were held spellbound until well into the small hours. But once alone in the flat he would shut the door on the world and remain in his room, often uncommunicative and deeply depressed. He was not the ideal flatmate.

Dr Riesenkampf later attributed Dostoyevsky's moods and eccentricities to the workings of a great mind wrestling with the sufferings of humanity and preparing to convey it to the world in his writing. In spite of this charitable evaluation, however, Dr Riesenkampf moved out of the flat before Dostoyevsky commenced writing his first novel.

Although Fyodor had been in no hurry to leave the military academy when his father died, he did not expect the military to become his life's vocation; rather, he used it to earn money and secure stability. However, in 1844 he discovered that this secure living was about to make serious inroads into his chosen career. A military career in the sophisticated city of St Petersburg was one thing; being transferred to the country was a different matter. He learned that he might be sent a good distance away from St Petersburg on an inspection mission, and so applied to be released from the military on the grounds of ill health. He succeeded. Finally, in October 1844 he was struck off the lists of the Corps of Military Engineers. Now writing was his only occupation – and his only income – so it became vital to get his work published, or at the very least to earn money by his pen; both journalism and translation beckoned. He had, of course, his own ambition to secure a reputation as an original writer, but in the first instance his ability as a translator was to provide him with some work and was also to influence his very first original novel.

Dostoyevsky was commissioned to translate the novella *Eugenie Grandét* by the French novelist Honoré de Balzac, and in some ways this was an appropriate training, for translating the work of another, much admired author would have given Dostoyevsky intimate knowledge of the text of *Eugenie Grandét*. The novel was the story of a woman, her miserly father and her poor judgement of men. Balzac, along with the Russian writer Gogol and, to some extent, Charles Dickens, was part of a movement of writers who were working towards the representation of realism in literature. Their intention was to *re-present* what they observed and to submerge the reader in the real world, albeit a world that the reader might not encounter in their own lives. These writers were known as the romantic realists. The collective pronoun 'romantic realists' referenced the legacy of Romanticism, which in Britain included the Romantic poets. These were the poets – Keats, Shelley, Wordsworth, Byron and others – who adhered to the idea that individual experience, particularly in face of the sublime of Nature, should be imbued with feelings of transcendence and enchantment. Thus in Romantic art the harvesters, butchers and farmers of quotidian scenes are presented as rosy cheeked, healthy people enjoying the hard work of the outdoors, accepting the challenge of survival with good health and much vigour. The view of their struggle to survive was romanticised both in art and poetry – a view that could be criticised as demonstrating an idealised view of what it is like to be poor.

The later group of writers defined as 'romantic realists' were less about the romance and more about the realism. They wished to eschew the aesthetic of the Romantic tradition, which told stories on an epic scale, with heroes and villains thrust into a world of natural forces rich with pathetic fallacy. The romantic realists intended to remain true to the structure of a traditional narrative but sought also to reflect life, to describe what they saw and present it in a more truthful style. Some critics construed that this meant the reader was treated to a list-like narrative that simply described surroundings and characters in a boring monotone, which just itemised what they looked like or did, without drama or romance. Although defined as a romantic realist, Balzac was of the opinion that realism could not be represented realistically lest it seem unbelievable; he genuinely believed that truth was stranger than fiction, and claimed that 'life would often seem implausible'. Donald Fanger asserts of Balzac's fiction that to overcome the paradoxical unbelievability of realism, to 'tell like it is', the writer resorted to dramatic caricature.[1] *Eugenie Grandét* features an old miser who is an exaggerated version of a parsimonious man.

He hides all his gold in one room, whilst Eugenie herself, his daughter, is without guile, an innocent. Her father is thus blackened by his caricature and Eugenie is brightened and radiates good. *Eugenie Grandét* is a moral parable about greed; and whether the story related, with trenchant irony, is more or less realistic than the world observed by the author, in its description of a controlling paternal figure, an unreliable suitor and the effects that poverty has on all its characters, it was worthy of praise and translation. It was a novel that Dostoyevsky came to know intimately. He wrote to Mikhail in September 1844 that he was writing a novel 'about the length of Eugenie',² and that he was well pleased with his work. Fyodor was inspired, and he was preparing to launch his own version of romantic realism on the Russian population.

Typically, Fyodor locked himself in his room for many hours at a time, furiously writing what would become his first novel, *Poor Folk*. His new flatmate was Dmitry Grigorovich, a fellow writer, who was understanding of Fyodor's lifestyle – and, better than that, he turned out to have influential friends.

Dostoyevsky said later that the novel *Poor Folk* just dropped into his mind when he was walking on the banks of the River Neva in St Petersburg. It was a bitter cold evening; his breath cracked in the air and the river was frozen. The sun was setting and it flamed the mist over the river, and in the swirling clouds of this radiant sunset Fyodor saw another city take shape. Living in this new city, in sadness and poverty, were his two protagonists: Deviushkin, a middle-aged civil servant, and Barbara, a penniless young woman. They wrote letters to each other, tracking the progress of their lives until the end of their doomed romance. Dostoyevsky went home and started writing.

The initial inspiration for this story was not so much the musings of another writer, such as Balzac, but the geography of the city that was Dostoyevsky's home. St Petersburg dominates Fyodor's writings from the moment the fictional Deviushkin puts pen to letter, and continues as a presence until the last 'Hurrah!' in *The Brothers Karamazov*. St Petersburg is the essence of Dostoyevsky's literary landscape.

The representation of the city almost as a character in its own right was evident in Balzac's work, where Paris dominates, and also in Dickens, whose characters inhabit a now famous version of industrial London, where poverty and Victorian figures stalk the landmarks of the Thames and St Pauls. Like these writers, Dostoyevsky constructed a set of stories out of the ancient streets of Russia's most European city. In fact, at the time St Petersburg was the subject of many portrayals; it competed for cultural importance in Russia with its compatriot Moscow. Alexander Herzen wrote an essay entitled *Moscow and St Petersburg,* countered by the iconoclastic Vissarion Belinsky's (of whom more later) *St Petersburg and Moscow.* These articles marked the beginnings of the travelogue genre, bearing descriptions in books and in newspapers of the people and places that made up the environment. St Petersburg itself was the centre of public discussion in Russia, particularly the debate surrounding patriotic adherence to Slavic principles, culture and origins versus the ever more powerful influence of Western Europe; transport and communication, along with St Peterburg's geographical proximity, was opening borders and changing minds. As Stefan Zweig summarised:

> The Russia of the mid-nineteenth century did not know where it was going, whether towards the west or towards the east, towards Europe or towards Asia, towards Petersburg, the 'artifical city', and civilisation, or back to the present smallholding in the boundless steppe. Turgenev pushed his compatriots forwards; Tolstoy held them back.[3]

Dostoyevsky's version of St Petersburg, like that of Dickens' London, is preoccupied not with the wealthy delights of rich city dwellers but with those who haunt the shadows, of the poor and poverty stricken, at the time when he was living and writing there. There was no definition of the new genre that he was developing. Tolstoy and Turgenev preoccupied themselves with 'landowners' literature': the epic canvasses of *War and Peace,* and even the more claustrophobic *Anna Karenina*, dealt with the miseries of the aristocracy, set against the backdrop of their wealth and land. The novels offered an insight into the world that most Russians could not access. Tolstoy looked back to the noble officers of the Russian gentry battling Napoleon. He depicted the dilemmas of landowners, problems of marriage and the existence of God. Turgenev's more agnostic and radical approach to Russian life came later, but was still preoccupied with the vast landscape of the Russian rural idyll and not with the onset of urbanisation. Turgenev and Tolstoy were in themselves objects of celebrity curiosity – they argued publicly and were so opposed that their relationship almost ended both their lives in a duel. Tolstoy, it seems, mentioned on one occasion that he disapproved of the manner in which Turgenev was bringing up his daughter. Offended, Turgenev threatened to punch Tolstoy on the nose. Insulted, Tolstoy left the scene but sent a letter demanding an apology, and when, as he thought, he did not get one, he challenged Turgenev to a duel. In fact, their letters had crossed in the post; Turgenev had apologised, after all, and the duel fizzled out. However, the two men did not then speak to each other for seventeen years.

Years later, Dostoyevsky was to lampoon Turgenev as the character of Karmazinov in *The Devils*. However, at this point the rivalries of these great Russian writers were yet to impact the literary landscape. In the meantime, the young Dostoyevsky was beginning to pioneer a new genre, the genre of the novel of the urban landscape, observed and lived in by the disenfranchised and the landless; the stories of the rich set against the grandiose landscape of their ownership and privilege was not a context that interested him. Perhaps without realising it, or because he set about exploring something different, the young Fyodor delighted in the chiaroscuro streets of the underbelly of his city; his writing was the *noir* of its time. His portrait of St Petersburg was full of shadows and shading; light illuminated the merest space; the inhabitants lived their lives by candlelight, hidden, obscured, as were their thoughts, feelings and their deeds. His first major characters were created for *Poor Folk*. Deviushkin was a copyist, a copyist no less of other people's novels, who lived behind a screen in a small flat, while Barbara, with whom he corresponded, lived in a slightly better-appointed room across the River Neva. So it is that the two protagonists communicate by sending letters across to each other, which becomes the novel's central narrative device. This is the story of two lovers trapped by their poverty into making declarations of love that have little hope of fulfilment. The novel describes in authentic detail the everyday living conditions of the poor. Fyodor uses the shadows of the city to represent the stark realism of urban existence and highlights the injustice of his characters' situation. He did not fail to move his readers. The story is both sentimental and anti-sentimental; it instigates the contradictions that were to underpin Dostoyevsky's literature throughout his life, the conflicts of love and justice. It is a tale of unrequited love in the face of utilitarian necessity, for Barbara must marry into money to protect her future, and thus Deviushkin's love, although acknowledged, is never accepted. This short novel was very different from the fashionable literature of the 1830s, which imitated German and Italian Romanticism. *Poor Folk* was something new, something different, and as such it had quite an impact.

Humiliation inhabits the text as it does throughout his work, for Dostoyevsky was to occupy his writing with the representation of the abject humiliation of the individual as a kind of painful precursor to either redemption or condemnation – in Deviushkin's case, a form of redemption. Deviushkin's humiliation is as painful as any modern satire. Deviushkin makes a mistake and is called to his boss to explain why he has missed a sentence from a novel he was copying, a serious error. Deviushkin is appalled and defeated, knowing that all is lost if he loses his job. He apologises profusely, but his humiliation does not stop there: a button from his battered jacket pings off and falls at the feet of his benefactor, and the reader is left with the vision of this defeated, poverty-stricken man crawling about on the floor trying to retrieve a button. All is not lost for Deviushkin, however: his boss is a decent man, given to donating money to his employees, and Deviushkin is in luck. His initial humiliation leads to his redemption as an employee – but not as a suitor. His failure is not as final as the humiliation and defeat of another character, Gorshkov, for nowhere else in the novel is an individual's downfall more poignantly charted.

This relates the plight of a colleague whose unfair dismissal goes to court. While he waits in misery for the court to decide his fate, his family begin to starve and he is forced to ask Deviushkin for money, who, despite his own shortcomings, obliges. Gorshkov is eventually exonerated, his job restored, and he returns home to celebrate with his wife and family, with Deviushkin in tow, who describes him as unable to sit still: 'He kept entering everyone's room in turn (whether invited thither or not), and, seating himself smilingly on a chair, would sometimes say something and sometimes not utter a word, but get up and go out again.'4 The evening progresses and Gorshkov remains in a state of agitation; at one point he forgets that his daughter Petunia has died. At last he goes to sleep, exhausted, but in the hour of his victory he dies, perhaps of a stroke. Whatever the cause, he is doomed only to have known failure, not success.

In the portrayal of this doom-laden scene Dostoyevsky differed, not just from his Russian contemporaries who were busy writing their stories of epic Russia, but from his more realist peers such as Balzac and Dickens. While both Balzac and Dickens attempted to represent, in some form, the eventual successes of their protagonists in their struggles, Dostoyevsky was preoccupied with their ultimate failure. *Poor Folk* is not the story of a poetic justice that sees Eugenie rewarded, even avenged, for her suffering and patience in Balzac's *Eugenie Grandét,* nor is it the pyrrhic victory of Oliver in Charles Dickens' *Oliver Twist* or Pip in *Great Expectations*. This kind of sentimental realism was not to be taken up by Fyodor Dostoyevsky. The resolution or equilibrium Deviushkin and Barbara seek is not for them, supplanted rather by a miserable separation, brought about by the utilitarian outlook that drives Barbara to risk her future on a bad-tempered husband who may be able to look after her, while Deviushkin, all too late, manages some kind of financial stability. Dostoyevsky's approach to realism lies not in the photographic reconstruction of reality, known as 'logical naturalism', but in the construction of conflicting emotions in the characters whose stories he relates, and of their eventual failure or remorse. Throughout his work Dostoyevsky was to repeat these themes of humiliation, redemption, and a remorse that resulted not in a restoration of a 'just' equilibrium but in a slow descent to disaster:

> From the murky squalor of these days something slowly emerges and takes definite shape; at last out of the visionary and crowded state of alternating anxiety and ecstasy there is born the first fruit of his imagination, the novel, *Poor Folk*.[5]

It was this capacity to characterise rather than to describe, and to embed these characters within the landscape not of the rural idyll of the Russian steppes but of the industrial discord of the emerging St Petersburg, with its Slavic and European contrasts, that caught the attention of the literary grandees of the time.

In the months leading up to its publication he wrote and rewrote the story, some of it during his summer stay with his brother at Reval. Once back in St Petersburg, Fyodor sent his newly married brother a commentary on how it was going, but he did not reveal anything to the ever-curious flatmate, Grigorovich, until he was sure that the much-revised manuscript was ready for its first reading.

One summer day he emerged from his room, having painstakingly copied out a neat version, and told his friend to sit down and listen. Within a page or two Grigorovich realised he was listening to a brilliant work. He interrupted Dostoyevsky to tell him so, but Dostoyevsky was too anxious to respond amiably to his friend's enthusiasm. He insisted that Dmitry sit down and listen without interrupting. Grigorovich did as he was told, and as he listened his conviction grew that here was a genius.

Grigorovich was acquainted with a young man of literary talent and entrepreneurial abilities, Nikolai Nekrasov, and he wasted no time in getting the manuscript to him for his opinion. At first they intended to read only a few pages, so that Nekrasov could get an idea of what it was like; but after ten pages they read another ten, and then ten more, until they had finished the whole novel in the small hours of the morning. When they came to the last scene, in which the lovers are forced to part, Grigorovich could no longer control himself and started to sob. When he looked up, he saw that Nekrasov too was weeping. The two could hardly bear to look at each other, for tears were streaming down both their faces. At four in the morning they returned to Dostoyevsky's flat to wake him up and tell him the great news that they loved the novel, and Nekrasov wanted to publish it. They would take it to Vissarion Belinsky, Russia's most influential literary critic of the time. They left Dostoyevsky pacing up and down his room, unable to sleep, nervously anticipating Belinsky's reaction. Recalling the scene later, Grigorovich admitted that it was probably a bit impetuous to wake Dostoyevsky so suddenly and give him the good news:

> I must confess that I had acted rashly. For I knew the character of my housemate, his morbid sensibility and reserve, his shyness – and I ought to have told him all quite quietly next morning instead of waking him in the middle of the night, and, moreover, bringing a strange man to visit him![6]

Dostoyevsky had read and admired Belinsky's work for several years, and all he could think of, after his visitors had gone, was that soon the great man would be reading what he himself had written. The tension continued for some time, for it was some weeks later that Dostoyevsky was called forward to meet with Belinsky. Nekrasov had to work hard to persuade Dostoyevsky to come, as despite the fact that, by then, Dostoyevsky knew that Belinsky also thought *Poor Folk* was a work of genius, he still could not see why the great critic would want to meet him.

Belinsky, or the 'Furious Vissarion' as his friends called him because of his passionate oratory, was the son of a navy doctor and the grandson of a priest. He was one of a new breed of

Russians known as the 'plebeian intelligentsia'. Belinsky was not of aristocratic birth and so had to earn his living. He did this not through the traditional channels of priesthood, medicine or the civil service, but through his education: he was a freelance journalist. Although catapulted into journalism by being expelled from university in 1832, he soon became an influential literary critic and socialist thinker. Belinsky believed that literature fundamentally should serve the aims of social justice; *Poor Folk* did exactly that. Belinsky received the novel enthusiastically and gave it, and Dostoyevsky, a good review.

Belinsky believed he had found the new genius of Russian literature, and Dostoyevsky soon came to agree: 'I go to see Belinsky very often. He is incredibly well-disposed towards me, and in all seriousness sees in me a demonstration to the public and a vindication of his opinions.'[7] So wrote Dostoyevsky to Mikhail in 1845. In fact, throughout that period Dostoyevsky wrote several times to his brother about Belinsky. Belinsky, he stated, 'loves me unboundedly' and 'declares that he is sure of me now'. As a consequence of this relationship Belinsky introduced Dostoyevsky to the Russian literary circle, which included the great Turgenev who, at the time, Dostoyevsky was delighted to meet. Turgenev apparently was friendly, and according to Dostoyevsky a 'highly gifted' writer – and all at twenty-five. He commended Turgenev's work to his brother, although, as time would tell, Dostoyevsky's relationship with Turgenev, like Turgenev's relationship with Tolstoy, was to turn out to be one of the most turbulent in Russian literary history. In the meantime, Dostoyevsky's name was on the lips of all in St Petersburg, and rumours of his novel grew as Belinsky propagated Fyodor's reputation. Fyodor struggled with censorship and with rewrites, but the Furious Vissarion lent his passion to the expectation of a new literary talent. In addition, Belinsky was not above giving Dostoyevsky practical advice on how to make a living out of literature; despite his socialist philosophy, or perhaps because of it, Belinsky told Dostoyevsky that for his 'soul's sake' he must not charge less than 200 roubles per sheet. As Dostoyevsky commented,

'He gave me a comprehensive lesson on how to live in the literary world.'[8] Dostoyevsky then worked out that his second novel, *The Double,* could fetch at least 1500 roubles.

Aside from their love of literature and their ambition to succeed as writers, both Belinsky and Dostoyevsky were men who were attracted to the ideas of the French writer Fourier. Fourier was a philosopher who had participated in and survived the French Revolution. Despite having had doubts about its progress, after the revolution he remained a teacher, philosopher and mathematician; he died in 1830. Fourier had stated that, because all current economic structures were riddled with injustice, only a complete destruction of the structures would result in any kind of social justice. These were the ideals of the French Revolution, if not the results. The people were to be persuaded to live in 'phalansteries' of about eighteen hundred persons in a single complex. This building would contain auditoriums, lecture theatres, dance halls and areas devoted to culture. In these phalansteries, social justice would be practised and a new, almost natural law would inevitably result, as inviolable as Newton's theory of gravity, a law of social harmony. According to Fourier, then, the barrier to social harmony was social injustice; it was institutions and governments, not human nature. This chimed with Belinsky, in particular. Russia in the nineteenth century was not a just society; in the eighteenth century, serfs had made up 45 per cent of the Russian population. They lived more or less without rights. Their owners could sell them without land, split up families, tell them who to marry and punish them at whim.

Dostoyevsky, keenly aware of the injustice inherent in the Russian feudal system, was attracted by the Fourierist solution. Through reading Zschokke he had come to believe in social justice as a Christian imperative; and Fourier's philosophy, although radical, spoke of economic, not political, reform. It did not seem to threaten the political structures of the Russian nation: phalansteries could be built without tearing down the existing system of government. Christianity could inform the construction

46

of a better society, but Christianity emphasised the nature of human inadequacy, of human sin, much more than did the utopianist philosopher so admired by Belinsky. While Dostoyevsky was enamoured of these philosophies he was not quite as convinced by the idea that an earthly social utopianism was possible without a religious imperative.

In addition, Belinsky's beliefs went far beyond Fourierism. Belinsky was also influenced by the rationalist philosopher Hegel, who argued that philosophical agreement could be achieved by the process of thesis, antithesis and synthesis: the presentation of an idea, the presentation of its opposite and thence the combination of the two towards a workable resolution. Belinsky was also an admirer of the theologian Feuerbach, whose book *The Essence of Christianity* suggested that all religion is the projection of humanity's wish to believe in God, and that that projection might be a necessary form of religion. However, by the time Belinsky and Dostoyevsky met, Belinsky had not only renounced Christianity but had come to regard religion as harmful.

In Russia, the Orthodox tradition had taught a passive faith for centuries. To many Russian socialists like Belinsky it seemed that the Orthodox Church colluded with a cruel and autocratic regime, and thus contributed to the oppression of the peasants. It offered colourful rituals and religious awe, reward in heaven, but no solution to the serf's poverty on earth. The offer of a future reward, based on compliant behaviour on earth, kept the status quo functioning in favour of those already privileged and already in power. It was this view of religion that led Marx to proclaim that religion was the 'opium' of the people. Belinsky had come to believe that religion was not even that. The people, he said, rejected religion. They used it as a superstition and held few priests in high esteem; it was harmful and divisive and was better destroyed. In order to be a true socialist, one must be an atheist: God had no place in the phalanstery.

Dostoyevsky later wrote of Belinsky: 'Still as a socialist, he had to destroy Christianity in the first place. He knew that the revolution must necessarily begin with atheism. He had to dethrone religion ...'[9] The Furious Vissarion argued his case cogently. He believed that if Christ had been born in Imperial Russia, he would have been effaced by the evil of the regime. Dostoyevsky did not go quite that far, for even as Belinsky spoke this way, he caught sight of Dostoyevsky: 'I am even touched to look at him,' he said, 'Every time I mention Christ his face changes expression, as if he were ready to start weeping.'[10] Dostoyevsky counterargued that if Christ had been born in their time, he would at least have joined the Left. This Belinsky conceded, unwillingly.

Belinsky's philosophical position was radical and he was a zealot in perpetuating his views. Dostoyevsky revelled in the attention that Belinsky had lavished upon him, but he was also aware that Belinsky's views might be too inflexible for a writer who wanted to explore all aspects of his art. Dostoyevsky wrote to his brother that Belinsky 'in all seriousness sees in me a demonstration to the public and a vindication of his opinions'.[11] Sadly, when Dostoyevsky demonstrated an opinion in his work that differed from those of Belinsky's, a division developed between the curious writer and dogmatic ideologue. Dostoyevsky had published *Poor Folk* on 15 January 1846 to a warm reception, and fired on by his success he published *The Double* on 30 January 1846. Thereafter, he promptly fell from grace.

4

DOPPELGÄNGERS
AND DREAMERS

The Double, subtitled *A St Petersburg Poem* though not technically a poem, is a novella that, like its predecessor *Poor Folk*, evokes the atmosphere of the urban cityscape of St Petersburg. However, it differs in one crucial respect in that the St Petersburg of *Poor Folk* addresses the characters in their domestic environs, while *The Double* navigates the city streets and the workplace. Dostoyevsky's new doomed character, Golyadkin, wanders the streets more readily than the Barbara and Deviushkin who seemed much more bound to their apartments. Golyadkin's tale is markedly not of their world:

> It was an awful November night – wet, foggy, rainy, snowy, teeming with colds in the head, fevers, swollen faces, quinseys, inflammations of all kinds and descriptions – teeming, in fact, with all the gifts of a Petersburg November. The wind howled in the deserted streets, lifting up the black water of the canal above the rings on the bank, and irritably brushing against the lean lamp-posts which chimed in with its howling in a thin, shrill creak, keeping up the endless squeaky, jangling concert with which every inhabitant of Petersburg is so familiar.[1]

In this setting of the onset of a Russian winter, Dostoyevsky's Mr Golyadkin navigates his way between his destinations until, on such a night by the Ismailovsky Bridge, he meets a stranger – an exact copy of himself. There follows an atmospheric journey through the streets of St Petersburg, a route that no doubt could be followed today using the technology of Google Street View, for such is every street named and every left or right turn described, as, to his horror, Golyadkin follows his doppelgänger back to his own flat.

Throughout most of the novella Dostoyevsky employs a third-person perspective, but occasionally the narrative switches and he deploys the second-person and calls the main protagonist 'our hero'. This use of what Richard Ayoade, director of a modern film version of *The Double*, called a 'quite intimate third person'.[2] Using the epithet 'our hero' is most likely a device to make sure the reader is clear who the protagonist is and who is the usurper. Perhaps also this idea of the 'intimate third person' is evident in the fact that in the opening paragraph of Chapter Four Dostoyevsky reverts to a first- and second-person narrative, taking on the persona of the first-person pronoun in 'I' and speaking directly to the reader when describing the party of his benefactor's daughter, Klara Olsufyevna, at which Veuve-Clicquot and oysters are served. Whether this slip into a different perspective was deliberate or the mistake of a hurried writer who constructed his work without an editor is unknown, but it does lend itself to the idea of the intimate narrator, and further one who understands St Petersburg well.

Events do not turn out well for 'our hero'. As the narrative progresses, Goladykin finds that he is being replaced by a better version of himself. The more 'our hero' Golyadkin beseeches those around him that he is being replaced, the less he is believed. The first Golyadkin is disadvantaged by an inability to socialise well. His first sentence in conversation, Dostoyevsky recounts, is often a 'stumbling-block', but nothing is a problem for the double:

> The figure that was sitting opposite Mr Golyadkin now was his terror, was his shame, was his nightmare of the evening before; in short, was Mr Golyadkin himself, not

the Mr Golyadkin who was sitting now in his chair with his mouth wide open and his pen petrified in his hand, not the one who acted as assistant to his chief, not the one who liked to efface himself and slink away in the crowd, not the one whose deportment plainly said, 'Don't touch me and I won't touch you,' or, 'Don't interfere with me, you see I'm not touching you'; no, this was another Mr Golyadkin, quite different, yet at the same time, exactly like the first.[3]

The original is a shy, unsociable man who is lost for words in social circumstances, blushes easily, is clumsy and, most of all, unconvincing. The double is a better version of Golyadkin himself; every quality the protagonist lacks, his double boasts; he is witty, efficient and attractive. Golyadkin not only lacks these qualities but also the confidence to grasp them; his timidity is exploited by the double, who bullies him. The doppelgänger is confident and more popular, and the more potent he becomes, the more the original is diminished, until Golyadkin senior ('our hero') is defeated and, in effect, dissolved into insanity.

The figure of Golyadkin's damaging double is part of what set Dostoyevsky apart from his contemporaries, but it is also what allows him to remain very much a part of the twenty-first century literary landscape today. Golyadkin's doppelgänger explores the anxiety of the self. The existential anxiety expressed by the binary representation of this character is a major preoccupation in much modern media, whether it be Harlan Ellison's novel *Shatterday* (1934), later made into a *Twilight Zone* episode starring Bruce Willis, where the alter ego of the protagonist haunts him, or whether it is Captain James T. Kirk fighting his own darker self from a parallel universe in *Star Trek*, or perhaps even the dark sides of Batman or Spiderman as they wrestle with the doppelgänger in their superhero realities. More recently, Jake Gyllenhaal has starred as a doppelgänger figure in *Enemy*, a film by Denis Villeneuve based on the novel by José Saramago, *The Double*, which concedes a debt to Dostoyevsky. Whilst in more fantastical science fiction the fear of the inhuman double is represented in *Invasion of the*

Body Snatchers, and discussions of the perfect double, or the more than perfect double, are recontextualised in issues of sentience and the rise of biotechnology. This latterday genre explores the concept that technology will one day replicate human thought processes, or even humanity itself, as demonstrated in the replicants of *Blade Runner* or the indistinguishable doubles that are the Cylons of *Battlestar Galactica*; all these modern preoccupations deal with the concept of *The Double*, the search for the authentic human self and how that self might measure up in the face of a more efficient doppelgänger.

In film and media the 'doppelgänger shot' is a standard semiotic trope that establishes the hidden identity of every character, from Killer Bob in *Twin Peaks* and Marion Crane in *Psycho* through to Richard Gere in the first moments of *Pretty Woman*: mirrors, windows, reflections all hint at the double within each individual. Dostoyevsky's story touches a modern nerve, one that Richard Ayoade filmed in his recent version of *The Double*, starring Jesse Eisenberg as the doubles. The story in this haunting film is as comfortable in the chiaroscuro universe of a 1984-style dystopia as it is in the streets of St Petersburg. The futility of existence, the need to establish identity in the face of numbing institutions that offer little status or comfort, the sense of poverty and uselessness: all are conveyed throughout the film, just as they were in the novella. The film is transposed to a modern parallel universe, where the loss of an identity card triggers the character's loss of identity, and the gradual takeover of his domineering alter ego begins. The story, thus updated, fits naturally into contemporary themes of anonymity, social impotence and the sense that all humanity is subsumed into a coldly mechanical universe, in which personal agency is reduced to complacency and human empathy replaced by a malign emptiness:

> But in the Dostoevsky [novella], it feels like the critique is more personal and existential. More about someone's buying into it themselves rather than how they are crushed by something without. To me, the Dostoevsky book feels more like Kafka,

which doesn't seem broadly particularly critical of the legal system. It's more a representation of what you fear about yourself if you would get into contact with something like that, and how you would crumble. It's kind of a manifestation of your own weakness – that seemed more interesting to me.[4]

The inadequacy of the individual, and thus the repressed desire for adequacy, is emphasised in the modern world by the collective fascination with and perpetuation of celebrity figures, who appear utterly capable and without flaw. Mr Golyadkin would crumble just as easily before the images of the 'perfect' celebrity as he does before the copy of himself that manages modern life so much more successfully. In *The Double* Dostoyevsky deals with humiliation and failure, the failure of the individual to measure up even to their own criteria of what they should be; Ayoade's version emphasizes this existential aspect, and more modern interpretations such as his, among others, all preserve some of the magical realism of the original as a device to assert the reality of human insecurity. However, this did not appear to be understood at the time, and the story was not received well, nor was its significance as an allegory considered appropriate for literary discussion.

When *Poor Folk* was published just a few weeks before, the influences of Dostoyevsky's heritage were noted in his work's relationship to Balzac and its treatment of realism. The Russian writer Gogol was also cited as an influence. Gogol's story *The Overcoat* presaged the poverty and humiliation of the Russian working man, a man who saves up for an overcoat that becomes his pride and joy and yet is then stolen from him, leaving him worse off than he was before. Further, in *Poor Folk*'s scene where Deviushkin loses his button, some similarities to a scene with a handkerchief in Gogol's *Notes of a Madmen* are evident. Critics decried *The Double* not just because of its magical realism, but because of this more obvious debt to Gogol. Under close scrutiny, the theme of a clerk in love with the patron's daughter, who then sinks into insanity, also echoed Gogol's *Notes of a Madman*; it seemed that Dostoyevsky was divested of ideas of his own. In addition, the idea of a vicious alter ego usurping an original was an homage or even a copy of the idea in Gogol's absurdist short story 'The Nose', where a sliced-off nose develops a personality and usurps its founder.

However, Dostoyevsky thought *The Double* was one of his better works. He certainly thought it was better than *Poor Folk* – in fact he told his brother it was 'ten times better than *Poor Folk*'.[5] The fact that it echoes or even satirises his predecessor Gogol, almost as if it was a reflection of some of his work, might actually be part of the joke – the idea of a double usurping Mr Golyadkin may be Dostoyevsky's small challenge to previous writers as he usurps their place in Russian literature. But the critical response to the novella grew more vocal, and some of the humour of the original idea was lost. Ultimately, while *The Double* is a disturbing, atmospheric tale set against the haunting backdrop of a wintry St Petersburg, it is also darkly funny. The nervous hero is comical in his responses to his challenger, an identical rival who falls into step beside him in the streets one night; Mr Golyadkin is, quite literally, beside himself. Later on in the story, as he tries to come to terms with his new version of himself, a night of drinking rum punch ends in a very accurate and funny description of being drunk: 'They reached their third and fourth glasses of punch at last, and then Mr Golyadkin began to be aware or two sensations: the one that he was extraordinarily happy, and the other that he could not stand on his legs.'[6]

Despite these moments of humour, by the end of the story Mr Golyadkin is outmanoeuvred, to the extent that he finds himself paying for eleven pies that his double has consumed, while he himself has only one; it is then only a matter of time before the Mr Golyadkin is completely diminished. However, it was not only Golyadkin who was to be diminished: Dostoyevsky too was to suffer a blow to his short-lived literary reputation. It was a setback from which he would find it difficult to recover, if not in terms of what he wrote, but in terms of how he evaluated his own work.

Vissarion Belinsky, the 'Furious Vissarion', lived up to his reputation and raged against the new novella; it was not a relevant social document, it was a useless exercise in fantasy and psychology. While Belinsky identified strengths in Dostoyevsky's representation of St Petersburg, he condemned it as repetitive: 'The point is there are far too many such wonderful places in *The Double*, and the same thing over and over again, however wonderful it may be, wearies and bores.'[7] However, Belinsky's agenda was clear: his praise for *Poor Folk* was underpinned by his credo that literature serve realism and realism reflect the plight of the poor, ultimately so that the plight of the poor may be changed. These were honourable requirements of literature, but they may have coloured Belinsky's reading of *The Double*. While the story can be read as the magical haunting of a man who meets his own ghost on the Ismailovsky Bridge – Golyadkin himself reflects, 'It began this way. It began on the Ismailovsky Bridge; that's how it began ...'[8] – it can also be seen as the realistic portrayal of the disintegration of the human mind. Early in the piece, Dostoyevsky describes the slightly obsessive Mr Golyadkin tidying and rearranging his flat. His shyness and anti-social demeanour all signal a disturbance of the mind that may be all too real rather than supernatural. However, Belinsky saw no purpose in such a portrayal: it did not address the injustice of poverty or the undeserved privilege of the rich. Art, Belinsky maintained, existed to serve the higher needs of public justice. In a utopia, art would serve the State; by contrast, fantasy and psychological analysis served no real purpose in the material world and therefore were not appropriate. Art that is not socially useful is not art. Moreover, the utopian-socialist mindset denies one of the fundamental aspects of the novel: that a human being could have an evil side as well as a good one. In the end, while Dostoyevsky proclaimed the need for social justice, and while he understood, perhaps better than all of his critics, the consequences of poverty, he could not bring himself to declare that human beings alone were capable of achieving a social utopia; somewhere deep in the psychology of the mind there was also the danger of sabotage, of evil.

Dostoyevsky soon found himself in a minority of one. While religious and philosophical differences might have underpinned some of his fall from grace in the Belinsky circle, arrogance and overconfidence also played a part. Dostoyevsky was carried away by the praise of his peers for *Poor Folk*, and he did not endear himself to his new found friends. He lorded it over other, more junior writers, or he reacted jealously to the attention they were getting. Dostoyevsky wrote to his brother that he was almost 'intoxicated' with his own fame.[9] Belinsky and Nekrasov began to think they had misjudged his genius, and they were not kind in their retractions. In a letter to Annenkov at the time, Belinsky declared:

> He has written other novels besides, but every new work of his is a new calamity. In the provinces they can't stand him, and in Petersburg even *Poor Folk* is abused; I tremble at the thought that I shall have to read this novel once more. We've all been taken in by our 'gifted' Dostoevsky![10]

Dmitry Grigorovich, perhaps not all that tactfully, reported all the gossip to Dostoyevsky. With *The Double*, Belinsky said, this genius had hit rock bottom. A cartoon portrayed Dostoyevsky as a red pimple on the nose of literature. An intense relationship with Turgenev, which had had the potential to become a lifelong friendship, turned sour almost as soon as it began. Turgenev rounded on Dostoyevsky and took the opportunity to mock him through a caricature of a provincial man who dreamed he was a genius. This caused such offence that, over thirty years later, Dostoyevsky and Turgenev had to be chaperoned at gatherings for fear of a row between them. Dostoyevsky got the point and left the group, never to join the Belinsky circle again.

Thus Dostoyevsky found himself out in the cold. The whole process had taken less than a month, and Dostoyevsky still had to earn a living. He had left the military and was relying upon his skills as a writer for money; without land he could not finance his pursuit, without publication he faced poverty of the kind he portrayed in *Poor Folk*. The answer for Dostoyevsky, as it is for many writers today, was journalism. At the time, there was a fashion for a new form of writing, known as the feuilleton, a type of article covering cultural events and current affairs not dissimilar to the writing of a column in a modern newspaper (a column, however, is usually contained within a newspaper where a feuilleton is a separate item).

The first feuilleton – it literally means a scrap of paper, an addition – appeared in 1800 in France in the *Journal des Debats* magazine. The fashion for feuilleton writing gained currency in 1836, when the French newspaper *La Presse* began to include a separate sheet, called simply 'Feuilleton', which was intended to develop observations and comments in short bursts of prose. In 1842 Eugène Sue published *Les Mystère de Paris*, which was a runaway success, and the practice took hold and spread quickly to Vienna, and from there to Russia, such that by the 1840s it had become a popular form of writing in St Petersburg.

There was a rash of publications on the subject of St Petersburg. Nekrasov wrote *St Petersburg Corners*, Krestovsky *St Petersburg Slums* and Butkov *St Petersburg Summits*; together these writers introduced to Russia a new journalistic genre akin to travelogue with the inclusion of creative non-fiction. The purpose of the feuilleton had developed such that it was to describe, observe and offer opinion on the ideas, places and people of the day. The style of writing, particularly in Russia, could combine fictional and satirical aspects as it commented on contemporary places and events. The feuilleton could further be argued to be the ancestor of the blog, as it allows the writer to explore topics more freely and according to their interests, rather than binding them to reportage alone.

Dostoyevsky had made one foray into the form when he wrote an announcement for a magazine, called *The Banterer*, to be published by Nekrasov. However, this did not succeed with censors: a phrase in Dostoyevsky's announcement, that 'the Banterer will laugh at everything deserving laughter', did not go down well with the authorities, and the enterprise was banned before it began.[11] However, despite Dostoyevsky's arrogance and tactlessness in Russian literary circles, and despite the damage to his reputation done by the Belinsky circle after the publication of *The Double*, Dostoyevsky got a job writing feuilletons for the *St Petersburg News*. Now Dostoyevsky could be paid for his work, and he was able to write about the city he loved and knew so well, a city that continued to inhabit his literature throughout his life. He wrote four pieces entitled 'A Petersburg Chronicle', one of which led with the phrase: 'Here is chaos, all miscellany' (1 June 1847).[12]

There is a sense of an early stream of consciousness technique as Dostoyevsky wanders through the streets of St Petersburg, reflecting on what is going on in the city. At one point he informs his readers that Jenny Lind (a famous Swedish opera singer) was going to London, and then he speculates as to why that would be relevant to anyone in St Petersburg, since few would know who she was and she was not heading to St Petersburg. In his earliest attempt, published on 1 June 1847, he reflects on the cliques and circles that inhabit the city, circles that do not always include him. He guides the reader through a description of these cliques and uses this guide as an opportunity to discuss themes of exclusion, isolation and loneliness. Dostoyevsky's feel for the urban landscape did not desert him; he had perceived the contradiction of an isolation juxtaposed against the close proximity of a thousand near neighbours: 'You die in the dark, at twilight, on a rainy day without a gleam of light, in full puzzlement.'[13] Dostoyevsky extends this mood by personifying the city itself: 'It was a raw misty morning and St Petersburg had got up ill-tempered and angry.'[14] Dostoyevsky compounds the conceit by suggesting that St Petersburg 'sulked' that the sun was too timid to shine on it, such that even at one o'clock in the afternoon the city is dulled with darkness, such that the clocks appear to be wrong. The 'Petersburg Chronicles' published in the *St Petersburg News* (sometimes called the *St Petersburg Gazette*) were not just a means to earn money through his chosen occupation: they were an opportunity to experiment with his own writing style and with his understanding of his home city and its population.

His depiction of St Petersburg as a lonely place, sometimes personified as a bitter personality, perhaps reflected his own approach to becoming a feuilletonist, which by luck or misfortune he had become because the previous incumbent had died suddenly. However, although that misfortune might have been Dostoyevsky's good fortune, he was still frustrated as a writer; while he wanted to earn his living, he also wanted to write his great novels. When he wrote to his brother in January 1847, shortly before he got his journalistic appointment, he described how he had heard that some considered *The Double* a powerful piece, more for the future than for the present. He reflected that this restored his confidence and speculated on what that speculative future might contain and when. He goes on to say that he is working on two stories, one he calls 'my *Mistress of the Inn*', which was later to be entitled *The Landlady* (perhaps so as not to be confused with Carlo Golden's play *The Mistress of the Inn*, premiered in 1753), and the other a novel, never to be finished, *Netochka Nezvanova* (translated 'nameless nobody'), about a poverty-stricken young girl who is adopted by a wealthy family and becomes infatuated with the daughter of the house. These novels and short stories were the purpose of his writing, they were the ambition that fuelled his soul to write; but earning money interfered with that purpose.

The Landlady was a story that was intended to reflect the form of a Russian folktale, written as a poem, that describes the desperate story of a woman whose father murders her mother and exerts such a power over his daughter, the landlady, that she is driven mad. Once again the story echoed stories before it, such as Gogol's *Nevsky Prospect* and the well-known tale, in imitation of a Ukrainian folktore, 'A Terrible Vengeance'. By offering

The Landlady to his public, Dostoyevsky was again affirming his dangerous love for the magical and fantastic, an element of his writing that many of his contemporary critics considered to be an unacceptable contradiction to his realistic outlook – but a contradiction that informed his life and populated his literature.

Contradiction was evident in the tale of Devuishkin and Barbara as they first professed their love for each other and then denounced it, and it is evident in Golyadkin as his own binary double invaded and destroyed his sanity. Contradiction is evident in the title of the short story 'White Nights', which is in itself an oxymoron and refers to the summer nights of St Petersburg, as the days grow long and the nights shorter – the sun rises at three thirty in the morning and sets at ten thirty at night. Though the temperatures are not unbearably hot, the population heads out of town to their dachas in the country to take best advantage of the milder weather and longer days. In those days the St Petersburg summer gave rise to the social phenomenon of the summer bachelor, not unlike the New Yorkers of the Fifties and Sixties whose wives headed to the Hamptons while the husbands struggled on through the city heat. In the same way, those who were left in St Petersburg either had to stay to keep the city running or otherwise had no property to retreat to in the country. In this context, Dostoyevsky chose to develop a character in 'White Nights' who is almost the binary opposite of his Golyadkin in *The Double,* an archetype that was to recur throughout his work: the *mechtatel,* the 'Petersburg dreamer'. This is an ethereal character that inhabits St Petersburg like Golyadkin's nemesis, shifting through the shadows and streets, almost without existence. The narrator of the story is just such an individual; in fact so ethereal is he in the deserted St Petersburg cityscape that it is possible to speculate he might inhabit the streets like a ghost, a spirit of the city, occupying it whilst almost no one else is there.

Dostoyevsky's work on the 'St Petersburg Chronicles' informed some of what he does in 'White Nights'. He explores the landscape of St Petersburg in more detail and develops his new archetypal character, one who floats across the surface of the city. Like

Golyadkin's double the protagonist of the story is ephemeral, so much so that when he has his first encounter with the heroine of the piece, she does not hear him and is unaware of his footsteps. The narrator (in this case Dostoyevsky used the first-person narrative) ascribes her lack of observation to the fact she appears to be crying. Thus, when he turns round to speak to her, he frightens her and she hurries away. Perhaps unwisely, he decides to follow her; understandably she perceives this as a threat. However, the real threat comes from another source, a drunken and unpleasant sex pest who has to be beaten off by the narrator's 'knobbly cane' – a cane not dissimilar to the one carried by Golyadkin's double. This incident effects an introduction and, ever the true gentleman, the narrator walks her home. Over the next four nights they enact a doomed romance in miniature, explore one another's histories, fall in love and fall apart. The dramatic plot itself is not necessarily significant; rather, it is the character of the narrator who assumes centre stage, a subject that foreshadows so much of Dostoyevsky's later work. In fact, when the young woman, Nastenka, interrogates her rescuer on the nature of his life and biography, he refers to himself as 'a character'. When she pursues this remark, he continues, saying that a character 'is a kind of freak'. He asks her, 'Do you know what a dreamer is?'[15]

The narrator's ensuing answer to that question suggests that the dreamer is, first and foremost, lonely. The protagonist lives alone, hiding in his room, knowing those around him but not known by them, and thus he dreams, or perhaps is preoccupied with his own inadequacy. The narrator of 'White Nights' describes himself as unable to make or maintain friends and unable to talk to women. He offers the image of a lonely man only comfortable within the geography of four walls, and has much in common with his predecessor Golyadkin. But he also foreshadows the greater heroes of Dostoyevsky's novels: Raskolnikov, Stavrogin and the Underground Man. However, the narrator's description of the dreamer does not stop there: 'A dreamer – if you must know its exact definition – is not a man, but a sort of creature of neuter gender. He settles mostly in some inaccessible place as though anxious to hide in it even from the light of day; and once he gets inside his room, he'll stick to it like a snail.'[16]

This character, while demonstrating a clear affection for Nastenka, having rescued her and befriended her, is not effectively connected to the physical universe, and thus he demonstrates an inability to communicate easily with other people. It is this space, between the internal imaginings of the dreamer and the way in which they attempt to relate to the physical world, that Dostoyevsky uses to explore the dissonance of existence. It is through this particular character, the *mechtatel* or the dreamer, that Dostoyevsky demonstrates the disconnect between the inner machinations of a fevered, sometimes hallucinatory mind and the effect this has on the person or people around them.

'White Nights' built on some of his more meandering thoughts expressed in his fourth feuilleton in the 'Petersburg Chronicles', wherein, just as he asks Nastenka whether she knows what a dreamer is, he also rhetorically poses the question to his readers. His answer is equally disturbing:

> '... and a man becomes at length not a man but some strange creature of an intermediate sort – a *dreamer*. Do you know what a dreamer is, gentlemen? It is a Petersburg nightmare, it is a sin personified, it is a tragedy, mute, mysterious, gloomy, savage, with all the furious horrors, with all the catastrophes, *péripéties* [adventures], plots and denouements, and we say this by no means in jest ...'[17]

Dostoyevsky conjures a Petersburg haunted by disconnected spirits, men unable to connect with the living world, and at the same time attempting to pursue an inner life; people who assert their right to existence but also wonder incessantly in what way they do exist. Dostoyevsky predicts not only his own later characters, but the existential elements that came to fore in early twentieth-century literature and philosophy, and perhaps as such he failed to connect as completely as an author with his own generation. This dreamer is specific to Petersburg: he is particularly Russian, and an urban inhabitant particularly from Petersburg. The dreamer is tormented and doomed. In 'White Nights', the dreamer-as-narrator enjoys his four nights with Natsenka while the relationship seems innocent, as they flirt and shiver in the dull, grey Petersburg nights. Dostoyevsky does not alleviate the mood with sunny settings, and the couple manage against the long-lit hours and the low temperatures of a Petersburg summer. Ultimately they must part when her real lover returns, and the *mechtatel* returns to the shadows or his room like a snail.

In his feuilleton writings and his short stories Dostoyevsky was able to observe and reflect on the world around him as a realist and a naturalist, but he was still attracted by the influence of the other-worldly and supernatural, and this placed him in opposition to the dominant trends of the time. Belinsky was a powerful influence and he still favoured the literal representation of the world for the purposes of changing that world.

Dostoyevsky was not entirely alone, however, and he did find some allies and admirers for his second novel, *The Double*. The young and talented Valerian Maikov not only liked *The Double*, he defended it publicly in his own review in *Notes of the Fatherland*. Maikov understood that Dostoyevsky was not just presenting a magical realist fantasia, but a psychological portrait of a human being's inner struggle. Thus Dostoyevsky also found himself caught up in a rivalry of publications that then placed him firmly on the side of Maikov, who by political outlook was a conservative and inclined to reactionary support of the status quo, a reformist in favour of better justice, than the all out revolutionary change advocated by Vissarion Belinsky. However, Valerian Maikov replaced Belinsky as chief literary critic of the journal *Notes of the Fatherland*, published by Krayevsky, who had also published *The Double*. Another journal was subsequently revived, one founded by Pushkin in its original incarnation, in order to rival *Notes of the Fatherland*: it was called *The Contemporary* and was run by rival publisher Nekrasov. Belinsky defected from *Notes of the Fatherland* to Nekrasov's new publication.

This division in the literary culture was a tangible representation of the division in philosophy and affiliation that divided the opinion-makers of St Petersburg at the time. These divisions were to define some of Dostoyevsky's choices and thus were to have a lasting effect on his future. However, not all of Dostoyevsky's decisions were governed by literary considerations: he already struggled with debt, and throughout his life, the matter of who he owed money to was to figure in how he functioned. Dostoyevsky had gained advances from Krayevsky and he could not pay them back, thus whether his literary decisions were governed by political agreement with the aims of *Notes of the Fatherland* or whether it was because he was in debt to Krayevsky is unknown. Krayevsky was a shrewd businessman and not open to negotiation on the subject of money. He went on to ruin a friend of Dostoyevsky's, whom he exploited so badly after buying him out of twenty-five years of national service that the young man died in poverty and despair. Thus Dostoyevsky was unlikely to have been in a position to defect to *The Contemporary* alongside Belinsky, even if he had wanted to, and even though Nekrasov did try to persuade him to do just that. Despite the reputation of *The Double*, Dostoyevsky still had currency in St Petersburg literary circles and was still much sought after; both Nekrasov and Krayevsky saw that. However, a move to the rival publication would have cost Dostoyevsky money he did not have, so he and Belinksy compounded their split by working with different publications.

Fyodor's loyalty to his publishers, bought or otherwise, and his need to be published drove him on. But the fact that he was ostracised from the Belinsky circle limited his social interaction. The literary cliques dominated and determined social success in the 1840s, and now Dostoyevsky could no longer shift easily between the different circles. His split with Belinsky was public, but in private they still maintained an amicable relationship for some time. In his autobiographical writings collected decades later, *The Diary of a Writer*, Dostoyevsky was to reflect on his relationship with Belinsky, perhaps with rose-tinted glasses. He claimed that he was then 'passionately following all his teachings'. Eventually, though, even their more tacit relationship was to end in an exchange of sharp words early in 1847, with Dostoyevsky stating in the *Diary of a Writer* that Belinsky had taken a dislike to him and the friends had parted ways permanently. Fyodor Dostoyevsky was in danger of being ostracised completely. He needed to find another social circle and quickly, but his next choice was also his doom.[18]

5

ARREST

The year after their final argument, Belinsky died. Death had denied Dostoyevsky the opportunity for further public debate with his old sponsor and it had denied them both the chance for a real reconciliation. The night he heard of Belinsky's death, Fyodor was staying at the home of his friend and doctor, Stepan Yanovsky. Yanovsky had recently become aware of Dostoyevsky's state of health, often treating him for apparent nervous disorders or for hallucinations. Yanovsky recalls that during the night after Belinsky's death Dostoyevsky suffered some form of convulsions, possibly an early indication of the epilepsy which was not to be officially diagnosed until nearly a decade later. Intellectual debate continued among Belinsky's followers, but never with the same heat that the 'Furious Vissarion' had brought to the discussions. Moreover, times were changing, and many, including Dostoyevsky, were soon to pay a high price for holding and expressing radical views.

Despite setbacks, Dostoyevsky was still a well-known author and not, as yet, a revolutionary. His main concern was his work and its reputation. His first novel had been an unqualified success, and although his second book, *The Double*, had had a mixed reception, Valerian Maikov had defended it in *Notes of the Fatherland*. Thus Dostoyevsky remained a respectable author.

Where Belinsky objected to the portraits of human beings that Dostoyevsky conjured in his more folk-influenced tales, Maikov saw portraits of the 'psychology' of human beings. When he compared Dostoyevsky and Gogol he conceded that they both wrote about the real world, but that where Gogol was 'primarily a social writer' Dostoyevsky was 'primarily a psychological writer'[1] – and such a writer represented the physical environment only as a context for the psychology of the characters. He perceived that Dostoyevsky could represent the inner man and that this, too, was an admirable talent. These allies soon sought Dostoyevsky out and invited him to join another literary clique.

Dostoyevsky could not be without a circle for long. Even in his feuilletons in his earliest 'St Petersburg Chronicles', he described St Petersburg as a city full of different little cliques that functioned to support one another, sometimes to include, sometimes to exclude. In order to offset his fall from grace he made his own attempt to set up a circle and began hosting dinners at the Hotel de France, inviting a few old friends to join him, including the Maikov brothers. Dostoyevsky was outgoing and passionate; he may have been a deeply psychological writer, but perhaps this introspective depth could only have developed from the way that he embraced all those whom he met, from those he gave money to in the street to those he entertained at dinner – and those with whom he discussed the most dangerous ideas. Nevertheless, his need for company and his passion for discussion were to lead him to a new circle, one that professed much greater radicalism than did Belinsky's. He was invited to join the Beketov Circle.

Necessity may have brought Dostoyevsky into contact with the Beketov Circle, but he now began to make lifelong friendships. The views expressed by the members of the circle, like Dostoyevsky's, took much more account of Christianity than had the atheistic socialism of the Belinsky group. Theirs was a Christian socialist utopia: Christ and Christianity demonstrated socialist principles as they were meant to be. Christianity made it a moral imperative for the believer to act justly and to work to improve the lot of the poor. Jesus Christ in this view became both a model for ethical behaviour and a rebuttal of Fourierism, with its teaching that moral corruption results from an unjust environment. Jesus, born in an occupied country, suffered the ultimate injustice and yet did not turn into a murderer or a criminal. He was not shaped by what had happened to him but maintained moral integrity in spite of his environment.

This may have been a humanist approach to Christ's teachings and example, but these ideas were congenial to the Dostoyevsky who, despite his later claims in *Diary of a Writer*, had been offended when Belinsky had condemned the character Christ and the function of religion. Had the Beketov literary circle lasted longer, Valerian Maikov's leadership and the propagation of his ideas might well have stabilised Dostoyevsky's own vacillating Christian opinions. The Beketev group, however, disintegrated a short time after Dostoyevsky joined them. On this occasion it was not because of philosophical differences, but the result of a tragedy: Valerian Maikov died in a drowning accident aggravated by sunstroke. The death of Maikov left Dostoyevsky bereft. Valerian had effectively saved Fyodor's career, and he had defended his literature and affirmed his reputation; he was a great loss. However, Valerian's older brother Apollon was to remain a consistent and lifelong friend, whose guidance and support Fyodor was to appreciate in the dangerous years to come.

The disintegration of the Beketov Circle meant that, once again, Dostoyevsky found himself without a milieu, isolated from the social scene that supported and fed the literary life of St Petersburg. Perhaps as a result of his need to socialise, both as an individual and for his career, Dostoyevsky was able to adapt his thinking, possibly doing so without thinking but imitating instead for social affirmation. At that time his ideas were fluid enough to be moulded by the strength of the characters that he met rather than his own strength of mind. His next group of friends was to be a dangerous mix of strong-minded radicals.

Mikhail Petrashevsky was an outrageous man. He sported both the arrogance and apology of privilege. He had been educated at one of Russia's most exclusive schools, the Alexander Lyceum at

Tsarskoe-Selo. He had just graduated and loved the dangerous and the radical. He was prone to pranks and was reputed to have turned up at an Orthodox Mass dressed as a woman; on another occasion when he was asked to cut his hair, he had reported to the authorities sporting a luxurious wig. He owned a large library, mostly of banned books, which he lent out. He was one of the authors of a clever book called *A Pocket Dictionary of Foreign Words*, which used the pretext of defining new words to communicate radical ideas without incurring the wrath of the censors. He was impatient with bureaucracy, insisting that the officials follow legal codes to the letter, in order to demonstrate the futility of constant form filling. Petrashevsky saw bureaucracy as a legitimate target. He was the same age as Dostoyevsky and, like Fyodor, he was heavily influenced by Fourier and the desire to achieve a more just system for the Russian peasant; like Belinsky he wanted a socialist utopia, which he tried to establish. He was a man of action and, in 1847, he built a phalanstery based on the Fourierist model and moved forty peasant families into their new home; it was burnt to the ground in one night. Unabashed, he decided that lack of preparation had been the issue, in that he had failed to sufficiently enlighten those involved or those observing as to the true purpose and benefits of the commune. He decided to remedy this by setting up his own circle to propagate the enlightenment to all those who needed to understand the new society. Thus the Petrashevsky Circle was formed.

Petrashevsky was an admirer of Dostoyevsky and made the first approach to the young and vulnerable writer. One evening while walking in the Nevsky Prospect, Petrashevsky, who had been talking with a mutual friend of Fyodor's, approached him and asked him what ideas he had for his next story.[2] Dostoyevsky was flattered and soon found himself under the influence of the charming and radical Petrashevsky. Petrashevsky's literary and political circle met on Friday nights, and Dostoyevsky wasted no time and joined straightaway.

Like Belinsky, Petrashevsky advocated the ideas of Fourier, David Strauss and Feuerbach. Strauss had written a life of Christ that investigated the role of myth-making in the historical story of Jesus, and Feuerbach had stated that all religion was, in effect, man's wishful thinking. Petrashevsky had a low opinion of Jesus' capabilities as a revolutionary and referred to him as a demagogue who came to an unhappy end. Petrashevsky clearly had ambitions to do better. However, religion was not the only matter for debate. Petrashevsky, like Belinsky, believed in the inherent good in human beings; evil, he thought, was caused by an unjust environment. He believed that, should he start chatting with a murderer on a railway platform while waiting for a train, a transformation would take place. The two men would describe each other's life stories and, as a result of their mutual understanding, Petrashevsky would be able to convince the murderer that his crime was a product of his oppression; that he was not to blame as an individual, but that, as an individual, he could redeem himself from his crime. The conversation would end in tears, the two men on equal terms: one repentant for his crime because he was forced by circumstances to do something against his nature, and the other glad to have freed that murderer of his responsibility and guilt, having taken some of it himself. Both men would then be able to anticipate an ideal life in a better world.

Much of what preoccupied the political landscape of St Petersburg in the 1840s was debate, idle discourse without decision. Writers, thinkers and activists formed circles within circles to present and discuss their ideas on how the future of their beloved Russia might be progressed. During this period most of the circles that Dostoyevsky attended were simply that – little cliques of literary enthusiasts, who maintained an interest in politics, literature and enlightened discussion. The activism of these groups was limited and they revelled in a sense of freedom in which they could discuss, without interference, the future of their country. This outlook transferred itself to the Petrashevsky Circle, but their discussions were more targeted, more direct. They discussed passionately the injustices committed against the serfs and they posited the active need for reform. The discussions of the various circles in St Petersburg, as elsewhere in Russia, were no doubt influenced by an increasingly restless Western Europe, for Western Europe underwent its own change of mood – a change of mood that was to impact the polite, if rumbustious, literary circles of the St Petersburg nightlife.

1848 in Europe was a year of revolutions, the culmination of a dissatisfaction that created widespread restlessness across the continent and toppled the political status quo. In the February of 1848 the middle- and working- classes of Paris took to the streets, dissatisfied with reforms offered by King Louis Phillippe. By 24 February, fearing another bloody revolution, the king had fled and France had declared its Second Republic. This set off a round of revolutions across the continent: in Germany Kaiser Wilhelm IV was forced to offer a Prussian Assembly, in Austria students and workers succeeded in setting up a Constituent Assembly, and in Budapest, Prague and finally in Rome, where in 1849 the Pope was temporarily deposed, autocracy was challenged and shaken. But it did not last. The authorities responded swiftly and effectively: the French objected to the defeat of the Pope, and the Austrian army overwhelmed revolts in Vienna, Budapest and Prague. The nascent liberal impulse was crushed, and very soon Louis Napoleon was elected into office in France and set about reinstating the power of the monarchy. The 'People's Spring' had failed and the impulse for democracy was defeated; but in 1848 in St Petersburg, the tsar and the Russian aristocracy watched events in Europe with increasing alarm. In 1847, Tsar Nicholas I had made tentative proposals towards some improvement in legal status for the serfs, to alleviate the injustice of their enslavement, but little was done, and with the onset of unrest in 1848 all talk of reparation was silenced. The tsar and the authorities were unnerved and they became more suspicious of apparently harmless literary circles. In early 1849 they placed the Petrashevsky Circle under surveillance, sending in a spy, Pyotr Antonelli, who reported back on the conversations he heard.

This was compounded with the fact that within the Petrashevsky Circle itself, some of the group were dissatisfied with mere discussion and were looking for more direct action. A few thought it was time to stop talking and to start to do something about injustice. Dostoyevsky himself, while usually focussing his discussions on the role of literature, was passionate in his concern for the serfs. He could not separate himself from his childhood awareness of the damage that severe poverty did to people; the plight of the poor still provoked his outrage. He understood very clearly the relationship between life and good health and money and welfare, and the serfs did not even have a right to their own homes, let alone access to wealth. He also could not stand the use of violence against the weak and impoverished, and had been enraged by stories of violence – one story suggests that while in the military he witnessed a soldier having to run the gauntlet and was angered enough at that moment to challenge all with a revolution in military behaviour. Thus when he did address the Petrashevsky Circle on a political topic it was to put the case for the defence of the serfs, and his articulate defence of the serfs and their plight attracted the attention of one Nikolai Speshnev. Speshnev had recently returned from five years in Europe studying communism, revolutionary politics and, significantly, the effectiveness of secret societies as a revolutionary tool.

Both Petrashevsky and Speshnev went to the same school, the aforementioned Alexander Lyceum, but Speshnev disdained academia and did not graduate, preferring the wisdom of his own opinion and travel, which he could finance himself. Speshnev was the only genuine member of the monied gentry in the group, the one who could afford to live without work. Speshnev knew Petrashevsky in school, but unlike Petrashvesky he was not an exhibitionist. Mikhail Bakunin, a contemporary revolutionary who met Speshnev in Siberia in 1860, described him as 'quietly cold', and the wife of another acquaintance described him as carrying a 'look of melancholy' and having 'finely chiseled features'.[3] He also carried the romance of combat experience, and was said to have fought as a volunteer with the liberal Swiss Catholics against the Jesuits in 1843 – if it was not true, the rumour certainly added to his romantic aura. The fact that Speshnev had travelled, that he may have seen action and, ironically, that he had the money to support his causes made him more, not less, radical than his more hard-pressed colleagues in the Petrashevsky Circle.

At some point in his personal journey Speshnev had crossed over from radical liberalism to communism, and his experience abroad had given him training in how to run a disruptive underground movement. His reading took him beyond the more sentimental reformist discussions of the propagation of knowledge and a reliance on the enlightened bourgeoisie to propose and implement a new democracy. His reading took him to violence and direct action; it led him to revolution. French revolutionary thinking at the time included the circulation of a book by Phillipe Buonarotti, *The Conspiracy of Equals* (1828), which became the handbook on how to run a secret society and how to begin to destabilise an unjust society. This was the basis of Speshnev's reading. Its philosophy was materialistic and atheistic, and it was entirely utilitarian in outlook, propounding self-interest as its motivation and reason as its method to raise revolution. Some in the Petrashevsky Circle were enamoured of Speshnev and his ideas, and he soon found supporters for his, or Buonarotti's, ideas on direct action. Dostoyevsky became one of them, especially after Speshnev shrewdly lent him five hundred roubles and then refused to take it back – Dostoyevsky commented to his friend Yanovsky that now he had his own personal 'Mephistopheles'. Thus Speshnev, Dostoyevsky and others joined a circle run by Sergey Durov and Alexander Palm, both of whom were impatient with Petrashevksy's dithering approach to political activism. They formed, in effect, a circle within a circle, a secret society with specific aims and goals, a secret oath and a call to arms, come the revolution.

Secret societies pose a threat to any regime but especially an autocratic regime. A strong enough oath of allegiance to a group in opposition to the government could be incriminating in itself; it is a covert loyalty that entraps the member and allows the society to maintain an iron grip or threat, using its criminality as a spring. Speshnev had become an expert in this kind of manipulation. The increasingly paranoid Tsar Nicholas I opposed all secret societies:

any allegiance to any such society could be construed as treason and carried with it severe penalties, even the death penalty. The barricades and call to arms Speshnev had planned for in Russia had become a reality in France, and in Austria and Italy, albeit briefly. The tsar had backed down on his promise to improve the lot of the serfs, but he was not complacent. Hungary, on the borders of Russia, for a short time expressed some very radical views, and in its April Laws of 1848 freed its serfs and allowed them to cultivate the land they lived on as their own. It seemed to Tsar Nicholas that Russia was the only stable government in Europe, and he intended to keep it that way. He lent a great deal of support to the Emperor Franz Josef, then only eighteen, to put down the Hungarian rebellion, and at home he set up a committee to monitor all publications and to apply strict censorship. Schools and universities were seen as breeding grounds of subversion, and it became increasingly difficult to publish anything but the most reactionary works in support of Russia and the tsar. Thus the sleeper agent Antonelli continued to report back to the secret service on the Petrashevsky Circle, although he was not so aware of the inner group, the secret society coalescing around Durov.

Throughout his life Dostoyevsky asserted that he did not support violent revolution and that he did not conspire to assassinate the tsar. To be sure, this claim could not be contradicted, for Antonelli could find no evidence to the contrary. Neither could he be sure of the existence of the secret society, nor name any possible members of that society – but the open activities of the Petrashevsky Circle were incriminating enough for the authorities:

At the meeting held on April 15 (1849) Dostoevsky read Gogol's correspondence with Belinsky, and notably, Belinsky's letter to Gogol. This letter summoned a considerable amount of enthusiastic approval ... especially at the point where Belinsky says that religion has no basis among the Russian people.[4]

In July 1847 Belinsky had written a letter to Gogol, which was a rebuttal of some of the arguments that Gogol had presented for discussion in his work, *Selected Passages*.[5] In this work Gogol presented a more reactionary view of the Russian state and a more pious leaning than he had hitherto presented in his more satirical and damning treatises, such as *Dead Souls*, published in 1842. Belinsky's letter to Gogol became notorious and was promptly banned by the authorities – a ban that remained in place in Russia until 1905.

Religion was implicated in the discussions of the Petrashevsky Circle, as was social philosophy and the topic of direct action. Trying to find a way to combine these elements proved hazardous, both philosophically and physically, even without the detection of the more extreme secret faction. Belinsky's letter to Gogol was a catalyst for discussion and a target for the censors. Those who had followed Gogol and admired his earlier works saw his comments in *Selected Passages,* particularly an essay entitled 'Easter Sunday', as a betrayal:

> Since few wish to be identified with the practical suggestions offered by Gogol in *Selected Passages,* the possibility that the work is indeed 'Gogolian' is rejected. At best, it is slighted on the ground that the man who produced such fictional monuments was simply not the same man who produced *Selected Passages.*[6]

The *Selected Passages*, published in early 1847, was meant to be a continuation of *Dead Souls*, and it was something that Gogol struggled with until his death in 1851. The crux of the discussion for many of the politically active individuals of the time was the role of Christianity in Russian life. In *Selected Passages* Gogol propounded the idea that Russia had a more peaceful relationship with religion; in fact, he appeared to state that only Russian Orthodoxy had a pure relationship with Christ. This was his response to Western Christianity, which Gogol had experienced abroad and which he considered corrupt. Russian Orthodoxy, as he stated in 'Easter Sunday', was compatible with the better society that the progressive-minded sought to create in the Russian state. For Gogol, Christianity had gently embedded itself in the politics and traditions of the Russian people and should therefore remain as part of the life of the nation – much to the horror of his followers. Gogol appeared to be recommending the status quo.

The radical feeling at the time, perpetuated by Belinsky and certainly advocated by Speshnev, was that religion was a mechanism for oppression. In this view, religion was the manner in which government perpetuated its own power at the cost of the people. The promise of heaven was a lie, the suggestion that individuals could not redeem themselves without God was deceit, and Russian Orthodoxy should be swept away to facilitate a new, more just order. Belinsky was outraged by *Selected Passages* and found Gogol's piety anathema to the movement that he had hoped would change Russian society:

> You, as far as I can see, you do not properly understand the Russian public. Its character is determined by the condition of Russian society in which fresh forces are seething and struggling for expression; but weighed down by heavy oppression, and finding no outlet, they induce merely dejection, weariness, and apathy. Only literature, despite the Tartar censorship, shows signs of life and progressive movement.[7]

Thus he accused Gogol of not 'properly' understanding the Russian public, telling Gogol that they were 'weighed down' by oppression and should look to literature as the hope of progression. This echoed Belinsky's criticism of *The Double*, wherein he did not see the work as a means to progress the debate on how to improve the lot of the oppressed peoples of the Russian state. Dostoyevsky in turn was alarmed by the utilitarian approach that Belinsky had adopted. Belinsky insisted on the merits of a materialistic social utopia without reference to the spiritual or the Christian. Dostoyevsky attempted to point to the historical Jesus and his own propagation of compassion and justice to demonstrate that a socialist utopia could function in a Christian context. However, for Belinsky the only important utopia was a socialist one, one that could be enacted in the physical lives of the oppressed at the cost of the oppressor. The representation of the poor in *Poor Folk* chimed appropriately with Belinsky's desire to see the oppressed represented realistically, but the magical realism of *The Double* seemed a pointless fantasy that could offer no solution – and literature must offer a solution. Dostoyevsky remained loyal to many of Belinsky's ideas, including the notion that literature could disseminate ideas that could change the world; and, although Belinsky's death was to disrupt any possible reconciliation between the two, his letter to Gogol was to bring about unanticipated consequences. Belinsky used the letter to condemn Orthodoxy, and by so doing he attacked the very root of Russian social structures and the authority of the tsar over his people. Dostoyevsky read the incendiary letter aloud to the group, thus disseminating subversive literature:

> Such are the problems that prey on the mind of Russia in her apathetic slumber! And at such a time a great writer, whose astonishingly artistic and deeply truthful works have so powerfully contributed toward Russia's awareness of herself, enabling her as they did to take a look at herself as though in a mirror – publishes a book in which he teaches the barbarian landowner to make still greater profits out of the peasants and to abuse them still more in the name of Christ and Church ... And would you expect me not to become indignant?[8]

Belinsky went on to proclaim that Russia's future lay in the exposition of humanitarianism, atheism and materialism. There was little hope for the 'barbarian landowner'. The letter was radical enough, but in addition to the content of the letter, which chimed with Dostoevsky's own sympathy for the serfs, Fyodor read this letter to the circle not once, but in all three times. He reported this himself in evidence given after his by then inevitable arrest: that he read it once that evening, then Petrashevsky dropped round for a few minutes and Dostoyevsky promised to read it at his group, then some more people visited and he read and discussed it once again. On this last occasion there was a suggestion that the letter should be reproduced and distributed to the public; this compounded the original crime by suggesting that the treasonous letter could be given to those who did not seek to discuss it, so that they could be convinced into political action.

When Dostoyevsky defended himself, he always assured the authorities that his interest in the circles was literary; that it was music, company and literature that he sought, and if he occasionally became passionate about issues this was always in the context of a discussion of literature. Throughout the ordeal to follow, Dostoyevsky remained loyal to his friends and said little or nothing to implicate them in any conspiracy.

Despite these protestations of innocence, nearly forty years later his old friend Apollon Maikov described how, as early as January 1848, Dostoevsky came to see him, and in conversation managed to write off Petrashevsky as 'an empty chatterer'.[9] Fyodor further divulged that he had been commissioned by an inner circle, the Durov circle, to set up a press to print and distribute radical literature. He explained that in this way they would avoid the censor by distributing their material direct and underground. Strict censorship, he said, meant that the people could never be educated about new ideas, that there could never be a popular movement for change because the people would not know how their situation could be changed. The printing press was to be constructed from separate parts ordered from different parts of the city; it was a well-organised attempt at sedition, but it was still pen-and-ink. Maikov, however, understood all too well the dangers and tried to dissuade Dostoyevsky from this idea: '... and I remember – there Dostoevsky sat, like dying Socrates in front of his friends, wearing a nightshirt with unbuttoned collar, and exerting all his eloquence as regards the holiness of this affair, our duty to the fatherland.'[10]

Perhaps Dostoyevsky's involvement was motivated by duty or perhaps by his financial debt to Speshnev, his 'Mephistopheles'.

Whatever the reason, Dostoyevsky was getting more and more involved in what would be defined by the government, made nervous by the presence of sedition and revolution elsewhere in Europe, as a conspiracy to overthrow the tsar. Maikov warned Dostoyevsky in their discussion that this could lead to serious trouble. What kind of revolutionaries, he asked, would poets and artists make? Dostoyevsky begged Maikov to join the group, but he refused, although he promised to say nothing about it. Maikov remained true to his promise, only naming the conspirators after their deaths years later.

Dostoyevsky was not unaware of the seriousness of his situation, and his health began to deteriorate. His doctor and friend, Stepan Yanovsky, noted that he saw Dostoyevsky often during his association with Speshnev and treated him for nerves, hypochondria, dizziness and hallucinations. Some of these symptoms again may have been precursors of his epilepsy. Opinions vary as to when the seizures started. His old flatmate Grigorovich stated that Dostoyevsky had a convulsion when they came across a funeral procession in St Petersburg:

> Sometimes he would even have a fit on one of our few walks together. Once we chanced to come on a funeral. Dostoevsky insisted on turning back at once; but he had scarcely gone a few steps when he had such a violent fit that I was obliged to carry him, with the help of some passers-by, into the nearest shop; it was with great difficulty that we restored him to consciousness.[11]

Perhaps this was a result of the sight of the trappings of death. Sigmund Freud suggested that Dostoevsky's epilepsy was brought on by his father's death, although it is unlikely to have presented itself as early as that or it would have ended his career at the military academy. Dostoyevsky himself did not document regular seizures until 1860, and from there on he seemed to experience one every three weeks – although he also would have bouts of double seizures. Yanovsky noted that Dostoyevsky's best guard against his early nervous attacks was prayer, which perhaps explains why even though Dostoyevsky became increasingly involved with the Durov group, he remained loyal to a belief in God. He still did not have real faith in human nature; he could not bring himself to believe in humankind as the architects of their own salvation. His political and religious beliefs were in conflict, and he still found comfort in retreat to faith.

Whatever the source of his ailments, as the Durov conspiracy became more and more demanding, increasingly Dostoyevsky was plagued by ill health. He was in debt to Speshnev, who had succeeded in securing Fyodor's loyalty in spite of his better judgment to avoid close contact. The debt, or favour, may have been why Dostoyevsky could not back away from involvement in the conspiracy; he owed it to Speshnev, but he also feared that Speshnev would hand him over to the authorities if he did not do what was asked of him. That being noted, Dostoyevsky was convinced that the plight of the peasant and the serf must be alleviated. There could be no Holy Russia if there was no justice. Dostoyevsky was trapped by ideology, debt and his own impetuosity. He was now a sworn in member of a secret society, and as such he could not leave Durov's group or disassociate himself from the Petrashevsky Circle.

On 7 April 1849 the circle met beneath a portrait of Fourier to celebrate the philosopher's birthday. Dividing up his book and distributing it among themselves in segments for translation, they were now most definitely indulging in the propagation of subversive ideas. It was on this occasion that Dostoyevsky went still further and read and endorsed the letter from Belinsky to Gogol. The informer, Pyotr Antonelli, reported this to his masters, and the authorities then took that information to show to the tsar personally. The order was given to smash the Petrashevsky Circle.

It was four in the morning of 23 April 1849, just after Dostoyevsky had gone to bed, when he was disturbed by somebody in his room. As he woke up, he heard the sound of military boots and the rattle of a sabre in its holster. He was addressed by his military rank, 'Engineer Lieutenant Dostoyevsky', and informed that he was under arrest. He dressed hurriedly, all his books and belongings were pulled down from their shelves and his letters and writings were sealed with wax to prevent tampering. By the end of the following day he was in solitary confinement in a cell in the St Peter and Paul Fortress, a prison reserved for only the most dangerous criminals.

6

THE SHADOW
OF THE EXECUTIONER

Take a soldier and put him in front of a cannon in battle
and fire at him and he will still hope, but read the same
soldier his death sentence for certain, and he will go mad
or burst out crying. Who says that human nature is capable
of bearing this without madness? Why this cruel, hideous,
unnecessary, and useless mockery? Possibly there are
men who have sentences of death read out to them and
have been given time to go through this torture, and have
then been told, 'You can go now, you've been reprieved.'
Such men could perhaps tell us. It was of agony like
this and of such horror that Christ spoke. No, you can't
treat a man like that!

The Idiot.[1]

The walls of Alekseyevsky Ravelin in the St Peter and Paul Fortress
were thick, damp and lined with mould. The ravelin, the strongest
fortification in the prison, had housed and seen Alexei, the heir
apparent to Peter the Great, murdered, either deliberately or
accidentally on the order of his father. Alexei had only returned
to Russia on the insistence of an ancestor to Leo Tolstoy, whose
opposition to execution probably made him a convincing errand
boy. He returned from safety in Naples, hoping to be allowed to

live out his life as a private citizen. It was not to be: his disappointed father first tortured and then facilitated the murder of his own son. Such was the history of Dostoyevsky's gaol. The St Peter and Paul Fortress had many dark secrets, and had borne witness to the bodies of those too weak, or too long incarcerated to last their stay, taken out of the fort by night and ferried down the river to their graves. It had presided over the doom of the rebel officers who had challenged Tsar Nicholas I when he first came to the throne. It had now opened and slammed shut its doors on Dostoyevsky and his friends.

The prisoners of the Petrashevsky Circle were each placed in solitary confinement with only rats for company and very little light, except that which came from a high and heavily barred window. The cells were always dim, and the prisoners had to burn candles continuously so that the eyes that viewed them from behind the long, narrow slit in the door could see what they were doing and ensure their misery. At the start of their imprisonment they were allowed no letters, no books, nothing to write with and no tea. They were allowed little or no human contact; for all they knew they had been buried alive and left to rot, not only imprisoned but forgotten. Their rebellion, little more than a conspiracy, had been thwarted before they could attract any real attention to their cause. There had been no heroic acts by which the people could remember them and they hoped, and even Speshnev probably prayed, that there would be no martyrs.

In July, when conditions were eased and Dostoyevsky was allowed to receive and write letters, he wrote to his brother Mikhail: 'If I am not allowed to write I shall perish. Better fifteen years in prison with a pen in my hands!'[2] While enduring that very deprivation, however, he had continued to use his imagination, planning novels in his head. Permitted to use a pen and paper, he occupied himself and his imagination with writing these out and, while still in the fortress, he wrote a short story, 'A Little Hero', first published anonymously in 1857 while he was still in Siberia.

Solitary confinement, poor food, lack of information and little stimulation took their toll on the prisoners. When they finally saw each other again, almost eight months later, they were thin and unshaven, some very ill and others worn down by loneliness and fear. However, despite the fact that Dostoyevsky entered prison already run down, suffering from nervous exhaustion and perhaps showing some symptoms of epilepsy, his health did not deteriorate as drastically under the prison regime as might have been expected. He was surprised at how well he coped with the prison routine and squalid conditions. He wrote to Mikhail: 'Meanwhile I am still alive and well, for all that … I expected much worse, but now I see that there is such a store of vitality inside me that it cannot be exhausted.'[3]

Perhaps imprisonment even came as something of a relief to the cantankerous Dostoyevsky. Stepan Yanovsky had already observed how nervous and tense he was just before his arrest and had diagnosed several of his problems as hypochondria; Apollon Maikov had noted that Dostoyevsky was very agitated when he arrived on his doorstep that January night to try to persuade him to join the secret society and contribute to the printing press enterprise. Apollon had painstakingly explained to him the dangers of his activities and, though Dostoyevsky did not take his advice, he could not have failed to understand it. He must have been aware that such a venture could only be doomed. Dostoyevsky's oblique references to Speshnev as his own personal devil perhaps indicated an underlying anxiety that indicated that he both feared capture and exposure but was relieved once it happened. Dostoyevsky had been all too aware of the seriousness of the situation prior to his arrest and it was the tension and anxiety that had affected his health. Once the worst had happened and the uncertainty was over, perhaps he found himself able to cope. Now, he had only to live through the consequences of his actions: imprisoned, he would probably be sent to Siberia, but that would be the end of it. He need no longer speculate as to the severity of his punishment or agonise when judgment day might be. It had now arrived – or so he thought.

Even if his nervous disposition improved, Dostoyevsky still faced physical threats to his health in the Alekseyevsky Ravelin. The water always tasted foul and so, not surprisingly, stomach problems were a constant complaint for most prisoners. Dostoyevsky suspected that he suffered from scrofula, a form of glandular tuberculosis, but in spite of that he was still able to maintain his stamina and his 'vitality'. He told his brother, 'There has never yet been working in me such a healthy abundance of spiritual life as now.'[4]

Fyodor was not the only Dostoyevsky arrested that night in April. His younger brother Andrei was also arrested and imprisoned, even though he had nothing to do with the Petrashevsky Circle and very little to do with his brother's activities. Mikhail, their oldest brother, was on the fringes of the group through Fyodor's involvement. He had attended some of the meetings and shared some of Fyodor's views and aspirations. It was therefore probably Mikhail that the authorities were after, but they arrested Andrei because he had briefly met with Fyodor in the street prior to their raids. The group was under heavy surveillance by then and an identification of Andrei as Fyodor's brother may have been enough to condemn him.

Andrei spent only a short time in gaol and consequently was accused by some of pointing the finger at Mikhail, who was arrested a short time later. Fyodor did not believe these rumours:

> I remember, my dear, I remember when we met (I think it was the last time we met) in the famous White Hall. Then you would only to have had to say one word to the right person and you would have been freed at once, as having been taken by mistake in place of your elder brother. But you listened to my representations and entreaties; you great-heartedly comprehended that our brother was in straitened circumstances, that his wife had just had a child and not yet recovered – you grasped all this and remained in prison, to give your brother an opportunity to prepare his wife and as far as possible provide for her during what might be a long absence.[5]

Fortunately, Mikhail did not spend much time in gaol either. He was released when the inquiry concluded that there was not enough evidence to link him with a deep involvement in the conspiracy. Fyodor, however, was a different matter.

Dostoyevsky's defence was a masterpiece of articulation. He did his best not to incriminate himself but was even more successful in not incriminating anyone else. When his questioners tried to force him to admit that the group held radical views on subjects such as serfdom, censorship or the Church, he replied that there was usually so much arguing over these issues that he was at a loss to identify any united view that the Petrashevsky Circle might have held, let alone publish.

The existence of the secret society centring around Durov was never discovered. The bulk of the evidence against Dostoyevsky related to the acts when he had read three times in public Belinsky's letter to Gogol, and his intentions to set up a printing press. The tsar regarded the letter as a seditious document – a slander on Orthodoxy, the Russian people and therefore on the tsar himself. Dostoyevsky defended himself on the grounds that simply reading out the letter was no indication that he sympathised with its views: 'Let him (the informer) recall whether there was in my judgements (from which I refrained) – or even in the intonation of my voice, or in my posture during the reading – anything that could in any way demonstrate my partiality to one party in the correspondence over the other?'[6] When asked whether he agreed with Belinsky's letter, Dostoyevsky said that he did not agree with the 'exaggerations' in it. In this way he neither incriminated himself nor betrayed his real view of the infamous letter to Gogol.

His split with Belinsky was also a useful tool for his defence. It was, after all, public knowledge that he and Belinsky had become enemies. Besides, he pointed out, in order to understand Belinsky's letter some reference had to be made to Gogol's views in the work to which the letter was a response. Indeed, Dostoyevsky had disseminated that information with as much eagerness as he had Belinsky's letter. This evidence, he suggested, could indicate that he agreed with Gogol and not Belinsky, that he was, in fact, a defender of Russian Orthodoxy.

All the prisoners, including Dostoyevsky, were interrogated alone before a court of six senior officials. There is no evidence that these sessions of questioning were brutal, or that they were tortured. Dostoyevsky suffered no significant hardships except those which separation and the denial of liberty imposed upon him. Apollon Maikov, who was taken in for questioning, remembered laughing with his interrogators as he tried to sketch out for them the architecture of a Fourierist phalanstery.

Petrashevsky, however, claimed to have been treated quite differently. According to rumour, apparently originating with Petrashevsky himself, the tsar was so incensed by the man's impertinent attitude that he himself got involved with the interrogation. The tsar reportedly had electrical wiring connected between his palace and Petrashevsky's cell, so that he could inflict electric shocks on the man from the comfort of his home. It was also rumoured that the tsar personally took Petrashevsky a poisoned drink, which the prisoner refused; suspicious of the liquid, he stuck his fingers in it and was burned. There is little evidence to support these stories. They were repeated by someone who met Petrashevsky on the road to Siberia and who claimed to have seen the burns on his fingers. Years later Dostoyevsky was to say that Petrashevsky was not in his right mind. He may indeed have told the stories, but it is as likely that he was suffering paranoid delusions. An exhibitionist in his youth, the ignominy of imprisonment may have led him to exaggerate his captivity.

Officially, the tsar was not an interrogator. Among those charged with prosecuting the case, opinion varied as to the seriousness of the conspiracy. One senator, Lebedov, found that the group was unconvincing as the perpetrators of a serious threat – he called them the 'child conspirators'.[7] However, the man in charge of surveillance, Liprandi, felt that their conspiracy posed a far greater threat to Imperial Russia than that of a student rebellion constructed by amateurs. Liprandi may have picked up some hints of the existence of the secret society centred on the Durov group, and he may have perceived a potential for subversion that went far beyond the plan to buy a printing press. However, with no hard evidence he sensed more danger than he could prove associated with the small discussion group.

Dostoyevsky's conditions in prison began to improve. There was now tea as well as new linen, and he was allowed writing utensils and some reading matter. He wrote to his brother asking for a Bible and the works of St Dmitry Rostovsky, Metropolitan of Rostov in the seventeenth century. Rostovsky was a storyteller, not a theologian: his stories of saints and martyrs perhaps reminded Dostoyevsky of his old Scripture teacher who had brought Bible stories to life. Now alone, without the pressure of his peers who attacked Christianity and sometimes mocked Christ, Dostoyevsky began to rediscover some of the old biblical stories and the teachings of his childhood faith.

It is hard to determine just what went through his mind at this time, but it is possible that he began to recommit himself to the Christian faith during his prison years. He stated in *The Diary of a Writer* that at the time of meeting Belinsky he had 'passionately embraced his teaching'.[8] However, from the evidence of his own later opinions it would seem that prison was a turning point for his Christian beliefs. His later writings tend to dramatise and simplify autobiographical material. By 1870 he interpreted his pre-prison beliefs as a sell-out to atheistic socialism and his post-prison beliefs as a commitment to Christianity. It was probably not as simple as that, for there is evidence to support the idea that he did have a commitment to Christianity even during his turbulent youth. He and Belinsky certainly disagreed on the subject of Christ, and even in all the excitement of making new friends and testing new ideas Dostoyevsky never abandoned his childhood practices of attending religious services and observing fast days. Prayer improved his health and he could never quite countenance the utopian idea of humankind's innate goodness. Later in life Dostoyevsky was to become very much a part of the establishment of Russia, and it would be convenient to write off his youth as an aberration and to espouse, without doubt, the orthodoxy of the Russian Church. Dostoyevsky had the option to reject the tradition of Russian Orthodoxy or to continue in it – but he had no need to be converted to it. Thus Dostoyevsky's relationship with organised religion was a lifelong tension between acceptance and rejection of the tradition into which he was born. His time in prison gave him the opportunity to sit and weigh the various influences and ideas in his life so far. Alone and unhampered by the pressure of other people's opinions, he could approach the question of faith and interrogate it independently in order to form and strengthen his own convictions. Faith in Christ may have been a source of comfort for him; though it could not be for his peers Speshnev or Petrashevsky, it may still in a very real way have been Dostoyevsky's salvation.

Dostoyevsky was tried before a military court, which demanded much harsher penalties than would a civilian court. The conspirators, including Dostoyevsky, were sentenced to death in their absence. An appeal for clemency was made, to which the tsar acceded, but not without one final act of cruelty that was to cost one man his sanity. The tsar secretly commuted the sentences of all the prisoners to varying lengths of imprisonment in Siberia, but he insisted that the death sentences should proceed as though they were about to be carried out.

On the morning of 22 December 1849, after almost exactly eight months in gaol, the prisoners of the Petrashevsky Circle were roused from their beds and ordered to dress. All they had available to wear were the clothes they had worn in April when they were arrested: light spring clothes were not suited to the heavy snow and subzero temperatures outside. They were placed in covered carriages and driven to Semyonovsky Square. When they were let out of the carriages they saw each other for the first time since their arrests. Some of their number were so changed that they were almost unrecognisable; others seemed undaunted by the months in prison. They greeted each other and turned towards the square.

There, in the centre of a waiting crowd, was a scaffold hung with black cloth. Nearby were three stakes placed in the ground and a firing squad. It began to dawn on the conspirators just what lay in store. 'It's not possible that we'll be executed?' Dostoyevsky asked Durov.⁹ The question circulated silently among them.

It seemed unbelievable when their only offence was to talk, but the evidence before their own eyes was clear enough. In the cold and gloom, shivering in their spring clothes, they listened to the death sentence being pronounced over them and they went through the rituals of the condemned. Swords were broken over their heads, a priest called on them to repent and confess, but none was willing to renounce his beliefs and confess guilt. However, though they would not confess, they did all bend to kiss the cross. Dostoyevsky first watched and then went forward himself. Later he said that he felt he had understood nothing until he witnessed how his companions could not bring themselves to trifle with the cross: its great significance and the enormity of what was about to happen to them kindled in them a last hope of faith:

> Today, December 22, we were driven to Semyonovsky Square. There the death-sentence was read out to all of us, we were given a Cross to kiss, swords were broken over our heads and our last toilet was made (white shirts). Then three of us were placed by the posts for the execution of the sentence. I was the sixth in order, we were called out in threes, consequently I was in the second batch and had not more than a minute to live.¹⁰

It was a long and excruciating minute. The first three were led to the stakes, and Petrashevsky, who was among them, tried to joke and yelled to his colleague to pick up his feet from the snow or else he would go to heaven with a cold. Soldiers tied them to the stakes and pulled the hoods of the shrouds down over their faces. Petrashevsky, however, managed to shake his free: he would see the last seconds of the dawn and the face of the man behind the gun.

The firing squad took aim and stood ready to fire. The minute stretched out, elongated until it was ready to split, and still no one gave the order to fire. The men at the stakes shook with cold and fear. Dostoyevsky turned to Speshnev and said that they would soon be with Christ. Speshnev replied that it was all 'a handful of dust'.[11]

The seconds stretched into another minute. Suddenly the prisoners heard galloping hooves and Adjutant General Sumarokov rode into view. From his horse, with a resounding stutter, he painfully stammered out the commutation of the death sentence on all the prisoners. Instead of death, their destiny would be Siberia. The prisoners were stunned. The crowd was silenced for a moment with shock, perhaps even disappointment, while at the stake Nikolay Grigoryev went mad.

7

REPRIEVE

'He remembered everything with the most accurate and
extraordinary distinctness, and declared that he would never
forget a single iota of the experience.'
                          Prince Myshkin, *The Idiot.*[1]

On that cold, clear morning just before Christmas, the sun suddenly
shone brighter for Fyodor Dostoyevsky. He had faced death and
he had never felt more alive. Even the sight of the ten-pound
chains that he was soon to wear night and day could not dampen
his newfound hope. He had been resurrected, allowed a second
chance, and the air tasted sweeter and the prospects looked better
than ever before. Life not execution, prison not death, exile not
oblivion – life was all that was important to him now; the rest was
of little consequence beside the fact that he had escaped the firing
squad. Years later, Fyodor was to recount the experience through
the words of his fictional character Prince Myshkin, who claimed
to have spoken to a man who had been reprieved from execution
at the last minute:

A little way off there stood a church, and its gilded spire
glittered in the sun. He remembered staring stubbornly at this
spire, and at the rays of light sparkling from it. He could not

tear his eyes from these rays of light; he got the idea that these rays were his new nature, and that in three minutes he would become one of them, amalgamated somehow with them.[2]

The detail that Myshkin uses when describing this event to his newly found lady friends is clearly wrought from the last-minute thoughts of the young Dostoyevsky; the detail and the tension are all palpable, as is the irony. When the young ladies ask Myshkin what the reprieved man did with his life, his new 'eternity of days', expecting to hear that obviously he would have made the most of his new opportunity and second chance, Myshkin replies that sadly the man did not use his time well, that he wasted many, many minutes and did not live as he had intended. Whether or not this would be true of Dostoyevsky is perhaps for history to judge, but what that reply does indicate is the underlying theme: human beings alone cannot make the most of what they are given, even if it comes in the guise of a second chance.

The second chance came in the form of harsh punishment. Now the real sentences were read to the prisoners: Dostoyevsky's punishment was to be four years hard labour in a Siberian prison, followed by four years as a private in Russia's army and an indefinite exile to Siberia. During this time he was forbidden to write or publish anything. His sentence would begin in two days.

The more dangerous Petrashevsky, by contrast, was allowed no goodbyes to any but those in the square. He was to be exiled to forced labour in the mines immediately. He and the others were taken to another part of the podium where, as a prelude to their own futures, Petrashevsky's chains were hammered on. This was not an easy task and the blacksmiths struggled with the chains, so Petrashevsky, in a final act of exhibitionism before a large crowd, snatched a mallet from their hands and beat down on his own chains, fixing them securely to his ankles. It was the act of a defiant man, a man determined not to let the authorities grind him down. Gripped by tension but under control, Petrashevsky staggered clumsily to each of his comrades, hugging them and wishing them farewell. He then turned and stumbled towards the waiting cart. Once by the horses, he turned to look once more at his friends, drinking them in as they did him, and then bowed with a flourish, entered the cart and was driven away.

Back in his cell Dostoyevsky paced up and down, singing. The room was too small to contain his excitement. He was alive! What could so easily have been taken from him had been given back, and with it came a new responsibility: 'Now, as my life changes, I am born again in a new mould. I swear to you, brother, that I will not lose hope and that I will keep my body and mind pure! I shall be born again to better things. This is my one hope, my one consolation!'³ Thus Fyodor wrote to Mikhail while he was waiting for his sentence to begin. Throughout his life he had feared death; in fact, many of his early convulsions had been associated with images of death. Now he had got close enough to death to taste it, and had been given back his life. He was ready to grasp the new start and hold on to it.

Fyodor was reminded of the work of another novelist, Victor Hugo, in his book *The Last Day of a Condemned Man*. Dostoyevsky had come to understand the condemned man's feeling that all that mattered was that he could see the sun. Nothing else was important – not material gain, not achievement, not fame. Dostoyevsky's brush with death could have made him too terrified to move or function, lest he bring the wrath of the authorities down on his head again. It did not. In fact it made him bold enough to face and survive Siberia.

He applied to see Mikhail one more time before leaving for Siberia. He had no idea what awaited him, whether he would be able to write letters, or read, or ever be released from his exile. He wanted to see Mikhail for one last time. He hoped that they might one day meet again, but if they did not at least their farewells would have been said. Permission was refused, and for a while the exhilaration of reprieve was dampened by the prospect of separation without a fond farewell to recall during the bleak years ahead.

However, Mikhail had also been asking to see his brother, and with more success. On the evening of 24 December Mikhail and a friend, Milyukov, gained entry to the prison to see two prisoners,

Dostoyevsky and Durov, to wish them well on their journey and exile. The prisoners were brought into the room where Milyukov and Mikhail waited. Durov had suffered more severely from the prison regime. He was gaunt and ill, whereas Dostoyevsky, although drawn and hungry, was still healthy.

The Dostoyevsky brothers hugged one another and Fyodor began to reassure the uncertain Mikhail that all would be well. They would see each other again, he said. He was confident he would survive his time in Siberia. Fyodor joked to Mikhail that his prison sentence was a good way to do research: it would give him plenty of copy for future books. Mikhail was not so optimistic.

Milyukov remembered the scene clearly: 'When the Dostoyevsky brothers took leave of one another, it was clear to me that not he who had to go to Siberia, but he who remained in St Petersburg, suffered the more. The elder brother wept, his lips trembled, while Fyodor seemed calm and even consoled him.'[4] The visit was over all too soon, and now the Dostoyevsky brothers would be separated for nearly a decade. Dostoyevsky would not hear from his brother once during his four years in prison, a source of deep frustration and hurt to him. When he was released from prison, his first letter to Mikhail was as full of reproaches for not answering his letters as it was conflicted over whether those letters or their replies ever got through:

> For God's sake, tell me why you have not to this day written a single word to me. Could I have expected this? Would you believe that in my solitary position, imprisoned as I was, I several times fell into actual despair, thinking that you were not even on this earth, and then spent whole nights brooding over what would happen to your children and cursing fate because I could be of no use to them?[5]

Once the visitors had gone, the two prisoners were taken to have their chains fixed to their feet. The ten-pound chains were to be a permanent addition to their bodies for the full extent of their gaol sentences. They were given winter clothes to protect them on their journey, and led to separate open sledges so that they could pose no threat to their guards.

In the cold of the St Petersburg night the temperature was well below freezing. They were driven through the snow-solid streets of St Petersburg at the dead of night. The streets were deserted: it was Christmas Eve and Christmas celebrations and parties were in full swing. The city did not brood about the fate of its 'unfortunates', as the prisoners of Siberia came to be known in Russia. The sledges passed by the heated houses of the rich and the happy; the churches were preparing for their Christmas celebrations; music and candles filled the incense-rich cathedrals. In the house of Dostoyevsky's publisher, Krayevsky, Mikhail's children had an invitation to play, perhaps to give Mikhail a moment of relief from relentless celebration on this grim day. If Mikhail had looked out later that night, he would have seen his brother, huddled in the prison cart, as the sledges and their passengers passed by first his house and then Krayevsky's, where the children played.

Fyodor wrote:

> We were taken past your flat and I saw Krayevsky's was all lit up. You had told me that they were having a Christmas party and that the children had gone there with Emilia Fedorovna and now by this house I felt cruelly despondent. I took my leave, as it were, of the children. I hated to leave them, and afterwards even years later, how often I thought of them, almost with tears in my eyes.[6]

The sledges pulled away from the city lights and took to the open road, heading towards the majestic Ural Mountains, the great geographical barrier between European and Asian Russia. The relentless journey had begun: nearly two thousand miles to cover in less than three weeks. It was bitterly cold, bleak and lonely – and it was Christmas Eve.

8

THE WIVES OF TOBOLSK

> It was a sad moment when we crossed the Urals. The horses
> and sledges had floundered into the drifts. A snow-storm
> was raging. We got out of the sledges - it was night - and
> stood waiting while they were dragged out of drifts. All
> around us was the snow and the storm; it was the frontier
> of Europe; ahead was Siberia and our unknown fate, while
> all the past lay behind us - it was so depressing that I was
> moved to tears.
>
> Dostoyevsky, 'Letter to Mikhail, February 1854'.[1]

The journey had been harsh and bitter. Dostoyevsky had had to sit in the freezing cold for ten hours at a time. Even though he had by this time been given a covered sledge, he was still frozen to the marrow. Even so, he had been luckier than many; prisoners often were forced to walk at least part of the way and, as a result, some died en route.

It was with mixed emotions that Dostoyevsky approached the great divide between Europe and Asia: relief because the journey was half over, apprehension at the unknown future, grief over what he had left behind. He was an urban European, a city dweller, about to enter a great expanse of wild and underpopulated country. Gone were the stone buildings, the comforting log fires, the horses and carriages and the familiar faces of St Petersburg. He was now over a thousand miles away from his well-decorated, well-insulated rooms, even from the less well-appointed St Peter and Paul Fortress, and he was still at least five hundred miles from his destination at Omsk. Ahead lay the eastern steppes, with their nomadic tribesmen, hunters and trappers, unfamiliar languages, hostile climate, and a different dominant religion.

Most European Russians did not cross over to the Asian continent unless they were exiled or serving punishment, seeking adventure or sent there by the military or civil service. Imperial Russia was thus divided into two separate entities. In the fourteenth century Asian Russia had been dominant. Mongol armies had penetrated as far as the borders of Moscow and from their capital at Sarai their 'khan' had ruled the empire. But by the fifteenth century their empire had weakened, driven back to Asian Russia by the combined, although not allied, forces of Orthodox Muscovite Russia and the Turks, who conquered in the name of militant Islam. Consequently much of what was later to become Asian Russia was Turkish ruled and Muslim. Half the population of Semipalatinsk, the town where Dostoyevsky was to do his military service, was Muslim, as were several of his fellow convicts; when Dostoyevsky was released from prison and allowed to write to his brother, among the many books he requested was the Koran. Four years in Eastern Russia had introduced him to the Islamic way of life, and while he never expressed any interest in following it, he was always interested in exploring other faiths.

In Asian Russia the Petrashevsky prisoners would encounter not only a different dominant religion but different races of people. Moving there as free men would have been challenging enough, but to go as middle-class prisoners, unused to physical hardship or discomfort, was daunting indeed. They were to exchange solid brick walls, well-heated homes and comfortable well-covered beds for thin prison walls and bunk beds with few blankets, none of which afforded much protection from ferocious winter cold or sizzling summer heat.

The horrors of the life awaiting them seemed too great a misery for the younger of the two other prisoners who travelled with Dostoyevsky to Siberia. Jastrzenbski, sentenced to six years hard labour and destined for a different prison from Durov and Dostoyevsky, was in despair. One night he announced that he had decided to kill himself. His life was in ruins – better to end it, he said. His two companions went into action to cheer him up: Durov negotiated with the guards for some tea, and Dostoyevsky produced some cigars that he had hidden and saved. The three men talked long into the night. The atmosphere was congenial and their conversation did not dwell on the miseries they were to face. They merely enjoyed one another's companionship and conversation, aspects of life that could not be spoiled by imprisonment or the prospect of a dismal future. Their companionship blocked out the sights they had already seen, of prisoners chained to a wall unable to move, thus punished because of their adjudged dangerous temperaments. It blotted out, too, the sounds of howls and drunken behaviour coming from the neighbouring cells of the prison in which they were temporarily housed. The three men who smoked and drank tea must have felt a little as though they were to be flung into the lions' den. They were not from the same class as most of the other prisoners, nor did they have the same physical strength or history of violence. They could hope for little camaraderie with the peasants and common criminals and certainly could expect no welcome from anyone. However, as the night deepened and they grew warm with the tea and cigars, Jastrzenbski changed his mind. He still had no illusions about what was to come, but he felt able to face it. Dostoyevsky's calm acceptance of his own fate soothed the younger man, and he parted with his friends in a much better humour. Jastrzenbski went on to serve and survive his sentence, and lived to tell the story of that night.

Now that Dostoyevsky and Durov had arrived at Tobolsk they were to make their last contact for four years with their compatriots from European Russia who valued freedom of thought and justice. Dostoyevsky wrote to his brother Mikhail:

> I wish I could tell you in detail of our six days in Tobolsk and the impressions they left on me, but this isn't the right place. I will only say that the sympathy and lively concern we met

with blessed us with almost complete happiness. The exiles of the old days (that is, not they themselves but their wives) looked after us as though we were their own flesh and blood. What wonderful people, tried by twenty-five years of sorrow and self-sacrifice! We had only a glimpse of them, for we were strictly confined. But they sent us food and clothing, they consoled us and gave us courage.'[2]

These 'exiles of the old days' were the Decembrists, men who had challenged Nicholas I upon his accession to the throne. Dostoyevsky knew of their rebellion and fate, and in some ways the aims of the Petrashevsky and Durov circles were not dissimilar; they were, in a way, taking up the anthem. The Decembrists themselves had been officers of the army who had tried to use their positions of authority to educate the mass of the army and persuade them, unsuccessfully, to rise against tsarism. The death of Alexander I had caught them by surprise, but an empty throne and a hesitating Grand Duke was too good an opportunity to miss. However, they were able to gather only three thousand men in the Senate Square. When the tsar tried to disperse the uprising without bloodshed they shot his negotiator dead. The tsar ordered his superior forces to fire on the protesters, and they fled to carry on a sporadic but doomed revolution.

The Decembrists are considered by many historians to be the first precursors of organised revolution in Russia. But this was not the first time the government in Russia had been challenged by its own people. Russian history is scattered with uprisings and mutinies, and the Decembrists may have been just another such mutiny. The Decembrist uprising in 1825 was the first mutiny to go beyond the point of a local and specific rebellion and thus to articulate aims and ambitions not just for themselves but also for the people as a whole. They were the first to possess a manifesto. Their rebellion was not motivated by dissatisfaction with a senior officer or by lousy pay, they had instead thought through a political agenda that would serve the people and make Russia a better place; their demands were not for themselves but for the people. Despite their noble ideals, they had not been able to disseminate their ideas sufficiently to convince the people they were trying to help, and so met with no popular support. After the uprising was crushed, the sentences given out ordered execution for five men, exile for life for some, and for the remaining participants hard labour or lesser periods of exile in Siberia.

When the survivors were sent to Siberia their wives followed, forsaking the comforts of the city for a harsh life on the border between Asian and European Russia. They were tough, faithful women and it was some of these individuals who now, at Tobolsk, Dostoyevsky's last major stop before prison, persuaded the authorities to let them meet with the prisoners and cook them some hot food. Among the women was Natalya Fonvizina, wife of General Mikhail Fonvizin. Natalya was nobility; she had come from a rich family and married a wealthy man in order to protect that wealth. She was pregnant with her oldest son when her husband was sentenced to hard labour, and it was from Dostoyevsky and Durov that she learned that that son, also named Mikhail and one of their circle, had died of consumption. She had been in Tobolsk for over twenty years, but she was undaunted. She had taken with her to exile a great love of literature. Dostoyevsky, a writer, was a kindred spirit, and through mutual misfortune and mutual interests they struck up a friendship that they were able to maintain through correspondence in future years:

When I last wrote, I was sick in body and soul. I was consumed with longings, and I daresay my letter was quite senseless. That long, colourless, physically and morally difficult life had stifled me. It is always grievous to me to write letters at such times; and I regard it as cowardice to force one's sorrow on others, even when they are very fond of one. I send you this letter indirectly, and I am glad to be able to speak with you quite unconstrainedly at last; all the more because I have been transferred to Semipalatinsk to the seventh battalion, and therefore don't at all know in what way I may be able to correspond with you in future.[3]

Besides food the women gave each prisoner a copy of the New Testament, the only book they were allowed to possess in prison and one that Dostoyevsky was to treasure for the rest of his life. During the four years in prison it was virtually his only reading matter, and when he died, thirty-one years later, it was clasped in his hands. When he left prison he wrote to Natalya Fonvizina describing to her something of the faith that he had rediscovered, perhaps partly through his many readings of that New Testament.

The Decembrists' wives' ministrations were not only of the spiritual kind. Inside each book jacket they slipped a ten-rouble note to give the prisoners some bargaining power when they arrived. They also provided information about the prison to which Dostoyevsky and Durov were going. The governor, they said, was a reasonable man, but they must watch out for Major Krivtsov, who was a drunkard and a thug. Dostoyevsky later described him as a 'brute in human form', who was given to punishing and beating prisoners at a whim. Dostoyevsky did indeed come across this man, and some have suggested that a punishment meted out by the Major caused Dostoyevsky's first major epileptic fit.

The wives also arranged for the prisoners to be carried by coach to their gaol and so not risk death by walking in the bitter Siberian cold. They promised too that they would write a letter to the governor of the prison requesting that these prisoners be given the courtesy due to their station. Unfortunately their letter arrived at the same time as one from the Tsar's office, stating that under no circumstances were these prisoners to be given any special treatment. The governor had little choice in the matter.

The meeting with the Decembrists' wives was over all too soon, a single episode of kindness and camaraderie that would soon be all that would sustain the two men through the hardships to come.

Dostoyevsky and Durov were taken in the driving snow to Omsk and their prison. As they left the town, Natalya Fonvizina and a companion made their way to the road where they had arranged with the sleigh driver to let them meet once more. The two men said one last farewell before ascending their sleigh again and, watched by the two figures wrapped tightly against the subzero cold, they disappeared into the white of the steppe.

9

THE 'UNFORTUNATES'

'Bring the rods!' was the cry when Fyodor was caught napping by the infamous Major Krivtsov. Here was a gift, an opportunity to administer a punishment to discourage the others and satisfy a drunken, sadistic urge. In fact, Dostoyevsky had permission to be resting as he was unwell, and it was against the law to punish or put to work sick prisoners. The cause of his sickness may have been an epileptic fit: a naval cadet nearby defended Fyodor on just that basis, and it seems possible that the fit came before and not after the proposed punishment. The punishment itself was never enforced, for the same cadet rushed off to get his commanding officer: 'General de Grave came at once to the guard-room and stopped the whipping; while to Major Krivtsov he administered a public reprimand, and gave orders that in no circumstances were ailing prisoners to be subjected to corporal punishment.'[1] Rarely does life present such satisfactory conclusions, although, no doubt, this incident did not endear Dostoyevsky to the brutal Major Krivtsov, whose punishment had been thwarted and whose pride had been publicly bruised.

Aside from avoiding confrontations with Krivtsov, Fyodor no longer seemed to be affectionate towards Durov. This was noted by Martyanov, who had been present at the St Peter and Paul Fortress when Dostoyevsky said goodbye to his brother, and who continued to research Dostoyevsky's time in prison for his own memoirs. He noted that the other prisoners saw no interaction between Durov and Dostoyevsky soon after they arrived. Gone was the camaraderie of Tobolsk, where they sat with their young companion prisoner, Jastrzenbski, and persuaded him to reject suicide and live through the hardships to come. Gone was the passion of the circle, the need to disseminate the knowledge of revolution to all around them. In fact, no one at Omsk saw Durov and Dostoyevsky speak to each other, and when they were placed in the same room they were monosyllabic. The recollections of other prisoners suggest that the two men had quite different personalities. Both wore the prison uniform of grey-and-white striped summer shirts with yellow badges on the back, and short sheepskin jackets for winter; but Durov wore his uniform with style and conducted himself with an open and friendly personality, whereas Dostoyevsky was less popular. He was monosyllabic to all – no one could recall seeing him smile – and he wore his cap over his eyes and was generally awkward with those around him. He could work hard and stay fit, but he may have been overshadowed by the ease with which Durov could relate to his fellow prisoners. Dostoyevsky kept to himself; any support he could have elicited from Durov he seemed to eschew. And, while he did not provoke dislike or malice, on the whole the prisoners avoided him.

Fyodor's prison term was a turning point in his life, and perhaps his rejection of Durov was an indication of his change of mindset. Such was the change in his circumstances – from minor noble and famous author to commoner stripped of all privileges, including liberty – that a change in his outlook was almost inevitable. In later years he was to trace many of his views about the Russian people and their faith to what he learned in prison. In Siberia he was compelled to live in close proximity with people he would never normally have met, and despite his reticence to communicate – one prisoner described him as a 'wolf in a trap'[2] – this forced an unexpected comradeship on him, and effected a profound change in his attitudes and his plans for the future.

Dostoyevsky arrived at Omsk gaol with a mixture of contradictory beliefs, beliefs for which he had sacrificed his freedom. Siberia, for all its hardships, was indeed a catalyst for his thought processes; as he had said to his brother when they had parted, there was much to be observed, much to be written about. However, his immediate task was to survive his new status as prisoner and peasant, not to plan for the future. He could do no more than hope that his old privileges and life would one day be restored, and that then he would then have the opportunity to assess and absorb what he was learning and experiencing.

The circumstances of Dostoyevsky's confinement were so dramatic that the urge to use them as material for a book was irresistible. In many of his novels he portrayed parts of his own life story and even parodied his friends and colleagues. Nowhere is this autobiographical detail more apparent than in the short novel many consider to be his first masterpiece, *The House of the Dead*, an account of his time in prison. Censorship rules prohibited his simply writing and publishing a straightforward autobiographical account of what had happened to him in prison, but he wanted to use what he had seen and suffered in his work. He wanted to give readers a chance to experience the reality of being an 'unfortunate', as the local residents called the prisoners. Thus he wrote a novel rather than a journalistic report and was thereby able to get his book published without offending the censors, clearing the way for further publications.

The House of the Dead was published in 1860, over a decade after Dostoyevsky was first put in chains. The book deals clearly with the subject of his prison years, without breaking the censorship laws. Just over a hundred years later, Truman Capote was to mix fact and fiction in his true-crime novel *In Cold Blood* about the murderers Perry Smith and Dick Hickock, who killed a family in Middle America in cold blood. Capote wove the real events and research gathered from interviews into a novel format in a new genre that became known as 'creative non-fiction'. Dostoyevsky got there first. *The House of the Dead* uses a simple fictional device: the narrator discovers in the belongings of a recently dead convict a manuscript describing that convict's time in gaol. This device is used by Peter Carey in *True History of the Kelly Gang*, also considered a masterpiece of the genre of creative non-fiction. In this case the convict is fictional, unlike Ned Kelly. Dostoyevsky's protagonist, Alexander Petrovitch, is convicted of murdering his wife and sentenced to ten years in prison in Siberia. The crime is different and the sentence is longer; but, once the narrative begins, the experiences described are those of Fyodor Dostoyevsky:

> Fearfully I raise my head and in the fitful candlelight gaze at my slumbering companions. I watch their unhappy countenances, their miserable beds. I view their nakedness, their wretchedness, and then convince myself that it is no nightmare but simple reality. Yes, it is reality. I hear a groan. Someone has moved his arm and caused his chains to rattle. Another is troubled in his dreams and speaks aloud, while the old grandfather prays for the 'Orthodox Christians'. I listen to his prayer, uttered regularly in soft, rather drawling tones: 'Lord Jesus Christ, have mercy on us.'[3]

The book did not violate the censorship laws, but its readers understood that the story was based on Dostoyevsky's own experience. The censors probably understood this as well, but the account is a good read – although the use of a fictional protagonist did rebound on Dostoyevsky, as he commented years later that some people still believed that he himself had been exiled for murdering his wife.

There were fifteen hundred posts in the prison fence at Omsk, and the prisoners used them to count off the days of their confinement. When a prisoner had counted them all, there was cause for great celebration. Prison conditions were hardly bearable. Thirty men were locked up in one long barrack room for the duration of the hours of darkness. Their beds were boards and they had little protection from the heat or severe cold. In winter they were issued sheepskin coats, which they wore during the day and slept under at night. The room was full of smoke and dirt, and it stank. The cold in winter was so severe that the one stove they had in the barracks could not thaw the ice, three inches thick, that was always on the windows. Looking back on it, Dostoyevsky was surprised that he ever got used to these conditions, but perhaps he was stronger than he realised.

The food was not so bad and the hard labour was not cruelly inflicted. He endured no individual torture, either physical or mental, and it is unlikely that he suffered any extra punishment. Other Petrashevskyites were treated as political prisoners, but in Omsk gaol Dostoyevsky was a common criminal: this made him anonymous and attracted less attention, attention in such situations usually being undesirable. His prison was not like the labour camps more recently portrayed in the novels of Alexander Solzhenitsyn; nor did he suffer the kind of brutality meted out in the 1970s and '80s to Anatoly (now Nathan) Sheransky, or the indignity of a psychiatric ward. Russian prisons of the nineteenth century were run with some sense of humanity, aided by geographic isolation and the harsh weather to make sure the prisoners understood they were receiving a punishment.

Nevertheless, to suffer the deprivation of liberty, in a place where the temperature can reach 40 degrees below freezing, to be deprived of the opportunity to write and, most important for Dostoyevsky, never, never to be left alone – this was harsh punishment indeed for the crime of reading out a letter and planning to buy a printing press.

It was the constant companionship of other prisoners that was hardest part of prison life for Dostoyevsky: 'Could I ever have imagined the poignant and terrible suffering of never being alone even for one minute during ten years? Working under escort in the barracks together with two hundred "companions": never alone, never!'[4] So spoke Alexander Petrovitch in *The House of the Dead*. For Dostoyevsky himself it was 'only' four years.

Occasionally the guards took the prisoners for a steam bath. This was a common tradition in Russia and remains so to this day, including the practice of self-flagellation. The heat was a good antidote to the winter weather and a good opportunity to sweat out the dirt. The prisoners sat or stood tightly packed in a steaming room. Dostoyevsky was found a seat, which he had to pay for, next to a fellow prisoner. He commented,

> The common people do not care to wash with soap and water; they prefer the horrible method of stewing and then douching themselves with cold water. Below I could see fifty bundles of twigs rising and falling; the holders were whipping themselves into a state akin to intoxication. The steam became thicker and thicker every minute, so that what one now felt was not a warm but a burning sensation, as from boiling pitch. The convicts shouted and howled to the accompaniment of the hundred chains shaking on the floor … It seemed to me that if ever we met in hell we should be reminded of this place.[5]

Dostoyevsky was one of only a few noblemen in the prison. Until he arrived there he had no idea how hostile the peasant classes and serfs were towards noblemen, however humble: 'Their hatred for the nobility is boundless; they regard all of us who belong to it with hostility and enmity. They would have devoured us if only they could.'[6] The peasants did not ask why such men were in prison; they saw all noblemen as oppressors and held them each personally responsible for the exploitation of their class.

One of the other noblemen was a prince, accused of having brutally murdered his father. The evidence against him was overwhelming; all of his local community was convinced that he did it, and he was serving a long sentence for the crime. Dostoyevsky, however, felt that the man seemed incapable of committing such a crime, and the prince himself claimed that he was innocent. There were very few convicts in prison who

Dostoyevsky felt were unjustly imprisoned, but this man did seem to have suffered an injustice. Years later, after a copy of *House of the Dead* had reached someone who knew of the case, Dostoyevsky learned that the prince had finally been vindicated. Another man had confessed to the crime and the prince was released, but the best years of his life were gone. In Dostoyevsky's last novel, *The Brothers Karamazov*, one brother, Dmitry Karamazov, suffers a similar fate. The evidence that he murdered his father is overwhelming and all those around him believe he committed the crime – his fate is sealed and prison is his destiny.

Apart from the prince and a few others Dostoyevsky had little noble company, and his relationships with the other men were always precarious. Occasionally he was offered reading material, but only accepted works by Charles Dickens, *David Copperfield* and the *Pickwick Papers*, which were to be his much-favoured novels in time to come. Pickwick, in particular, may have influenced Dostoyevsky's character of Prince Myshkin in *The Idiot*.

Work assignments, especially at the beginning of his sentence, were where the difficulties were most apparent. He did not shirk his duties and could put in a good day's labour, although that may not always have been appreciated. The convicts did as little work as they could get away with and did not welcome help from a nobleman. Instead, they behaved like a gang of schoolchildren who have decided to ostracise one of their number. Early in his sentence, Dostoyevsky was sent with a party of convicts to dismantle a barge. This task was performed slowly, until the convicts were told they could go back to the barracks as soon as it was done. Then, said Dostoyevsky, the convicts became suddenly 'intelligent' and got on with their work efficiently and quickly. As for him, however, 'I seemed all the time to be in somebody's way ...'[7] A barrage of unhelpful and mocking remarks was flung at him. He was told to 'clear off' or 'get out of the light', sworn at and informed that he was not wanted. In the end he gave up and sat down. It was no comfort that he had had a restful day, for prison could only be bearable if he could make friends with the men, or at least be tolerated by them. However, his habit of pulling his cap down over his face and being taciturn with his comrades was not likely to endear him to them. Some, however, did recall him as a popular soul and as the producer of the prison play, which turned out to be a great success; some of the prisoners' performances, Dostoyevsky claimed, were the best he had ever seen.

Even so, he made few individual friends in prison – and not always on the terms he would have liked. One man adopted him as his master and took pains to serve him tea and generally look after his needs – all whilst robbing him incessantly. Others simply avoided him, and whatever had happened between him and Durov never healed. This erratic behaviour and other similar examples of capriciousness no doubt contributed to a change in Dostoyevsky's view of humankind: he came to prison a martyr for a socialist cause, a cause convinced that people are fundamentally good, made evil by their environment. Socialism propagated the idea that a man who was beaten, starved, unjustly treated and denied access to a better life could not be held responsible for his character. Given better circumstances, he would be a better man; if food, good treatment, education and justice were made equally available to all, then strife and warfare would disappear. Dostoyevsky had never been completely convinced by that argument, and what he saw in prison did not disabuse him of the underlying philosophical conviction that man was inherently inclined to sin.

When Dostoyevsky left prison, he was more certain that evil came from the inner man, not his environment:

During many years I never remarked the least sign of repentance nor even the slightest uneasiness in a man with regard to his crime, and that most of the convicts considered neither honour nor conscience, holding that they had a right to act as they thought fit. Certainly vanity, bad example, deceitfulness, and false shame were responsible for much. On the other hand, who can claim to have sounded the depths of those hearts given over to perdition, and to have found them closed to all light? It would seem indeed that during all those years I should have been able to detect some indication, however fugitive, of some regret, of some moral suffering. I positively saw nothing of the kind.[8]

Despite this, Dostoyevsky had not lost his faith in justice or in his desire to fight for fair treatment for all human beings. But the philosophy that had been at the centre of his socialist thinking collapsed. No longer could he believe in the man who would willingly be unenvious, loving and content in one of Fourier's phalansteries. Dostoyevsky was now convinced that humankind was a fallen race.

His prison experience also made him more critical of the penal system. Prison, he said, was not an effective means of rehabilitation: a prison term did more to reassure society than to benefit the prisoner; hard labour only reinforced feelings of hatred, pride and anger. The only 'rehabilitation' that the inmates themselves wanted was to find ways to make money, most of which they spent on drink: 'The convict is greedy for money, to the point of madness, and if he throws it away he does so in order to procure what he values far above money – liberty or at least some semblance of liberty.'[9] Convicts thought up all sorts of ways to make money such that even the prison dogs were not safe: one very endearing animal friend of Dostoyevsky's finished up as the lining in a pair of boots that were sold to the wife of a local official.

Very little was sacred among the prisoners, but Dostoyevsky noticed that they respected each other's religions. When they took part in church rituals they did so with respect and dignity, in contrast to their often petty and drunken behaviour. In *The House of the Dead* Dostoyevsky recalls the way the prisoners prostrated themselves with fervour at Lenten services.[10] They found particular significance in the fact that Jesus had saved the thief on the cross.

Dostoyevsky watched them as each went forward with his farthing to give for the collection or for a candle. Through their actions and their piety they seemed to say, 'I too am a man.' He speculated that as they said their prayers, not only before God but before the noblemen and the free men of the town, they may have said, 'Before God we are all equal.' Of the services themselves, he wrote, 'The Lenten services, familiar to me from early childhood in my father's house – the solemn prayers, the protestations – all stirred in me the memory of things long, long past, and awoke my earliest impressions to fresh life.'[11]

In prison, nevertheless, holy days and feast days were not happily anticipated. The men drank, gambled and brawled their way through their time off, and the guards kept clear of them as they grew steadily drunker and more argumentative. Dostoyevsky wrote of one holiday: 'I could never understand how it was that within five minutes of the governor's departure the room was full of drunken men, all of whom had appeared stone-cold sober as long as he remained.'[12] Drunkenness often turned to violence. After one particularly brutal Easter-day brawl, he records in his *Diary of a Writer*, he went back to his barrack room and lay down on his bunk feigning sleep to avoid being bothered by fellow prisoners. This gave him time to recall that summer's day in Darovoye when he ran for comfort to the peasant for fear of the wolf. Peasant Marey's kindness to him that long-ago day showed him that, while a pleasant environment might not make a person righteous, a harsh environment did not necessarily make him evil. This realisation left him with a basic contradiction in his view of human nature: people could do evil without provocation, but they could also do good in the face of provocation. His later portrayals of men such as Raskolnikov in *Crime and Punishment* illustrated this dilemma: in one man both tremendous evil and tremendous love can be expressed: in one world both destruction and salvation are at work.

Dostoyevsky, then, gave up the Romantic idea of man as a 'noble savage', but he did not give up on the human race. Now, even though he believed that humanity lived in a state of sin, he also came to love and respect the common people much more than he had before. Their resilience in the face of a society loaded against them was much to be admired. Even though he withdrew from many of those around him because he deplored their behaviour, he saw in them a simple, unquestioning faith that he came to believe was the essence of salvation. He was not necessarily conscious of these changes in his worldview while he was still in prison. It was with hindsight that Dostoyevsky came to terms with much of what he had learned in prison and thence organised it into a coherent creed.

10

FREEDOM IN EXILE

One afternoon, when the drum beat for work, they took the
eagle, tied his beak (for he assumed a desperate attitude),
and took him out on to the ramparts. The twelve convicts
forming the gang were extremely anxious to know where he
would go. It was a strange thing; they all seemed as happy
as though they had themselves obtained their freedom.
Dostoyevsky, *The House of the Dead*.[1]

Dostoyevsky received a form of freedom in February 1854, but
although his prison sentence was completed, his punishment was
not over. In March of that year he was given the rank of private and
was sent to join the Seventh Siberian Regiment in Semipalatinsk,
an outpost town close to the Russo-Chinese border.

Semipalatinsk had a population of about six thousand,
approximately half of who were Muslim. Outside the town the
Kirghizes, nomads of the steppe, camped, coming in to more
permanent homes only during the winter months. There were
seven mosques in the town and one church. Like most frontier
towns, the people were hardened by their harsh living conditions,
and money and self-interest dominated their lives. The Orthodox
Church seemed to have little relevance to their daily struggle to
scratch a living out of the tundra.

In this difficult town, nicknamed 'The Devil's Sandbox', Dostoyevsky resumed his career in the army. His length of service had been set at four years but the confiscation of his civil rights was indefinite. Dostoyevsky had a long way to go before he could call himself a free man. His first act on leaving prison was to write to his brother Mikhail in St Petersburg. In this letter he first of all reproached his brother for not having answered his letters to him, not knowing whether to blame Mikhail for not replying or to blame the authorities for intercepting or failing to deliver the letters.

He told his brother all he could about the past four years, describing prison conditions and some of the difficulties he had suffered. Despite it all, he reassured Mikhail that he was still reasonably healthy and looking forward to his new start. Finally, and inevitably, he asked his brother to send him some books, including the Koran and Kant's *Critique of Reason*.

Dostoyevsky had been almost totally without books for almost four years. Work had been relentless; time to read the Dickens he had managed to get his hands on was limited, and his only respite was the times spent in hospital where he could read. Dostoyevsky devoured his reading matter voraciously and secretly. He came to admire Dickens, and his own literary representations of the poor have often been compared with those of Dickens. The two writers' descriptions of the living conditions of the urban poor had a similar impact on readers: for the first time the more affluent gained some insight into what it was like to be poor in Dostoyevsky's Russia or Dickens' London. Sometimes when Dostoyevsky stole some reading time, he was genuinely sick, but sometimes he got a little extra time in bed and a little reading, courtesy of a sympathetic doctor. His enthusiasm to read overcame his repulsion at having to endure hospital routine and, most particularly, hospital garments:

It [his dressing gown] exhaled a most offensive odour which contact with my body helped to bring out. It smelt of plasters and medicaments of all kinds, and seemed as though it had been worn by patients from time immemorial; the lining had, perhaps, been washed once, but I would not swear to it. Certainly at the time I put it on it was saturated with lotions and stained by contact with poultices and plasters of every imaginable kind.[2]

Dostoyevsky sent his first letter to Mikhail through unofficial channels because its contents gave away too much about prison conditions, and it would have been intercepted and censored by the authorities if it had been posted in the ordinary way. (All Dostoyevsky's post was to be monitored for many years to come.) However, he asked Mikhail to reply through the normal post, probably in the hope that such a reply would take less time to arrive and attract less attention.

In Semipalatinsk Dostoyevsky was a prisoner on the outside. He still wore the red cap showing he was a convict soldier; he still could not publish; and he definitely could not leave Asian Russia. He lived in barracks with the other soldiers of the regiment, who were mostly peasants, exiles or convict soldiers like himself. There was little difference between these conditions and his environment in prison. However, very soon he was granted permission to live outside the barracks. He rented a small room in a house occupied by the landlady and her two daughters, who were most impressed that he had once been a nobleman, however minor. His room was a typical peasant dwelling, with mud walls lined with benches and faded calico curtains dividing the living area from the sleeping area. There were some dismal, dark red curtains hung at the window where some straggly geraniums grew. The room was lit by candles, which he had to use almost all the time because the small window let in little light, and the whole dwelling was infested with fleas. Despite all these drawbacks, the accommodation had one major advantage over barracks: there he could be alone.

Dostoyevsky was not unsuited to the military life. His time at the Academy of Engineers had prepared him for parade drill, military discipline, nights on watch and exercises. Moreover, he was fitter now than he had ever been. Hard labour and rationed food had made him lean and strong, and he had plenty of stamina. He had suffered the stomach problems endured by almost every convict in prison, but his health had not been broken. He was more fortunate than the others: Durov had suffered badly both physically and mentally, and had hardly been able to walk when he left prison. Petrashevsky himself, Dostoyevsky wrote to his brother, was not in his right mind. Dostoyevsky, by contrast, was ready to start again, and he faced the uncertainty of an indefinite period in Siberia with equanimity, even optimism.

He had left prison with many of his previous ideas about human nature, the role of socialism and the Christian faith challenged and changed, but he had not, as yet, begun to build any coherent belief system of his own. The society of Semipalatinsk did not encourage him to intellectual activity; as an ex-convict, Dostoyevsky was on a par with the commonest peasant, and during those first few months few educated people were willing to give him the time of day. Thus in order to continue his education, Dostoyevsky depended on the parcels and letters he received from home. He also took the opportunity to write to Natalya Fonvizina to thank her for the New Testament that she had given him at Tobolsk and which he still treasured. She was a religious woman, noble and well educated, and thus he felt that he could tell her about his emerging faith. She, at least, would enter into a discussion with him. In his letter, he started to come to terms with his faith and analyse the changes in his ideas and beliefs: 'I believe that there is nothing lovelier, deeper, more sympathetic, more rational, more manly and more perfect than the Saviour,' he wrote, 'I say to myself with jealous love that there is no one else like Him, but that there could be none. I would even say more: If anyone could prove to me that Christ is outside the truth and if the truth really did exclude Christ, I should prefer to stay with Christ and not with the truth.'[3]

This comment in his letter to Natalya Fonvizina is hard to fathom and is, in some ways, controversial. It is probable that he was searching for a new creed. He had found socialist and utopian theories inadequate in the face of the reality of human evil. He had also come to believe that claims by religion and politics to possess 'absolute truth' were dangerous, because a definition of absolute morality somehow bound Christ and God to obey it. In Dostoyevsky's view, most religious creeds or 'absolute truths' were flawed. In Christ, by contrast, Dostoyevsky saw a perfect man who had given the world a great philosophy. In his life and teaching, Christ combined all the justice, love and strength that was required of humankind. Christ's teaching seemed to work in the real world and, where a set creed might fail, Christ's essential character was still credible. It seemed more important to come to know and love the character of Christ than to adhere blindly to a creed purporting to be the truth. Even so, Fyodor's expression of a revitalised faith seemed to be conflicted; he eschewed blind fundamentalism and yet clung to Christ. His views held that humanity was flawed, but not Christ. Perhaps his attraction to the person of Christ was indeed a human one: Christ could be the only man who could live up to the utopian socialist ideal, that mankind could build its own just society on earth.

Much of Dostoyevsky's later work was to deal with this very conflict between absolute morality and the unfathomable character of God. In one potent scene in *The Brothers Karamazov*, for example, Alyosha and Ivan discuss the morality of God. Alyosha asks Ivan if he could build the most beautiful building in the world if he knew beforehand that it would entail the death of a child. The brothers both decide that they could not do so; and yet this is what they charge God with so doing. He, with full foreknowledge, has created a world in which many children die. Absolute morality would suggest that such a venture was not worth the suffering it caused, but loyalty to God might require accepting that suffering.

In 1854, though, Dostoyevsky was not so preoccupied by philosophy. He had become enamoured with Christ, but he was still living through the suffering that was to make his later novels deal so candidly with eternal questions. The comfort of Christianity became a potent influence in his life. His experience of isolation in prison, the hardship, and the separation from his family and friends could not have failed to motivate him to seek comfort in faith as well as books. His post-prison self is more rooted in ideas of Orthodox Christian faith, but he had not fully deserted that faith before his imprisonment, even though in his search for a just Russia he found commonality with the radical, atheistic circles of St Petersburg. Some of his post-prison behaviour suggests some form of reaffirmation of his faith. However, a conversion is probably too strong a description of his renewed fervour. Dostoyevsky had to build a new life using new points of reference.

Dostoyevsky's tendency to remain faithful to Christianity did create an inconvenient blot on what was otherwise a pure revolutionary career. Dostoyevsky's place in the annals of Russian literature, particularly in the communist years, has been uncomfortable. While he was a revolutionary, he was also a man of faith; he never professed to be atheist or entirely socialist.

Not long after his release into the army, his loneliness was alleviated. A companion from the familiar world of European Russia arrived. Baron Alexander Wrangel was a person with whom Dostoyevsky could speak on level terms and with whom he could develop a friendship – not only that Baron Wrangel was a committed fan. In December 1849 this young man, then seventeen years old, had stood in Semyonovsky Square and watched the mock execution. He had read Dostoyevsky's work and felt deeply for the writer as he witnessed the trick perpetrated on the conspirators. While Dostoyevsky served his sentence, Baron Wrangel embarked on his career as a public prosecutor. Like many young men, he wanted to travel and he applied for a transfer to Semipalatinsk. That way he could combine his quest for adventure with an opportunity to meet the writer he admired.

He went first to Mikhail to pick up books, letters and gossip, and as soon as he arrived in Semipalatinsk, he sent for Dostoyevsky. He describes their first meeting:

At first he did not know who I was and why I had asked him to come; so he was in the beginning very reticent. He wore a grey military cloak with a high red collar and red epaulettes; his pale, freckled face had a morose expression. His fair hair was closely shorn. He scrutinised me keenly with his intelligent blue-grey eyes, as if seeking to divine what sort of person I was.[4]

Both men recalled the meeting vividly. Dostoyevsky, nervous at being called to the district attorney's office, thought he might be in some sort of trouble. Wrangel, on the other hand, was deeply apprehensive at the thought of meeting this great but tragic figure, and could only hope that they might like each other. Wrangel offered him the letters he had brought from home, and Dostoyevsky sat down and read them. The atmosphere was now more relaxed since Wrangel had explained himself, but as Dostoyevsky read the letters he began to cry. It was perhaps not only the letters but the fact that, for the first time in four years, he had been treated with respect. His tears moved his young admirer, who also had some letters from home, which he began to read. In a moment they were both crying: the young man far from home and facing a new independent life, and the older man not knowing whether he would ever see his family again. From that day on the two men were firm friends.

Baron Wrangel's arrival changed Dostoyevsky's life in the small frontier town. Suddenly he was no longer persona non grata. Under the young baron's guidance and through his introductions he was accepted into the higher society of Semipalatinsk, such as it was. The friendship of the two men did not go unnoticed by the authorities but, despite initial suspicion, they interfered little: 'I grew fonder and fonder of Dostoyevsky,' wrote the Baron, 'my house was open to him day and night. When I returned from duty, I often found him there already having come to me from the drill-ground or the regimental office.'[5]

Baron Wrangel was a man of traditional Christian faith. By contrast, although Dostoyevsky was in the process of reaffirming his understanding of the person of Christ, he did not go to church. He had no respect for the Siberian priests and not much more respect for the priests of European Russia. He was enough of a socialist to understand the role played by the Church in the oppression of the serfs and the peasants. The collection of riches and the failure of the churches to alleviate the suffering of their flock with those riches obviously predicated the delayed promises of heaven that were a betrayal of the love of God as represented by Christ. In his view, the Church should be doing more on earth to offer justice to the oppressed. The baron, however, wisely kept clear of discussing such controversial subjects with the writer: 'He seldom spoke of religion. He was at heart religious, though he rarely entered a church; the popes, and especially the Siberian ones, he could not stand at all. Of Christ he would speak with moving rapture.'[6] Dostoyevsky was cautious now that he was rebuilding his life and beliefs. He did not want to return to prison.

Baron Wrangel rented a small cottage outside the town for the summer. This was a retreat for both of them and, as often as they could get away, the two men retreated to the cottage, where Dostoyevsky gardened assiduously. He managed to grow dahlias and carnations – difficult to do on the tundra: 'I can see Dostoyevsky now, watering the young plants,' wrote the Baron, 'he would take off his regimental cloak, and stand among the flower-beds in a pink cotton shirt … He was quite fascinated with gardening and took great delight in it.'[7]

Baron Wrangel loved riding, and after much persuasion managed to convince Dostoyevsky to learn. He was a bit awkward on horseback at first, but once he got used to it he enjoyed their rides on the steppe. Riding gave him a feeling of freedom. The gentlemen at the house even received the occasional lady visitor. They also encouraged two snakes to come and visit by putting out milk for them, although the snakes did not mix well with the ladies.

Friendship, a hot summer, opportunities to read, write and discuss life – these went a long way towards improving Dostoyevsky's state of mind and his health. By now he was thirty-three and had been a long time out of the regular company of women. His rehabilitation may have been going smoothly but he would soon run into trouble again, this time of the emotional kind: Dostoyevsky fell in love.

11

LOVE AND MARRIAGE

Maria Isayeva was twenty-eight when Dostoyevsky first met her. She was married to a drunk, one Alexander Isayev, who was attempting to hold down a job as a customs official in the Russian civil service. Although Alexander Isayev was not actually cruel to his wife, his heavy drinking reduced the couple to near poverty. The couple had a son, Pasha, who was seven years old when Maria met Fyodor.

Dostoyevsky later portrayed Alexander Isayev in *Crime and Punishment* through the comical, if tragic, figure of Marmeladov: 'He was a man over fifty, bald and grizzled, of medium height, and stoutly built. His face, bloated from continual drinking, was of a yellow, even greenish, tinge, with swollen eyelids, out of which keen, reddish eyes gleamed like little chinks.'[1] Although Marmeladov may not be an exact copy of Isayev, his drunken behaviour led to the death of his wife, the consumptive Katerina Ivanova. Alexander's wife, Maria, Dostoyevsky's Siberian love, was already showing signs of the tuberculosis that was to claim her.

Baron Wrangel, who watched the relationship between Dostoyevsky and Maria develop, had no great respect for Maria, whom he regarded as capricious and jealous. Had he realised how seriously Dostoyevsky was in love with her, he might have made more effort to help his friend avoid a mistake. Thinking this was only a casual flirtation, he was persuaded by Dostoyevsky to connive in the couple's meetings. More than once he got Isayev drunk to keep him out of their way.

Wrangel, however, perceived immediately what turned out to be the fatal flaw in the relationship: what Dostoyevsky took for love, was in fact Maria's pity for him as an ex-convict. Perhaps also she encouraged him because she needed affection; Fyodor's kindness and attention compensated for the aggression and ignorance that she got from Alexander Isayev. 'I do not think that she highly esteemed him,' Wrangel later wrote as he recalled the couple's initial meetings, 'it was more that she pitied him. Possibly she was attached to him also; but in love with him she most decidedly never was.'[2]

Wrangel reported that Maria said Dostoyevsky was a man with no future. She felt sorry for this writer who had once been famous, but was now reduced to living in little more than a hut in Siberia and still faced at least a four-year stretch in the army and an indefinite period in the tundra. She saw Fyodor as a man whose future was behind him: he was now trapped in Siberia and could expect little from life other than the simple pleasures and another man's wife. She, on the other hand, gained his kindness and a small measure of social standing because of her association with a once famous writer and revolutionary. She had little doubt that Fyodor's fate was sealed and he should see out his days in Siberia. She underestimated Dostoyevsky's tenacity in regaining his civil rights, getting out of Siberia and eventually making an honest woman of her.

This was not the first time Dostoyevsky had been in love, nor was it the first time he had mistaken fondness and affection for something deeper. It was not even the first time he ignored the fact that the object of his affection was already married. Avdotya Panayeva, wife of Ivan Panayev, had been a society hostess in St Petersburg when Dostoyevsky was enjoying his fame after publishing *Poor Folk*. Dostoyevsky wrote to Mikhail that he thought he had fallen 'quite seriously' in love with her. She was his ideal woman, both beautiful and clever, and it was well known that her marriage was a little lacking in lustre. Her husband's infidelity gave many men, including Dostoyevsky, the hope that she might look in their direction for comfort. She was kind to him and probably liked him, but she was never in love with him. Moreover, Dostoyevsky also wrote that he was 'intoxicated' by his fame, this being the period in his life when *Poor Folk* had been published to acclaim from Belinsky;[3] a week later he was to publish *The Double* and such thoughts of fame and infidelity were to recede. His hopes were never fulfilled, and soon after this first passion Dostoyevsky was to find himself in gaol, separated from regular female company for nearly five years.

It is not surprising, then, that upon his release Dostoyevsky was quick to fall in love and tempted to interpret any affection he got in return as a mutual passion, especially when Maria's loneliness and ill-treatment at the hands of her husband made her crave, in return, the affection Dostoyevsky offered. At first, the affair consisted only of visits to the Isayevs' dwelling, where the couple developed their intense and furtive relationship. The desperation of their situation made Dostoyevsky love Maria all the more; the fact that she was inaccessible was compelling, and in her turn she was all the more grateful for his attention and generosity.

Then Alexander Isayev moved from Semipalatinsk to Kuznetsk some four hundred miles away. Isayev had got a job as a caretaker of an inn, which promised a new start for the family, whether or not he had any inkling of the affair is unknown but likely; the upshot was that the illicit couple were separated. Dostoyevsky was devastated. The restriction laid on him by the army meant that he would not be free to visit very often, if ever. There was a heartrending farewell at which Baron Wrangel reluctantly cooperated and got Isayev too drunk to notice the passionate parting that took place between his wife and Fyodor.

Dostoyevsky, desperate that Maria had gone, lost motivation and gave up working on *The House of the Dead*. He began to consult a fortune teller, looking for a quick fix and some hope in his still dire situation. The notion of another dimension of spiritual beings fascinated him, and the thought that he might divine what the future held for him was very tempting. His life thus far had been an indiscriminate mixture of success and disaster; if he could learn what was to come, perhaps he could better prepare for it. In later life he was to renounce unequivocally his interest in any kind of spiritualism or occult practices, but for this moment all he wanted to know was whether there was any future for him and Maria, and he did not care how he found out.

He felt that he could not live without her, and her letters to him did not help him to bear their separation. She described in detail her poverty, Isayev's drunkenness and the fact he was in increasingly bad health; Dostoyevsky in return sent Maria money and wrote soothing letters to her. But this was not enough. Once again he involved Wrangel in a deception so that he could see Maria. This time, Wrangel told Dostoyevsky's army superiors that Dostoyevsky was ill, while Dostoyevsky travelled halfway to Kuznetsk where he had arranged to meet Maria. When he arrived, however, she was not there. She had sent a message to say that she was nursing her sick husband and could not come. In fact the combination of sickness, drunkenness and despair finally proved too much for Alexander Isayev, and not long after Dostoyevsky's futile journey, he received a letter saying that Alexander Isayev had died. Now Dostoyevsky had new hope but no way of consolidating his advantage, for Maria was in Kuznetsk and he was in Semipalatinsk. He feared that she would fall in love with someone else – as, of course, she did.

Dostoyevsky's first rival was a fictitious wealthy official, of whom Maria wrote to make him jealous. His second rival was no fiction but a schoolmaster, younger than both of them but with a regular salary. He did not drink and was probably more suited to the ailing, selfish Maria and her son than was Dostoyevsky. Maria's behaviour at this time only served to confirm Baron Wrangel's misgivings, but Dostoyevsky was undeterred. Letters to Dostoyevsky describing this man and her affection for him sent

Dostoyevsky shooting out of Semipalatinsk to Kuznetsk on an illegal and risky diversion from military business to dissuade her from marrying the schoolmaster.

In early March 1855, while Dostoyevsky was preoccupied with his affairs of the heart, something significant happened that was to give him the opportunity he sought to restart his career: Tsar Nicholas I died. The death of the tsar was sudden and unexpected: just fifty-eight, a mild cold had progressed to a severe case of pneumonia in the space of a day. He left Russia in the grip of the Crimean War, which was ultimately lost to the Ottoman Empire, supported by the British and the French. The late tsar had resolved none of Russia's internal injustices, such as serfdom; he left the empire to his son Alexander with the words 'Serve Russia'. In Siberia, his death was a glimmer of hope for Dostoyevsky: perhaps now he could appeal to a more merciful tsar, a tsar who had no personal involvement in his case. Rumours spread that the new Tsar Alexander II, who was reputed to be more liberal, might grant an amnesty for political prisoners. Dostoyevsky and Baron Wrangel attended a solemn Mass for Nicholas, to begin the evidence of Fyodor's rehabilitation.

Nicholas I's death prompted Dostoyevsky to send the first of many missives to those in authority in European Russia, pleading his case for the right to publish and to return across the Urals. First he sent a poem dedicated to Nicholas's wife, the tsarina, expounding the virtues of her late husband. Then he wrote a poem on the coronation of the new tsar. Both poems were unashamedly flattering and intended to prove that Dostoyevsky would now use his writing talent to the benefit, and not the detriment, of the tsarist regime.

To General Eduard Totleben, the engineer hero of the siege of Sevastopol in the Crimean War and brother of his old flatmate, Adolph, Dostoyevsky wrote:

I was guilty, and am very conscious of it. I was convicted of the intention (but only the intention) of acting against the

Government. I was lawfully and quite justly condemned; the hard, painful experiences of the ensuing years have sobered me, and altered my views in many respects.[4]

This was intended to spread the word amongst the senior elements of Russian aristocracy that Fyodor Dostoyevsky was a repentant man.

Soon after the tsar's death, Baron Wrangel's term of duty as district attorney expired and he was forced to return to European Russia. In effect, this meant that Dostoyevsky would have a friend and ally pleading his cause in St Petersburg, but it also meant that he was, once again, alone and isolated in Siberia. 'Our parting grieved me bitterly,' wrote Wrangel, 'I was young, strong, and full of roseate hopes; while he – great, God-given writer – was losing his only friend, and had to stay behind as a common soldier, sick, forsaken, desolate – in Siberia.'[5]

The letter to Eduard Totleben had the desired effect, though, and in the autumn of 1856 Dostoyevsky was promoted to second lieutenant and given permission to commence writing with a view to publication, so long as what he wrote came within the law. This was good progress and gave the lie to Maria's perception of Dostoyevsky as a man without a future. In 1857 he published the short story written in the Peter and Paul Fortress some years before, 'A Little Hero', and in 1859 two novels, *Uncle's Dream* and *The Village of Stepanchikovo*, were published. He had established that he could once again get into print.

Just as persistence earned him the right to publish, it also won him the hand of Maria Isayeva in marriage. The wedding took place on 6 February 1857 in Kuznetsk, but it was a hollow victory. Fyodor was worn out with the battle to win Maria's hand. Perhaps, too, he understood the selfishness of her affection for him. And Maria was ill, very ill. Finally, within days of their wedding, Maria was witness to Dostoyevsky's most severe epileptic fit to date; the fact of his fits was something that Fyodor had omitted to mention when they were courting. Maria was appalled.

While Fyodor's fits at this stage were no doubt inconvenient, especially to Maria, and the exact origin of his convulsions unknown, there is no doubt that later in life Dostoyevsky was plagued by them. However, he used them creatively and endowed many of his characters with epilepsy, including Prince Myshkin, hero of *The Idiot*, whose life is saved from a murderous attack by a conveniently timed epileptic fit, while the servant Smerdyakov in *The Brothers Karamazov* uses his fits as an alibi. In particular, Dostoyevsky's descriptions of Myshkin's epilepsy give insight into how he viewed his own affliction. Anna, his second wife, later described vividly how it appeared to others. This is how one seizure began:

> Suddenly he broke off in mid-syllable, turned white, started to get up from the couch and began leaning over toward me. I looked in amazement at his changed face. And suddenly there was a horrible, inhuman scream, or more precisely, a howl – and he began to topple forward.[6]

The practical consequences of his epilepsy, apart from the ever-present fear of having a seizure in the street or injuring himself severely during a fit, were the depression, confusion and loss of memory that followed. He lost more than one friend because he failed to recognise them after a fit. He wrote copious notes on the characterisations and plots of his novels so that he could remind himself of what he was working on if a seizure interrupted the flow.

Convulsions seemed to come haphazardly, although alcohol could provoke a fit and he believed certain types of weather also had an effect. Moreover, he often knew when a fit was coming on even though he was helpless against it – an aspect of the malady he gave to Smerdyakov in *Karamazov*. One significant feature of his epilepsy was the feeling of ecstasy that immediately preceded a seizure:

> Then suddenly some gulf seemed to open up before him: a blinding inner light flooded his soul. The moment lasted perhaps half a second, yet he clearly and consciously

remembered the beginning, the first sound of the dreadful scream, which burst from his chest of its own accord and which he could have done nothing to suppress. Then his consciousness was instantly extinguished and complete darkness set in.[7]

His ill health may have contributed to the strain of mysticism to Dostoyevsky's religious thought. Some Romantic artists – Coleridge among them – sought religious experiences through the use of drugs. They believed that drugs could break down the inhibitions of the rational mind and bring the dreamer closer to God, and Dostoyevsky wondered whether his epilepsy could have the same effect. While it no doubt coloured his vision of heaven, it did not cure him of the fear of death. All his life he feared sudden death brought on by a convulsion.

To his first wife, Maria, his epileptic seizure was terrifying. She was less stoic than Dostoyevsky's second wife, Anna. Maria now realised that not only had she married an ex-convict, she had married one with a severe brain disease. She had never seen anything like his fits before and she contacted doctors immediately, thus alerting the authorities to his medical condition. Epilepsy was officially diagnosed and Dostoyevsky was released from military service on grounds of ill health.

Two years after his marriage in 1857, after further appeals, Dostoyevsky's noble title was restored to him. By July 1859 he was given permission to leave Asian Russia, cross the Urals and live in the European region. He first settled in Tver, but Tver offered few opportunities to make the living he needed as a writer in order to put his stepson, Pasha, through school. It was clear to Dostoyevsky and Maria that only St Petersburg offered them chance of making a success of his new life. His brother Mikhail had set up a magazine in the city, thereby presenting Fyodor with a chance to work in his beloved field of literature, if he could only get back home. The problem was getting permission to live there. Permission to return to European Russia was one thing; permission to return to its major historic cities was quite another. Moscow and St Petersburg were forbidden to him. Once again, he wrote to General Eduard Totleben asking him for just one more favour: to get him out of Tver. Five months went by with no response, but then, in December 1859, ten years after he left the city in chains, Dostoyevsky was back in St Petersburg.

12

THE TOWER OF BABEL

They say it is spring in Petersburg. Is it? Still, perhaps it is.
Indeed all the signs of spring are there. Half the town is
down with 'flu and the other half has at least a cold in the
head. These gifts of Mother Nature fully convince us of her
renascence. So it is spring!

Dostoyevsky, 'Four Essays'.[1]

Dostoyevsky loved St Petersburg: it was the foundation of his
life and literature, and it was to be his home for the rest of his
life. In later years he left unwillingly to travel abroad for the sake
of his journalism, his second wife and his health, but he always
returned to the city he loved. Under the rule of Alexander II in the
late 1850s and early 1860s, St Petersburg was a marginally more
relaxed place to live than before Dostoyevsky's imprisonment.
Legislation was being prepared that, to Fyodor, must have seemed
an answer to prayer, for the Tsar was planning to free the serfs.

The long-awaited liberation happened in 1861. Russia was at
last a liberated modern country that had abandoned its feudal
ways and joined the modern world – or so many thought. But it
was a liberation without land and an emancipation without means.
In Russia land ownership has always been less important than land
control. Emancipation liberated the serfs from the personal and

individual control of the landowners – no longer could they split up families, force marriages or punish their workers directly – but they still controlled the land, at least for the time being. The emancipated serfs were instructed to buy back the land on which they had worked all their lives at terms agreed between the landowner and appointed arbitrators. This left the workers with large mortgages, payable in money or services to the landowners just as they had had to when they were serfs. Eventually, of course, they could hope to own and control their land – but the success of the scheme and the prosperity of the liberated serfs depended heavily on the fertility of the land and the type of work required, which, in turn, depended on the landowner's discretion.

Moreover, emancipation meant that the landowners were released from any obligation to their workers. Before 1861 they were responsible for the physical and spiritual welfare of the 'souls' who lived on and worked their land and gave back to them its produce. After 1861, they had workers who were independent of them in every way except that they were privately buying the land. The landowner had no duty of care, and many ex-serfs found themselves working just as hard as before on the same land, with little or no time to plough and cultivate the property they were buying, now quite without the help or protection, or indeed obligation, from their overlord. It was a compromised emancipation, calculated to keep the landowners pacified, and it betrayed the serfs and lost forever the support of the workers. Within a few years the system's inadequacies were plain to see and unrest in Russia deepened. In 1881 Tsar Alexander II was assassinated.

However, when the new legislation came in, Dostoyevsky welcomed it. It removed the last great barrier between himself and loyalty to the tsar, and it appeared to establish that the tsarist regime could dispense justice without having to be dismantled. Although very soon the inadequacies of the system began to show, the practice of serfdom had, at least in principle, been abolished, and thus Dostoyevsky's loyalty was won.

Just a year after the emancipation, however, in 1862, a series of pamphlets appeared on the streets of St Petersburg urging the population to revolution. 'To the axe!' the pamphlet exhorted, calling on the people to strike at the Imperial Party without restraint in the city squares, in the houses, in the narrow streets.[2] The pamphlets caused Dostoyevsky much distress. They appeared just as a number of fires broke out in St Petersburg with no apparent cause. How the fires started is not known but many people, including Dostoyevsky, attributed them to revolutionary activity. Now that he was a reformed revolutionary, Dostoyevsky felt obligated to warn others of the error of their ways and so to save them from his fate or worse. There was a great difference, he felt, between attaining justice and instigating a revolution: the two were not compatible.

Like many others in St Petersburg, he assumed that a well-known radical, Chernyshevsky, was either responsible for the fires or able to influence the perpetrators. Dostoyevsky decided to visit Chernyshevsky to see if he could help stop the fires. He took a big risk in visiting the radical – if he had been seen by the authorities he might well have lost his freedom and doomed his brother's magazine, *Time*, on which he worked. Chernyshevsky recalled Dostoyevsky's visit as somewhat hysterical, while Dostoyevsky said he made a calm and considered approach. Whatever the manner of the conversation, Chernyshevsky denied having anything to do with the fires and Dostoyevsky went away reassured. Nevertheless Chernyshevsky was arrested, tried and found guilty of instigating them and, although the evidence was flimsy, he was sent to Siberia.

Dostoyevsky later published a cruel satire, 'The Crocodile', depicting a political radical having been swallowed by a crocodile but still spouting his philosophy from inside its stomach. When readers protested, Dostoyevsky denied that he was caricaturing Chernyshevsky, although the piece was so pointed that it was difficult to make any other interpretation of it. Possibly, as an ex-prisoner himself, he realised he should have had more sympathy for his fellow 'unfortunate'. Chernyshevsky did not fare so well as

Dostoyevsky had: he spent most of the rest of his life in Siberia, only returning to his hometown of Saratov to die in 1889.

A widespread political confusion was dominant in Russia after the emancipation of the serfs. Dostoyevsky's mood, like that of many of his contemporaries, went from elation to despair at the situation. His loyalty to the tsar and Russia's autocratic regime never wavered, but it soon became obvious that this liberation had not ushered in justice; in fact it compounded the injustices of serfdom. Emancipated serfs were no less bonded to their masters than they had been before. Dostoyevsky was to document mercilessly the effects of poverty on the human psyche. He would observe and explain the motivations of the revolutionary, the atheist, the nihilist and the anarchist in the face of a cruel political regime and an inadequate explanation of God and His justice. However, he limited his comments to a discussion of the problem rather than proposing any radical solution. His speculative focus on the human response to poverty, injustice and the problem of evil were to help evade the unwanted attention of the authorities for the rest of his life, while still allowing him the expression of a free writer.

Against this background, his brother Mikhail continued editing the journal *Time*, which he had set up in 1858 just before Dostoyevsky's return. Fyodor, though not permitted to edit any journal, was a contributor to the magazine and, unofficially, had much involvement behind the scenes. In addition, he involved himself in many other activities. He was elected a member of The Society for Assisting Needy Authors, and immediately arranged a loan from the Society to his fellow prisoner, Durov, now dying in Odessa, a gesture which conflicts with the witness accounts of the two of them not speaking to each other during their prison years. Perhaps Dostoyevsky felt guilty or he had mellowed over the years; perhaps their separation in prison had been the result of a minor argument, now forgotten, or a calculated attempt to avoid accusations of forming conspiracies while in prison. Whatever the reason, Fyodor did his best for Durov at this time. He thus flung himself enthusiastically into a fundraising event, a performance of Gogol's *The Inspector General*, playing his part as the postmaster with gusto, despite the fact that another member of the cast was Turgenev, with whom he was still not speaking after their row over *The Double*.

Dostoyevsky supported the Sunday-school movement, which had initial government backing, as a way of reassuring the authorities that his conversion to the status quo was genuine. However, he later came to think that the schools were being used as a method of subversive education, and so Fyodor quietly retired from his duties there. These endeavours involved Dostoyevsky in the fight for justice without involving him in actual revolutionary struggle. He had not lost his keen desire to see human beings better treated but he worked now within the framework of government-approved, legal enterprises.

Dostoyevsky was preoccupied with his and Mikhail's journal, *Time*. The magazine was feeling its way towards a more conservative position than that taken by their competitor, *The Contemporary*. The two magazines represented and polarised the two strands of thought that were beginning to dominate the Russian political debate. *Time* lauded Russia as it stood: it was loyal to the regime and only recommended change that was endorsed by that regime. It saw its role as to reveal to Russians the injustices that still existed in their country, but also to highlight the pride they could take in the progress that had already been made. Gradually *Time* began to take on a particularly nationalistic stance, a tendency that Dostoyevsky was to develop into a creed of his own in his later political writings. By contrast, *The Contemporary*, edited by Nekrasov and contributed to by Turgenev, applauded the Westernisation of Russia and advocated the subordination of Russian nationalism to the values and culture of the West.

Nekrasov initially underestimated his old friend and rival Dostoyevsky. He stated that Dostoyevsky was finished, that his post-prison stories would not save his career or his reputation; but once again Fyodor was dismissed too soon, for he had only just begun. He opposed Westernisation because he felt that the result would be secularisation, perhaps an intentional side effect wished for by those who had at one time flirted with atheistic socialism and who saw Orthodox Christianity as an oppressive yoke. Dostoyevsky, now more than ever a believer, did not want to rid Russia of religion for the sake of modernisation, he wanted to combine modern Russia with a quintessential Russian approach to religion. However, he did not know what he was up against. To rectify this, he decided to travel to Europe to see the Western way of life for himself, and to examine how religion fared in the Western world.

He went alone, without Maria; their marriage was now a sham, a marriage in name only. Baron Wrangel's fears had come to pass, and added to that Maria hated St Petersburg and Dostoyevsky's family had never really accepted her. She was aware of this obvious dislike and found that the St Petersburg air aggravated her tuberculosis, so in November 1863 they moved to Moscow, where she was looked after by friends and servants. Dostoyevsky visited her occasionally, but his heart was not with his wife and he remained in St Petersburg. Perhaps understandably, whenever they were together she bickered with him and accused him of neglect. Maria lived only for attention, and Dostoyevsky's mind was on his career. His marriage was a mistake. All his friends and relatives knew it and he did too within months of marrying Maria, but he did look after her and he never shirked his obligations towards her and her son.

Dostoyevsky saw in Europe all that he dreaded. Shocked at the conditions under which the English poor were forced to live, he described London in Dickensian terms. The Crystal Palace, he thought, was a monument to the anti-Christ, the Tower of Babel:

> It is a Biblical sight, something to do with Babylon, some prophecy out of the Apocalypse being fulfilled before your very eyes. You feel that a rich ancient tradition of denial and protest is needed in order not to yield, not to succumb to suppression, not to bow down in worship of fact, and not to idolise Baal.[3]

Western Europe, he perceived, was selling its soul to Mammon in the form of science and materialism. When he returned to Russia he wrote about his travels in *Time,* under the title 'Winter Notes on Summer Impressions'.

Speaking no English, Fyodor was in London for 'all of eight days', and he did not see St Paul's. He stayed with an exiled revolutionary journalist called Alexander Herzen, who was a lively personality and acted as a guide, not just to Britain but to European culture, which he shared in Dostoyevsky's view as considering corrupt. Dostoyevsky may well have been influenced by him: certainly his trip to Europe did not seem to broaden his mind on the subject of other cultures – quite the opposite, it nurtured an increasing xenophobia, which only emphasised the growing gulf between himself and Nekrasov and Turgenev of *The Contemporary,* the very people who had started him on his career. True to form, he had moved into a new circle.

Time was gaining ground in Russian literary circles and re-establishing Dostoyevsky as both a writer of fiction and a journalist, but luck was not on their side, and in 1863 disaster struck. In January of that year a rebellion broke out in Poland. The struggle, which was to last a year, would lead to the more aggressive Russification of Polish institutions and the tighter rule of Russia over its Polish territory. Russification – the process by which Russian systems of government, bureaucracy, law and control were imposed on other countries, a form of covert Russian expansionism – provoked a variety of responses, and Dostoyevsky felt obliged to make some comment. He commissioned one Nikolai Strakhov to write an article for *Time* on the subject. Strakhov was a keen reactionary, anti-West in stance and a great influence on the writers of his time, including Tolstoy and Turgenev. Strakhov later became one of Dostoyevsky's earliest biographers. He should therefore have been a good commission for the magazine. The article was supposed to toe the government line, but instead somehow Strakhov failed to get the balance right. The censors took offence and the magazine was closed down.

This was indeed a calamity, not only because it took away the platform from which Dostoyevsky was re-establishing his career but also because it placed a great financial burden on the brothers. Mikhail had been so confident in the continuing success of the magazine that he had just sold his cigarette factory when the blow struck; this left him with no means of supporting himself or his family. Fyodor had fewer responsibilities, but his epilepsy was growing worse and he wanted to make another trip abroad. The pretext for his last trip had been medicinal, and the change of air had seemed to improve his epilepsy. Moreover, one or two medical experts had recommended a second trip in order to make permission easier to obtain. Now that he was no longer needed at *Time* he reapplied to go abroad, this time with a companion.

Apollinaria Suslova, or Polina, was the second great disaster of Dostoyevsky's love life. A student, she had met him at an evening gathering, where he had read excerpts from *The House of the Dead*. Polina was impressed with his dramatic delivery, his voice that shrieked with passion and whispered with tension. But she was a modern woman, a believer in free love, not one to ally herself with just one man.

The affair began earnestly enough and they arranged to go away together. However, Dostoyevsky was not able to travel with her immediately and she went ahead to wait for him in Paris. Unfortunately, Dostoyevsky waited too long before he followed her. By the time he reached Paris she had met, fallen in love with and gone to bed with one Salvador, who swept her off her feet and disappeared just as fast. After his conquest, this one night stand sent her a note saying that he had typhus and that this was probably farewell. This ruse might have worked had Polina not seen him in the street while he was supposed to be dying. When Dostoyevsky arrived in Paris he found a note telling him that it was all over and she must return to Russia, but Polina had not been quick enough to leave. Dostoyevsky found her and was able to confront her. There followed a difficult discussion, during which the scorned Polina threatened to cut Salvador's throat;

Dostoyevsky managed to calm her down and they agreed to travel on together as brother and sister.

The nature of the relationship proved difficult to maintain. Dostoyevsky sublimated his dissatisfaction and began gambling addictively. The addiction surprised his old friend Baron Wrangel, who never saw him gamble in Semipalatinsk although opportunities to do so had been plentiful. Nevertheless, the casinos of Europe were an aspect of Western life that attracted Dostoyevsky, and like all addicted gamblers he lost hopelessly. Polina spent the rest of the trip lending him money, pawning her jewellry and moving out of hotels under dubious circumstances. In spite of this she stayed with him – until they met the exiled Russian radical, Herzen, and Dostoyevsky passed her off as a near-relative. Disgusted, Polina went back to Paris to find Salvador.

It would be easy to dismiss the importance of this relationship in Dostoyevsky's life because of its brevity and failure, but Polina was a firebrand and their mutual attraction was powerful. While they had parted, they remained in contact, and Dostoyevsky kept up a correspondence with her that would later make his second wife feel insecure. In the end the correspondence and the friendship faded, but it is probable that Polina was the love of his life in spite of the destructive effect they had on each other. The relationship was, at best, stormy, and neither behaved very honourably towards the other. Polina went on to hold virulently fascist and anti-Semitic views.

Dostoyevsky was attracted to fiery personalities but his demands of women suited more compliant personalities than Polina, and he had yet to approach the kind of woman with whom he could build a successful relationship. He did, however, use the experience in his writing to portray the power of a destructive relationship. The character of Nastasya Filippovna in *The Idiot* is thought to reflect Polina, and the relationship Nastasya suffers with Rogozhin powerfully portrays the effects of a destructive attraction.

After Polina had gone, Dostoyevsky stayed in Europe gambling. He was soon urgently called back to Russia, however: he received word that his wife, Maria, was dying.

13

UNDERGROUND MAN

Maria Dmitryevna Dostoyevskaya rocked herself constantly in the rocking chair at her apartment in Moscow. Her husband sat and watched her. Like many in her situation, she found it hard, in fact impossible, to face up to her own imminent death. Her conversation avoided the subject. She and Dostoyevsky made plans for the future. They spoke of summer holidays, of getting better, of anything but tuberculosis and death.

When Dostoyevsky suggested that her son, Pasha, should visit her, she panicked and accused him of intimating that she was dying. 'She will not see him,' Fyodor wrote to Mikhail:

> You can't blame a consumptive for her state of mind. She has said she will send for him to give him her blessing when she feels she is dying. But she may die this evening, and meanwhile this very morning she was making plans for spending the summer in the country, and removing to Taganrog or Astrakhan in three years' time. It is impossible to remind her about Pasha. She is terribly apprehensive and will take fright at once and say, 'That means I am very ill, I am dying.'[1]

Occasionally she was lucid; at times she hallucinated. She saw demons in the room and would go into an hysterical rage until the doctor opened the window and shooed the demons out. There was no comfort for her, and nothing for Dostoyevsky to do but wait. When she finally took to her bed for the last time, he sat at a desk in her room, listening to her ever-shallower breathing and occasional ramblings, staying with her so that he could be with her at the end. While he waited he thought and he wrote:

> I'm writing this just for myself, for even if I do address myself to imaginary readers, I do it only because it makes it easier for me to write. It's just a matter of form, nothing else, for as I said before, I'll never have any readers.[2]

Thus wrote Underground Man, protagonist of the short novel *Notes from the Undergound*, written while Maria was dying. In it Dostoyevsky created, or rather recreated, a character he had explored before: his Petersburg dreamer, his man of the city. But this time, unlike his portrayal in 'White Nights', this time the dreamer was a dark anti-hero with a selfish taint. This dreamer was a man with an unredeemed nature.

In 'White Nights' Dostoyevsky described the events of four summer nights in Petersburg, where his narrator and protagonist engaged in a brief but doomed romance with a young woman waiting for the return of her fiancé. Ultimately, even though this love triangle ends in the inevitable outcome of unrequited love, his protagonist harbours no ill will towards Natsenka and reconciles himself to her loss by wishing her well. However the significance of the story derives not so much from the plot but in its characterisation, and it is the character of the narrator, the Petersburg dreamer, that Dostoyevsky reimagines for his much darker story of urban dissonance in *Notes from the Undergound*. In this story the dreamer is indeed an 'underground man': like his predecessor he inhabits the darkened rooms of a solitary existence, but unlike his predecessor he is less enamoured with romance than he is with lust, less preoccupied with the benefits of caring for someone else than he is with his own selfishness. Underground

Man's own perception of himself is not flattering; from the start he introduces himself as a man who enjoys humiliating others: 'Whenever people used to come to my office on some business, I snarled at them and felt as pleased as Punch when I succeeded in making one of them really unhappy.'[3] Despite telling this story, he reneges on the comment and claims to have been exaggerating; he denies that this makes him a spiteful man. He does, however, say that he has always considered himself as cleverer than anyone else in the world (although he also suggests that he probably deserves a slap in the face). However, in referencing his own superiority he presages the attitude and arrogance of one of Dostoyevsky's greatest anti-heroes, Raskolnikov in *Crime and Punishment*, who takes the idea of his own superiority to extreme lengths.

The language of *Notes from the Undergound* centres on the protagonist in St Petersburg and perpetuates the feeling of the underground by references to rooms like caves, already, in some way, literally underground. Underground Man's room 'is a dreadful horrible hole'. He refers to his work place as a 'funk hole', a place where he has been for four years, and he uses a conceit of the man as a mouse, a mouse who has lived in a 'subterranean hole' for forty years nursing its own spite and bitterness. The mouse, its age and attitude bear a startling resemblance in history to the Underground Man himself. He speaks of the 'dark cellar' that he lives in, and hints at a vile and lonely man who avoids contact with human beings, is unable to make appropriate relationships with his fellow office workers; one who at night pursues his 'vile amusements', while during the day he carries 'the dark cellar about with me in my soul. I was terribly afraid of being seen, of meeting someone I knew, of being recognised, I frequented all sorts of rather obscure dens of vice.'[4] His predecessor, protagonist in 'White Nights', describes the dreamer-*mechtatel* figure as sticking to his room like a snail, and in the 'St Petersburg Chronicles' Dostoyevsky describes the dreamer as a 'Petersburg Nightmare'. Underground Man personifies the nightmare. He is a man who confines himself to his room in an atmosphere of bitter disappointment, peppered with complaints about his health, a living declaration that humiliation and degradation are in some masochistic way to be enjoyed.

While much of Dostoyevsky's observations of Underground Man owed something to the prototype in 'White Nights', his subsequent experience of human nature in prison may have informed this less attractive inhabitant of St Petersburg, whose experience of the city is not that of 'White Nights', but of wet snow which has been falling for days and which demands that he retreat to his dark and dank room. In addition to observing the behaviour of men and women in prison, Dostoyevsky drew on Dickens, and in Dickens found a kindred spirit, another writer who was inclined to set his stories in the grim inner-city atmosphere, which in the latter's case became known as Dickensian London. It was this urban landscape, rather than the estates and grounds of the aristocracy, that was Dickens' currency. The mists that dog the Thames, that cover Magwitch and haunt Pip in Dickens' *Great Expectations*, are suggested in the wet snow and dark corners of the Nevsky Prospect next to the River Neva in Underground Man's unredeemed St Petersburg. Dickens expresses the city of London as an extension of the marshes from which Magwitch rises – an extension that is, in a sense, both geographically and morally true for Dickens. The dreariness of the English grey sky and the swamp that London sits on follows Pip even as he tries to impress the unimpressed Stella or succeed as a gentleman in higher society – thus even the ever-optimistic Pip describes everything as 'dismal':

> We entered this haven through a wicket-gate, and were disgorged by an introductory passage into a melancholy little square that looked to me like a flat burying-ground. I thought it had the most dismal trees in it, and the most dismal sparrows, and the most dismal cats, and the most dismal houses (in number half a dozen or so), that I had ever seen.[5]

Dickens deliberately personifies the square as 'melancholy', whereas Dostoyevsky is less direct in his descriptions of St Petersburg as perceived by Underground Man. He sets the story against an atmosphere of depression, a depression brought on by exaggerating the evidence everywhere of poverty as a norm. Dostoyevsky does however differ from Dickens in his treatment of his characters. Dickens perpetuates the imagery of mists until the end of *Great Expectations* when, as Pip steps forward with Estella, the mists rise and the shadows disappear; he sees no shadow of another parting with her. But there is no such clearing of the mists for Dostoyevsky's characters; their fate is much more mired in a context they cannot escape. It is using this dramatic conceit that he suggests no intelligent man can succeed; in such a world, only a fool survives unscathed: 'Yes a man of the nineteenth century must be, and is indeed morally bound to be, above all a characterless person; a man of character on the other hand, a man of action, is mostly a fellow with a very circumscribed imagination.'[6]

Underground Man addresses the reader directly as 'gentleman' and is unapologetic in his discussion of himself. His rhetorical questions both articulate and enact the subject of the novel: he asks what does a 'decent chap' talk about, and answers 'about himself' – and so he talks about himself. The arrogant, disappointed, embittered man who considers himself clever, precisely because he is someone who cannot finish anything that he has started, cites this as evidence of his superiority; being indecisive is to demonstrate more clarity of thought, not less.

In common with much of what Dostoyevsky had written before, *Notes from the Undergound* was an answer to another author's previous works, in this case Nikolai Chernyshevsky's *What is to be Done?* Chernyshevsky's novel posited the idea that a better world should be propagated by the educated classes, forming small communities that practised and spread a more equal and utopianist model of society: phalansteries. *What is to be Done?* has been cited as one of the most influential treatises in nineteenth-century Russian revolutionary philosophy. Indeed, Leo Tolstoy finished his life living on a commune modelled on these utopian principles. However, Chernyshevsky's new society relied on a belief in the innate goodness of human nature. Dostoyevsky was not so convinced, and Underground Man was his answer.

This St Petersburg dreamer delighted in the humiliation of others, took a masochistic pleasure in his own pain, and is one who considers laziness an attribute to be admired. Not much about Underground Man is likeable, and this was the way that Dostoyevsky intended his protagonist to be received. He was to be the Alf Garnett of his day. However, like Alf Garnett, the irony of the character escaped some of the audience in the reading. In the same way that the figure created by Johnny Speight in 1967 and broadcast on BBC 1 was supposed to expose and mock the vicious racism of the time, perpetuated by Enoch Powell and before him Oswald Moseley, so Underground Man was supposed to deflate the utopian hopes of Chernyshevsky with a satirical and uncooperative representation of an irredeemable human being. In both cases, not everybody saw the joke: 'The trouble was, the ignorant bigots embraced Alf as their spokesman. They memorised his racist rants and parroted them back. Speight may have wanted *Till Death Us Do Part* to give prejudice a kicking. In fact it gave it a platform.'[7]

In the same way, Underground Man was not perceived as a satirical character but as the representation of an unpleasant anti-hero. In order to avert this Dostoyevsky wrote a footnote that clarified the idea that Underground Man was to be read as an ironic character – not someone to be emulated but to be mocked: 'Both the author of the Notes and the Notes themselves are, of course, fictitious.' But Dostoyevsky goes on to say, 'He is one of the representatives of a generation that is still with us.'[8]

Perhaps Underground Man reflected the way Dostoyevsky felt about himself at the time. He, like his protagonist, had failed in love. His marriage had been a disaster. Maria's life had been shoddy from start to finish and he had done little to improve things for her. Underground Man's cynical and harsh tone may have reflected Dostoyevsky's guilt. He was, in a sense, a portrait of guilt and what it does to a human being. Unlike his successor anti-heroes, such as Raskolnikov and Svidrigailov in *Crime and Punishment*, or even Stavrogin in *The Devils*, there is nothing to like about Underground Man. In this respect he is more like old Karamazov, father of the brothers Karamazov in the novel of that name, than the almost likeable and compelling villains Stavrogin and Raskolnikov.

Underground Man takes pride in humiliating other people. He then feels guilty about it while resenting the fact that he is hated because of it. He enters a sado-masochistic cycle of mental torture. If he tries to make things better, he always ends by making them worse. He attends a party at which he is quite clearly not wanted. He forces his way past the protesting but compliant guests, but then, instead of settling quietly down to enjoy himself in their company, he fulfils their worst apprehensions by abusing the guest of honour. The friends he followed to the party make their escape, pursued by Underground Man, who is desperate to apologise. The friends elude him and he settles for a night with a prostitute, whom he proceeds to humiliate by describing to her the ghastliness of her future:

> You're in debt to them, and you'll remain in debt till the end – till the time when the customers refuse to use you. And that's not as far off as you think, for you'd be wrong to rely too much upon your youth. Time moves very fast indeed here. They'll kick you out soon enough.[9]

Notes from the Undergound is a deeply depressing description of the self-destructiveness of the human psyche. In some ways it may have been a catharsis for Dostoyevsky. He knew what it felt like to go to parties where he was not wanted. His fall from grace after the publication of *The Double* had seen him edged out of the top literary cliques, partly because of his own arrogant behaviour. His relationship with his wife was one of guilt-ridden failure. He had pursued her to the altar and then abandoned her, only really returning to attend her death.

In addition to the personal significance that Underground Man may have had for Dostoyevsky as an expiation of his own guilt, he is also one of the first detailed characterisations of that most famous kind of fictional hero: the anti-hero. The term anti-hero is a modern term applied to a kind of character that some believe to be Dostoyevsky's invention. While he may not have been the first ever to use such a character, many of his creations are archetypal anti-heroes, major characters with no traditionally heroic qualities. The anti-hero is not a good man, but his motivations, characteristics, past and present actions are described with subjective interest. This character may be familiar to modern consumers of media and film: the anti-hero is the character who gets things done, in spite of, or perhaps because of, the flaws in his or her personality.

In the late 1970s one particular director along with a new young actor decided to explore this character and his faults in more detail, and perhaps to take the self-indulgent thinking of Underground Man to its inevitable conclusion. The director was Martin Scorsese, the actor Robert de Niro and the character that so closely resembles Underground Man is *Taxi Driver*'s Travis Bickle:

> I felt close to the character by way of Dostoevski. I had always wanted to do a movie of *Notes from the Undergound*. I mentioned that to Paul [Schrader] and he said, 'Well this is what I have – *Taxi Driver*.' And I said, 'Great this is it!'[10]

The story of the disenfranchised taxi driver who traverses the urban streets of 1970s New York, then a very dangerous city, who befriends a child prostitute and descends into a character collapse prompted by his own contradictions, reflects a reimagining of Dostoyevsky's anti-social, introverted Underground Man. Dostoyevsky's protagonist hides in the streets of urban St Petersburg, making similar observations about himself and his surroundings, albeit descending into a less Americanised chaos than does his twentieth-century counterpart, Travis Bickle.

While Underground Man berates the prostitute Lizaveta for selling her favours:

> You give your love to be outraged by every drunkard! Love! But that's everything, you know, it's a priceless diamond, it's a maiden's treasure, love – why, a man would be ready to give his soul, to face death to gain that love. But how much is your love worth now? You are sold, all of you, body and soul, and there is no need to strive for love when you can have everything without love. And you know there is no greater insult to a girl than that, do you understand?[11]

Travis Bickle offers the same observation in less delicate language to Iris, played by the young Jodie Foster: 'You walk out with those f**king creeps and lowlifes and degenerates out on the street, and you sell your, sell your little p*ssy, for nothing, man! For some lowlife pimp!'[12]

Like his literary predecessor, Travis records most of his thoughts in a journal, and the character, through the medium of voice-over, narrates its entries. Travis inhabits the underground of New York: he drives through its dark streets, he is the audience's guide through the sleazy underground of its sex-work community, although he does not participate in it. Like Underground Man, he confines himself to his room, where the gun and the mirror provide Bickle with his own personal doppelgänger and he rehearses the pleasure of the power of the gun – a truly American form of indulgence – in one of the most quoted scenes in cinema history: 'Are you talking to me?' Bickle rehearses his power over individuals with his voice and a gun in hand; Underground Man also retreats to his room and dreams of influence worthy of his imagined power:

> On the contrary I longed passionately to show all that 'rabble' that I was not such a coward even as I imagined myself to be. And that was not all by any means: in the most powerful

paroxysms of my cowardly fever I dreamed of getting the upper hand, of sweeping the floor with them of forcing them to admire and like me ...[13]

Underground Man befriends Lizaveta and yet humiliates her by attempting to buy what she was willing to give freely; so Travis humiliates Betsy (played by Cybil Shepherd), dating her and yet taking her to a pornographic movie and then abusing her publicly when she refuses to date him any more.

Both men inhabit the underbelly of their society, and both men bewail the fact they might have stomach cancer. Underground Man is a dark St Petersburg *mechtatel* and Travis is a New York nightmare: both men loathe what they see and experience and loathe themselves for their inability to rescue themselves or anybody else from its worst excesses. Travis writes in his journal that he is 'God's lonely man', an epithet that could be applied to many of Dostoyevsky's protagonists, who feel themselves alienated from society partly by the idea that they are somehow able to see more clearly, judge more effectively the moral compass of their degenerate surroundings. However, neither is able to resist a descent into further chaos in the hell-like urban *mise en scène* in which they live:

> Despite any legitimacy to their moral outrage, the Underground Man and Travis ultimately seethe with an insidious misanthropy and also self-loathing, which prevent them from becoming 'heroes'. The justified moral outrage begets effective satire on hypocrisy and sound invectives against vice, but the erosion to the fabric of society does not justify our archetype as he himself becomes anti-social.[14]

While Travis descends to violence and attempts suicide, Underground Man remains more aloof from the concept of direct action. Neither believes himself to be a 'hero' although both are offended by the urban condition: 'Dostoyevsky's protagonists loom as an inescapable subtext for any subsequent tale of a marginalised urban figure, and the influence of *Notes* on *Taxi Driver* results from a literary and cinematic lineage of underground men leading from Dostoyevsky to Scorsese.'[15]

Underground Man's prototypical anti-hero had his roots in the *mechtatel* that inhabited Golyadkin's double, and the less disturbing inhabitant of the summer nights of St Petersburg in 'White Nights', but the character had yet to develop. He was to become the central character or the pivot around which at least two major novels Dostoyevsky was to write were to revolve: Raskolnikov, the central character but villain of *Crime and Punishment*, and Stavrogin of *The Devils*. Frequently the godly counterparts of such characters suffer by comparison. The power of goodness is difficult to portray because good characters tend not to fight dirty and can appear weak in the face of evil opposition. All of Dostoyevsky's characters struggle to represent the good as effectively as they represent the nightmare. Just as Hamlet appears weak in the face of his murderous stepfather, so Shatov and Kirilov are little match for the evil Peter Verkhovensky and Stavrogin, the anti-heroes in *The Devils*.

While Dostoyevsky sat beside his dying wife, he explored the depths of his own selfishness in *Notes from the Undergound*, and he interrogated his own behaviour and the prospects for a better world, a better human being. The counter to the evil that he was so good at representing came, he felt, from self sacrifice, from Christ's command to 'Love others as much as you love yourself'. Dostoyevsky saw selfishness in his behaviour towards his wife and felt drawn to the idea that a better man would be less selfish, as indeed a better woman would be less selfish, and therein lay the solution for much of humanity's woes, as well as a solution to his literary dilemma to portray the good as well as the evil. From the time of Maria's final illness, Dostoyevsky felt that selflessness held the secret of salvation. As he watched his wife dying, however, he developed the idea that to destroy the self would make sense only if there was an afterlife. If there were no future life then the only reasonable approach would be to live entirely for one's own gratification, because nothing in the future would compensate for the self-sacrifice. Christ's commandment, then, was proof in itself and pointed to life after death.

Underground Man was a selfish man with a great self-love. In the context of belief this made him a sinner. Other Dostoyevsky characters would represent the purity of self-sacrifice and counter this evil of the urban nightmare. The character of Sonya does this in *Crime and Punishment*. Her sacrifice is great for she becomes a prostitute, sacrificing her worldly reputation and purity to feed the family who loves her. According to Dostoyevsky, such a sacrifice would be meaningless without immortality. By contrast, Stavrogin in *The Devils* demonstrates the logical consequence of the failure to believe in immortality: perhaps Dostoyevsky's greatest sinner, he is given over to the flesh and the desires of self.

Dostoyevsky's last novel, *The Brothers Karamazov*, expresses this idea most succinctly when Miusov quotes Ivan Karamazov:

> But that is not all: he wound up with the assertion that for every individual, like myself, for instance, who does not believe in God or in his own immortality, the moral laws of nature must at once be changed into the exact opposite of the former religious laws, and that self interest, even if it were to lead to crime, must not only be permitted but even recognised as the necessary, the most rational, and practically the most honourable motive for a man in his position.[16]

While Fyodor Dostoyevsky was sitting at his wife's bedside, Mikhail had got permission to publish another journal to replace the now defunct *Time*. The new journal, whose first issue was published in March 1864, was called *Epoch*. Mikhail sent a copy to Fyodor to read and evaluate. His first response was not encouraging; he felt that there was still much work to be done. 'Here is my impression,' he wrote, 'the production might have been rather more elegant, the misprints are so numerous that it amounts to slovenliness.'

Neither did Fyodor appreciate the work the censors had done on his own contribution, the first part of *Notes from the Undergound*: 'Those brutes of censors. Where I made a mock of everything and sometimes blasphemed for form's sake, that is passed, but where I deduced from all this the necessity of faith and of Christ – that is suppressed. Are the censors in a plot against the government or something?'[17]

The new journal had to be very careful not to offend the censors: Mikhail had sunk all he had into its production and, since he had sold his cigarette factory, the magazine was his only chance to make a living. Unfortunately, it was proving extremely difficult to guess what would please or offend the censors. The article that had brought down *Time* had been the victim of an unfavourable interpretation. Suspicious-minded censors had read into the piece something that the publishers had not intended to say, and they were not given the benefit of the doubt. Consequently *Epoch* was desperate not to publish anything that might be misinterpreted. However, they paid a price for their careful publishing, for many readers of the old *Time* felt that *Epoch* blunted its effectiveness by compromising too far. Whereas *Time* had had a good following of regular subscribers, few of its old readers remained faithful to *Epoch*. *The Contemporary, Time*'s old rival, was back in the marketplace after having been banned for nine months and, with the combined talents of Nekrasov and Turgenev backing the journal, it attracted much more attention and many more readers than *Epoch*.

Despite this, Mikhail did get Turgenev to write a piece for *Epoch*, even though his main outlet was *The Contemporary*. This did not mean that the rift between him and Dostoyevsky was in any way made narrower. (It did not help that payment for Turgenev's piece was long delayed.) On the contrary, political and religious differences, reflected in their respective journals, aggravated their relationship. Turgenev still represented the view that art must have some function beyond just being art, that it must be subordinated to higher social causes such as socialism or Westernisation. They no longer argued the point as they once did. The different writers simply got on with their individual work and thus presented their different approaches to the public through their journals and books.

However, to say that Dostoyevsky did not want to express any message through his work would be inaccurate. He did not want to represent the world exactly as people experienced it but to externalise his characters' personal and moral battles through fantasy, dream sequences and supernatural occurrences. His greatest novels were yet to come and they would have much to say, much to discuss.

In April 1864 Maria Dostoyevskaya died. Her death represented one of Dostoyevsky's greatest failures. He had failed to make a good marriage with her and he had failed to make a good death for her. It was with sadness and regret that Dostoyevsky kept vigil at her bedside, and when she died he reflected on the nature of their love. To his old friend Baron Wrangel he wrote:

> I will tell you everything when we meet, but now I will only say that although (because of her strange, mistrustful and morbidly fanciful nature) we were decidedly unhappy together, we could not cease to love each other ... I had no idea how empty and aching my life would be when the earth was strewn on her coffin.[18]

Dostoyevsky packed up his notebook jottings and short novel about Underground Man and left Moscow for St Petersburg to try to make a go of the new journal *Epoch*. This, however, was not to be.

14

LOSS

The strain of restarting a magazine and trying to live without a secure income told on Mikhail Dostoyevsky. Despite early indications of illness, he was desperate with anxiety over the need to make money and so he worked until he dropped. Three days after having been rushed home he was diagnosed as suffering from a liver infection. Mikhail died on 10 July 1864, less than six months after Maria. This was a devastating blow to Fyodor. He had lost his most faithful friend and brother as well as a business partner and supporter. His death not only left Dostoyevsky bereft, it also loaded him with a whole new set of responsibilities. Mikhail had to use the capital from the cigarette factory to live on and to start the new journal. Not only had the money all gone, it had not been enough. *Epoch* was deeply in debt. Dostoyevsky could not officially edit it, nor could he make enough money from it to service the debts and satisfy his own needs; and yet Mikhail's family assumed that Fyodor would now be responsible for them and would take on Mikhail's debts as well as his own. This he did, but it was a heavy burden for he had also committed himself to supporting Pasha, Maria's son.

In the first few days after his brother's death he could choose either to continue to publish *Epoch* or to wind it up and assign it to creditors. He tried, for a few days, to continue publishing it.

In making that decision, he took on all the magazine's business debts as his own: 'What a pity I did not decide on the first', he wrote to Baron Wrangel, for in the end he had no choice but to cut his losses and assign Epoch to creditors.[1] It was better to concentrate on his work and hope that he could finance everybody through his personal writing. He needed to move fast to find a publisher and to develop a novel that would bail them all out.

In the months following the deaths of both his wife and Mikhail, Dostoyevsky urgently needed companionship. Maria's death was more of a reproach than bereavement, but the loss of Mikhail was devastating. Without his friend, his confidante, brother and business partner, Dostoyevsky had to struggle to rebuild his life alone. It must have seemed a bitter blow to survive Siberia only to lose Mikhail after such a short time back together in the same city. It was also hard to face the complete failure of their dreams for literary fame. They had been sidetracked by their army careers and by his exile; only now were they beginning to realise their dreams, and Mikhail was lost. The only lasting monument to Mikhail's life was a needy family and a mountain of debts, and Fyodor had pledged to take all this on.

Dostoyevsky had no one he could depend on. He sought female companionship and his thoughts turned to remarriage. But, as ever, his choices and attractions did little to provide him with a more stable environment. Martha Brown was a young woman with a nomadic lifestyle who had travelled extensively in Europe and had lived with various men. She was Russian by birth – her name was Elizaveta Andreevna Khlebnikova, but 'Martha Brown' seemed more convenient. Upon her return to Russia after her travels, Dostoyevsky gave her some work on *Epoch* and may have asked her to live with him. Her free manner and liberated behaviour attracted him, but she felt that he was not the right partner for her. They wrote to each other for a time until she married an American sailor.

Friendships such as this could not help him solve the difficulties of his day-to-day life. A far more serious relationship developed between Dostoyevsky and one Anna Krukovskaya. Anna was born of a noble family: her father was a general and her sister, Sophia, was an accomplished mathematician. Anna, like so many women who became involved with Dostoyevsky, was deeply moved by him, but was probably more fascinated by him than in love with him. She was impressed by his character, his fame and his misfortune. She had sent some stories to Dostoyevsky, which he published, and they entered into a correspondence until her father discovered that she had accepted money for the stories. Anna won her father over to a continued, if censored, correspondence; she was eager to meet this both famous and infamous writer. Her parents did not view such a prospect with equanimity. Dostoyevsky was a man of limited and uncertain means. He was twice as old as Anna, an epileptic and an ex-convict. An involvement with such a man did not bode well for the future of their daughter.

Anna was a persuasive woman and her parents finally agreed to a chaperoned meeting, probably thinking that this would do less harm than an illicit correspondence. Anna's mother was present at this first exchange, which was not a success. Dostoyevsky was irritated by the older woman's presence and as a result was rude and discourteous. He spoke only in monosyllables and made no attempt to hide his annoyance about being chaperoned. When the agonisingly embarrassing meeting was over, Anna ran to her room screaming at her parents, 'You always spoil everything!'[2]

Dostoyevsky, however, was not to be beaten as easily as that. The next time he and Anna met he contrived to make an unscheduled call, when everyone except Anna and her younger sister Sophia happened to be out. Although the meeting was discovered, the two sisters and Dostoyevsky were in such good spirits that the girls' parents invited him to lunch.

For their daughters' sake the senior Krukovskys did their best to welcome Dostoyevsky into their home, but his behaviour left them anxious and perplexed. At one dinner party he began to describe, in detail, the seduction of a young girl by one of his heroes. In the middle of his recital Mrs Krukovskaya cut in, 'Fyodor

Michailovitch! For pity's sake, the children are listening!'³ Sophia, who was more deeply infatuated with Dostoyevsky than was Anna, later said that her mother need not have worried – she had had no idea what Dostoyevsky was talking about.

According to Sophia, Dostoyevsky was preoccupied with her sister. He wanted only to speak to her and came to their house for that reason alone. Anna's parents noticed his intensity. At another dinner party Mrs Krukovskaya, once again, felt obliged to rebuke him, this time for monopolising her daughter and keeping her away from all the other guests. Anna's mother need not have worried that her daughter was spending her affections on an unsuitable partner: Anna herself soon realised that their relationship could not lead to any serious commitment. They simply were not compatible.

Anna was an independent woman, a believer in women's rights and not eager to assume the traditional role of the wife. Dostoyevsky's view of the role of women was more conservative, even though so far he had been attracted to few women who would willingly have conformed to that role. Anna's political views remained firmly within the context of utopian socialism, and Dostoyevsky was moving further and further away from that philosophy. The revolutionary who had been sent to Siberia was now more reactionary than Anna could stand. Anna was young and keen for adventure. Fyodor and Anna argued constantly. Once again, Dostoyevsky found that he was more in love than he was loved, and their relationship bickered its way into exhaustion. Anna left Russia in 1866, when she met and married a Frenchman by the name of Victor Jacquard; the couple became deeply involved in the construction of the Paris Commune, and also became friends of Karl Marx. After the failure of the commune they returned to Russia where they occasionally reconnected with Dostoyevsky. Fyodor and Anna continued to write to each other for a while and renewed their friendship in the late 1870s shortly before Fyodor's death.

Anna was not the only woman Dostoyevsky was courting at that time. In the summer of 1866 he went to his sister's country estate at Lyublino to try to complete *Crime and Punishment*, which was already being serialised in *The Russian Messenger*. While there, he met Elena Pavlovna, a married woman whose husband was dying. Closer to Dostoyevsky in age than was Anna, she was much more willing to subordinate herself to his demanding nature. However she was not, as yet, free to marry. She and Dostoyevsky agreed that once her husband died they would marry, but Dostoyevsky was to break that promise, because he fell in love with someone else. He later wrote to the wife he chose, Anna Snitkina, 'Elena Pavlovna has taken it all pretty well, and only said to me, "I am very glad I did not consent in the summer or say anything definite, or I should have been shattered." I am very glad she has taken it like this, and I am now quite reassured on that score.'[4]

The romance with Anna Snitkina flared quickly, fanned during a period in which Dostoyevsky was in a mess and unable to control his business interests properly. He was about to fail and to fail badly. Apart from writing *Crime and Punishment*, Dostoyevsky had already committed himself to write another novel that he had to submit by November 1866 to another publisher, Stellovsky. Desperate for money, and not blessed with a good head for business, Dostoyevsky had agreed to deliver the manuscript of *The Gambler* on this tight deadline for a ridiculously small amount of money. Not only that, he had agreed to pay a penalty should he fail to deliver by that deadline. Penalties for failing to meet deadlines are not uncommon, but this one was severe: in the event that he failed to deliver *The Gambler* on time, he would hand over the publishing rights of all his works to Stellovsky for the next nine years. Dostoyevsky fell increasingly behind on this novel, and as the November deadline grew closer it looked more and more likely that Dostoyevsky would lose his only livelihood to an unscrupulous man.

Dostoyevsky was in despair. With four weeks to go he did not believe it was physically possible for him to write a novel and deliver it. Friends offered to write a chapter apiece if he would set out the plot and plans, but he was both too honourable and too proud to let them do that. However, another friend, Milyukov, had a more practical idea and suggested that he dictate his work to a stenographer. Dostoyevsky was skeptical about this but had little choice; it was his last hope, and so he agreed. Milyukov approached a stenography tutor, Pavel Olkhin, and asked him to provide Dostoyevsky with his best student. This turned out to be Anna Snitkina, then aged twenty. When Olkhin told her that he had recommended her to Dostoyevsky for the task she was flattered but not convinced that she was up to the job. Her father, who had died not long before, had been a great admirer of Dostoyevsky's writing: Anna and her family had all read his books.

Anna was both delighted and excited. For her, the prospect of working for this great writer was daunting, and the night before she was due to meet him she could not sleep. However, she was ambitious to earn her own way in the world, and this was a good opportunity for a serious-minded young person to get experience, contacts and a reputation as a reliable and accurate stenographer. Things were not to turn out quite as she had envisaged during her training; the independent career that she so coveted was not to be, but the ambition and competence that fuelled her young aspirations were to stand her in good stead in the years to come, because she saved Dostoyevsky's career.

'To tell the truth,' she wrote of their first meeting, 'at first sight I did not at all take to him.'[5] As soon as she introduced herself he forgot her name, and she noticed that his eyes did not match: one pupil was constantly dilated, the result of a seizure. He was just as nervous as she was and completely unused to dictation. He launched into a speedy delivery of a test piece and she could not keep up. When she read it back he thoroughly scolded her for missing a full stop. The only positive comment he made was that he was glad that she was not a man, as men tended to drink. That night she returned promptly at eight with a neat and perfectly worded version of the morning's dictation. Dostoyevsky began to relax.

Once the initial awe and awkwardness of their first meeting wore off, they began working well together. Anna Snitkina, like

Fyodor Dostoyevsky, Semipalatinsk 1858,
Dostoyevsky Museum, Moscow.
(Courtesy of SPUTNIK, Alamy.com)

Anna G. Dostoyevsky from the collection of
the Museum of Moscow.
(Courtesy of SPUTNIK, Alamy.com)

A page from notes on *The Devils*, by Dostoyevsky. (Courtesy of INTERFOTO, Alamy.com)

Above: St Peter and Paul Fortress, St Petersburg. (Public Domain www.pixabay.com)

Below: St Petersburg White Nights. Church of the Saviour on Blood on Griboyedov Canal (Public Domain www.pixabay.com)

Above: St Petersburg White Nights. Church of the Saviour on Blood on Griboyedov Canal. (Courtesy of Anton Balazh, Shutterstock.com)

Below: The Great Trinity Monastery in Sergiev Posad near Moscow. (Courtesy of Viacheslav Lopatin, Shutterstock.com)

Samtliche Romane Und Novellen (Novels and Novellas) 1921. (Courtesy of
Internet Book Archive, © Flickr.com)

Above: Dostoyevsky's Office, House Museum of Dostoyevsky, Staraya Russia. (Copyright Konstantin Pukhov, Dreamstime.com)

Below: Museum of Dostoyevsky, Omsk, Russia. (Courtesy of H. Galina, Shutterstock.com)

Above: Grave of Dostoyevsky, Nevsky Monastery, St Petersburg, Omsk, Russia. (Courtesy of dimbar76, Shutterstock.com)

Below: Moscow Metro Mosaic. (Copyright Vovez, Dreamstime.com)

Fyodor Dostoyevsky antique print 1899.
(Copyright Georgios Kollidas,
Dreamstime.com)

Monument to Dostoyevsky, Tobolsk, Russia.
(Courtesy of Elena Mirage Shutterstock.com)

so many women before her, found herself feeling sympathy for the rather sad man who employed her: 'For the first time in my life I had seen a man unhappy, deserted and badly treated, and a feeling of deep compassion and sympathy was born in my heart.'[6]

Their meetings were intense. They had a deadline to meet – a common enemy – and their feelings for each other deepened and developed. Five days before they were due to meet their deadline and so stop their working partnership, Dostoyevsky confessed that he would miss her and said he would like to see her again. Anna arranged for him to come to tea and meet her socially in the presence of her family, but she was afraid of the kind of impression her family might make on him. They were not rich: her father had been an administrator in the tsar's palaces, and the family owned a few pieces of land on which stood some houses, but these were mortgaged. An added complication for the contemplated afternoon tea was that a friend insisted to Anna that she too should come to tea to meet Dostoyevsky. Anna felt forced to lie to the girl:

> But how to get rid of her, seeing she had invited herself? I thought for a long while and was greatly worried about it; and then I decided on a feminine stratagem: to call her on Thursday morning and to tell her that Dostoevsky had paid us a visit the previous night, on Wednesday, and so was not coming Thursday. That little lie was disgusting to me; but what could I do if I feared her rivalry so much?'[7]

While the couple were falling in love they were also completing their assignment. The day came when the manuscript was complete and ready to deliver, on time, to the publisher. Stellovsky, probably anticipating a last rally on the part of Dostoyevsky, had left the country and so was not available to receive the manuscript. Moreover his offices were closed. After a desperate search for someone to take it in they finally persuaded an Inspector of the Police to accept it on Stellovsky's behalf and to give Dostoyevsky a receipt for it as proof of delivery. It was ten o'clock at night: they had found a legal recipient just two hours from the deadline. The couple decided to push the boat out and go off for a cup of coffee to celebrate.

Anna was eager to partake in this small victory celebration, but she was also worried that accepting a cup of coffee from Dostoyevsky might not be proper. She did not want to get a loose reputation. Moreover, she held some feminist views: 'As a girl of the sixties, I had a prejudice against all such marks of attention, as the kissing of a woman's hands, or the putting of an arm round her waist in helping her to get out of a cab.'[8] Consequently when he tried to help her out of the cab she informed him promptly that she was all right and would not fall out. Unabashed, he replied that he would be delighted if she did, for then he could catch her and hold her. His intimacy was declared.

A few days later, Fyodor proposed to Anna. He did not go down on one knee and ask her to marry him but presented his proposal in the form of a story. He said he wanted her advice on the plot of a new novel. A young woman called Anna (and to begin with Anna Snitkina thought he meant Anna Korvin Krukovskaya) is less than half the age of the man who wants to marry her. Would such a marriage be right? The man, in this case, is worried about the age gap, the sacrifices the young Anna would have to make in her career and life. Anna assured him that the sacrifice would be nothing if she loved him and that the girl would mature quickly. The story progressed, and she gradually came to realise that he was proposing to her. She accepted:

> Dostoyevsky's face expressed so much agitation, such anguish of heart that I at last understood that it was not simply a literary discussion, and that I should be dealing a death-blow to his pride and *amour-propre* if I gave an evasive answer. I glanced at his agitated face, so dear to me, and said, 'I should answer that I love you and shall love you all my life.'[9]

They were married in February 1867, in St Petersburg's Trinity Cathedral. This ceremony was a far cry from the shabby wedding to Maria in the outpost town of Kuznetsk in 1857. However, history was to repeat itself in at least one aspect of their honeymoon. Alcohol often precipitated fits and, as a result of drinking too much champagne, Dostoyevsky had two consecutive epileptic fits. Consequently Anna, like Maria before her, had to face the terror of his illness very early in their marriage. However, unlike Maria, she soon came to terms with it and was even able to see the funny side of it:

> This time he did not come round for a rather long time, and when he began to do so – however bitterly and painfully I felt, I had a desire to laugh, for any words he uttered were spoken in German. He said: '*Was? Was doch? Lassen Sie micht*', and went on with a long string of German phrases.[10]

Anna Snitkina had married an ex-convict twice her age who suffered from an incurable condition. He had an unreliable and demanding stepson and a mountain of debts. However, if not rich, he had also just become extremely famous. *Crime and Punishment* was the first of his four great novels to be published and, after he had spent over fifteen years in the literary wilderness, it was to re-establish him as a major literary figure. Typically, though, it was also to create some controversy. *Crime and Punishment* did not receive rave reviews – if anything, it was greeted with anger. Like Dickens, Dostoyevsky had portrayed the conditions of the poor. He brought to lurid life the agonies of poverty in the slums of St Petersburg. In this respect, his realistic approach was merciless: drunkards, beggars, women dying of consumption, and children – dirty, ragged and beaten – stalked the streets of the city amidst the dust and grime of an oppressive Petersburg summer, and through this dismal landscape walked the haggard figure of the *mechtatel* Raskolnikov.

15

THE RAISING OF RASKOLNIKOV

In 1866 came *Crime and Punishment*, which brought
Dostoyevsky fame. This book, Dostoyevsky's Macbeth, is
so well known in the French and English translations that
it hardly needs any comment. Dostoyevsky never wrote
anything more tremendous than the portrayal of the anguish
that seethes in the shoulders of Raskolnikov, after he has
killed the old woman.

Maurice Baring,
An Outline of Russian Literature.[1]

Raskolnikov was a student who had fallen on hard times. He was
an educated man, who valued that education to the extent that
he saw it as the bedrock of his superiority. His education had
introduced him to the ideas and philosophies of a socialism
radicalised with anarchy and nihilism. His was an atheistic view
of the world and, as a natural consequence, he lived for himself
and for the exercise of his own free will. Raskolnikov's decision-
making made no recourse to a higher moral authority or to other
people; Raskolnikov existed and that was that. If God did not
exist then humanity was earthbound, like 'underground man',
and decisions about life and death had to be made on utilitarian
grounds. In a letter of 1878 to N. L. Osmidov, with whom he

was corresponding over the merits of Christianity, Dostoyevsky clarified the initial ideas that Raskolnikov expressed:

> Now suppose that there is no God, and no personal immortality (personal immortality and God are one and the same – an identical idea). Tell me then: Why am I to live decently and do good, if I die irrevocably here below? If there is no immortality, I need but live out my appointed day and let the rest go hang.[2]

This was the debate that now preoccupied Fyodor: why be a moral human being if there was no reward in heaven? It was not that Dostoyevsky felt that doing good should be motivated by self-interest, merely that he did not think humanity was capable of being good consistently without that motivation. His portrait of Raskolnikov is a dramatisation of that debate. Raskolnikov employs the logic of a young man, convinced by the cold rationalism of a socialist utopia, and his character and will were the outworking of the best of humankind; Raskolnikov is the logical conclusion of Nikolai Chernyshevsky's *What is to be Done?* But Raskolnikov's logic led him to evil ends. Raskolnikov stalked the proposed socialism of Belinsky's politics, where human beings would perpetuate a better world and where they would release the oppressed from the injustice of their subjection. The commune of Petrashevsky was to be peopled with the poor, who would finally be treated with the deference they deserved, and civilisation would progress to an inevitable utopia – but Dostoyevsky was not convinced of that and never had been. Raskolnikov was his answer. Despite claiming in *The Diary of a Writer* that he had 'followed passionately' everything Belinsky said, Dostoyevsky remained faithful to the Christianity that informed Russian history and to the idea that Christ and the interaction of human beings with God was the only hope of better behaviour on earth. Raskolnikov thus needed a dramatic conceit, a salvation, so at the opening of *Crime and Punishment* he is a godless man who commits a dreadful crime.

Raskolnikov does not rise into the streets of St Petersburg from nowhere: he is the continuation of those strange St Petersburg dreamers, the *mechtatel* who haunt the darkness of the city streets, alienated and spiteful. He is an underground man, gradually succumbing to his lesser self, the self that Dostoyevsky sees as dominant and as a threat to the utopia that so many Russian idealists hoped to build: 'It was remarkable that Raskolnikov had hardly any friends at the university; he kept aloof from everyone, went to see no one, and did not welcome anyone who came to see him, and indeed everyone soon gave him up.'[3]

Raskolnikov is isolated. He has no one to discuss his ideas with, and so his logic is placed before the reader, in the same way Underground Man challenges the reader directly, describing himself as the kind of boss who likes to mock his employees, challenging the reader to dislike him. Raskolnikov, often called by Dostoyevsky the 'young man', is a student, but one without the usual student social life. He backs away from company and only rarely does he seek it out; sometimes, like any student, he gets drunk. Thus secluded in isolation Raskolnikov builds a logic that leads him to murder.

Raskolnikov's crime stems from his atheism and his appeal to a utilitarian logic. Raskolnikov's chosen victim is an old pawnbroker and, accidentally, her sister. The young man, as Dostoyevsky defines him, builds a logic based on his own right to rid the world of those he considers inappropriate to live in it. The pawnbroker is a parasite: she lends money at a high rate, she shows no compassion for those who borrow from her, and thus she deserves her fate. Raskolnikov believes it is his prerogative to commit the crime, for then quite logically enough the world will be a better place. However, his thought processes are not rigorous and thoroughly contemplated – it is an overheard conversation that sparks his idea and provides him with the victim: 'Kill her, take her money and with the help of it devote oneself to the service of humanity and the good of all. What do you think, would not one tiny crime be wiped out by thousands of good deeds?'[4] It is not Raskolnikov who makes this point but two drunken gentlemen in a bar discussing their dissatisfaction with the pawnbroker and, more particularly, her sister, Lizaveta. Raskolnikov is at once resolved upon it, but the reader is only half aware of his plan. Dostoyevsky plays with the psychology of his protagonist, just as Valerian Maikov had said, in defending Dostoyevsky's *The Double* in 1847, that he was now offering sophisticated portraits of the inner psyche of his characters. This was a reality that, whilst it was rooted in the physical universe, remained at the mercy of the irrational impulses of the mind of man.

Thus, in the chapters that lead up to the crime Dostoyevsky offers a psychological profile of a lonely student with few friends, alarmed by a letter from his mother about his sister whose suitors for marriage are both inappropriate. His landlady stops sending him meals because he has not paid the rent on his top-floor apartment (as was the convention in St Petersburg at the time, social success was then defined by the floor on which you lived; the higher up the building the less affluent the tenant). Plagued by hunger, loneliness, debt and the anxious expectation of the arrival of his mother and sister in St Petersburg, Raskolnikov is troubled by dreams. In one dream he sees again the cruel treatment and death of a horse that could not pull its cart, laden with expectant people. Consequently, her owner Mikolka becomes enraged and, embarrassed by the horse's failure, he and others in the group proceed to beat the horse with whips and sticks, in front of a tearful seven-year-old Raskolnikov and his father. Mikolka defies all interference from those around him, including the boy and his father, repeating that the horse is his 'property'; and so at last, when the animal kicks again in defence of herself, he beats her to the ground with a club. The horse collapses, barely alive; the words 'Fetch an axe' and 'Finish her off' echo in Raskolnikov's dream. Mikolka does the deed, still proclaiming that the horse is his property, while others accuse him of not being Christian. Thus the contrast between the utilitarian impulse, that all things must be of use, and an appeal to Christian compassion is symbolised in Raskolnikov's dream and foreshadows the crime he is about to commit. He wakes in a sweat, asking himself whether he shall really take an axe, whether he shall really go through with it. He fears that he cannot even though the utilitarian calculus seems to him to be as clear as 'arithmetic'. However, the reader is yet to really understand what crime it is that he will commit. The St Petersburg dreamer heads out into the urban landscape of a hot and uncomfortable summer so that, on one those by now archetypal 'White Nights', Raskolnikov can kill.

Anyone reading the account of the crime cannot fail to be impressed by the tension, the subsequent ineptitude and ultimately the brute fact that he has to kill not one but two people – two women. Moreover, getting out of the flat unnoticed does not prove easy and is not without its surprises and misdirection; for all his ability to explore the forensic psychology of his young man, Dostoyevsky is a master too of physical tension and suspenseful storytelling, for which, in all of the discussion of the greater themes, he get still gets little credit. The crime, however, is the catalyst: it is the tool by which Dostoyevsky can explore the themes of the nature of man, free will and the possibility of social utopia when that man is given over to his 'arithmetic'. However, it is this logic that finally sets the young student apart from his compatriots; he progresses from a lonely student with a limited social life to someone who is set apart by his crime, and who for a while believes that to be the correct order of thing:

> But Raskolnikov has placed himself outside of society consciously through his concept of the superman and of man-made reason and will-controlled morality which discounts all tradition and feeling, and unconsciously through his crime.[5]

Like Dickens, Dostoyevsky sometimes used names to indicate something about the characters he created. The *raskol*, or 'old believers', were a sect who refused to accept the new liturgy and the few modernisations to the Orthodox faith imposed by Patriarch Nikon in the seventeenth century, seeing such concessions as a compromise with Rome. Raskolnikov seems to have little in common with the beliefs of this strange sect, but one theory posits that Dostoyevsky saw the behaviour of extremists, be they political or religious, as analogous. A political sect differed from a religious sect only in the nature of its beliefs. Eventually the word *raskol* came to mean division or schism; in this way, a 'rascal' may well have a double. However, *raskol* may also have had personal significance to Dostoyevsky. Perhaps Raskolnikov represented Dostoyevsky's own 'old beliefs' or his own lifelong contradictions and beliefs. Raskolnikov may have been the ultimate realisation of what Dostoyevsky believed became of those who held to the socialist and anarchist political systems he had once embraced.

Another character, a friend of Raskolnikov's, is called Razumihin. The name has its root in *razum*, meaning 'reason', and there is no doubt that Razumihin is a sensible and decent friend, but one who, ironically, eventually comes to understand Raskonlnikov's crime by instinct not by reason. Sonya is a derivative of the name Sophia, which in Slavic languages is a form of divine love, a fourth love almost as divine as that from the trinity, and a redemptive love which in essence is the core both of Sonya's character and the theme of the book. The sense of the divine is emphasised by the use of light: Sonya lives in an apartment surrounded by windows, and sunshine follows her throughout the novel, whereas Raskolnikov inhabits the dingy streets of St Petersburg and his room is a 'closet'. Svidrigailov, a lesser character in the plot but also deeply corrupt, is literally nocturnal, nurturing his lechery for Dunia, Raskolnikov's sister, and allowing his musings on little girls to drive him to suicide.

Dostoyevsky was fascinated, not so much with humanity's capacity to do evil, although he had become a master at portraying such evil, but with their impulse to do good and the dilemma of how they might redeem themselves from such evil if they could. He had spent almost a decade in Siberia, some of that time in prison alongside men who had committed evil deeds. The propensity of humankind to commit evil had become a familiar aspect of his life. It was probably part of what confirmed his belief that humans alone could not construct a social utopia, that somehow the flawed impulse to do evil would always damage the longed for Crystal Palace that his friends of the 1840s had so dreamt to build, and which was still gaining traction in the philosophies of the nineteenth century. The solution to the problem of evil itself was a harder construct to approach than simply building communes or challenging governments. Dostoyevsky resorted to faith and salvation, and he was coming to believe that the only motivation to do good must lie in a belief in God.

Thus it is Sonya, the woman who loves him and with whom he falls in love, who shows him the path to redemption, one founded on Christian salvation. Under Sonya's influence Raskolnikov comes to renounce what he has done and, to an extent, what he has believed. Sonya, however, is an unlikely source for the Christian message: she is a prostitute who sells her body in order to support her drunken father's wife and children, who would starve without her money. Her holiness is derived from her self-sacrifice, which purifies her lifestyle as a prostitute; the spiritual, not the physical, is her path to salvation. She reflects the sacrifice of the prostitute in *Notes from the Undergound*, but in this case the Petersburg *mechtatel* or dreamer is redeemed. He does not abuse her choices, nor does he disrespect her affection nor use it; her love, her divine love, becomes the source of his redemption.

A central scene in *Crime and Punishment* portrays Sonya reading to Raskolnikov the story of the raising of Lazarus. It introduces the motif of resurrection: Raskolnikov must die to his old beliefs, and therefore to his crime, and be raised a redeemed man. In this way Dostoyevsky rescues Raskolnikov from the consequences of his belief in atheistic socialism. In later novels Dostoyevsky was not to be so generous to some of his anti-heroes, but Raskolnikov steps back from suicide without really knowing why. Like Shakespeare's Hamlet, he is afraid to take the decisive step and so end his 'sea of troubles' because, like Hamlet, he fears that the dreams of such a sleep may be terrible. He may have an immortal soul, but he may also be required to answer for his actions. This is surely a fear he would not have if he were truly an avowed atheist.

When Raskolnikov, still unrepentant, comes to Sonya to confess his crime, he confesses not just the act but the reason, that is the sense that he may have considered he was committing the act on principle because he was entitled to rid the world of inferiority – but ultimately he has to recognise that in fact his tendency to evil was much more basic:

> 'I wanted to find out something else; it was something else led me on. I wanted to find out then and quickly whether I was a louse like everybody else or a man. Whether I can step over barriers or not, whether I dare stoop to pick up or not, whether I am a trembling creature or whether I have the right...'
> 'To kill? Have the right to kill?' Sonia clasped her hands.[6]

On hearing of his deed, a matter about which she has had some doubts, she demands he confesses, that he 'kisses the ground in Siberia' and makes his penance. He must denounce his crime, his arrogance as a man and student, and he must submit to the judgement of his fellow men and enact penance before God. Unless this is done, Dostoyevsky suggests, there is no hope for real social justice on earth; utopia will always be sabotaged by utilitarianism. Divine love, the impulse to redemption and the need for penance are crucial to ensuring a better world.

Many reviewers said that the first half of the book was brilliant but after that it degenerated into a kind of morbid self-examination. Many more saw it as an insult to the young people of the time; they thought it implied that St Petersburg's young men were so influenced by nihilistic and atheistic ideas that they were all potential murderers. Critics condemned the link Dostoyevsky made between radical ideas such as social utopianism and the tendency towards crime. Dostoyevsky had attempted to draw a line through the original thinking of his former radical circles to the logical consequences of such philosophies. His depiction of this lost young man drew a great deal of attention. A major critic of the day Dmitry Pisarev wrote a lengthy sixty-page review of the novel. Pisarev, like Belinsky before him, believed that literature served a purpose to educate and enlighten, so his review of *Crime and Punishment* served to point out the way in which the portrait of Raskolnikov did serve, rather than defeat, the ideas of the social realists. He demonstrated that it was Raskolnikov's poverty that leads him to lose his reason and commit the crime to clear his debts and thus help his sister, Dunia, avoid an unpleasant marriage. For Pisarev, the representation of the conditions in which Raskolnikov lived and the way his character is treated are evidence of Dostoyevsky's talent as a realistic writer, and as such the characters serve the main purpose of any art form, to reflect and expose the injustices of the social world in order to invoke improvement.

Nikolai Strakhov was more impressed with the novel and understood it as a more complete piece. He perceived that it was an exercise in annihilating nihilism; he did not see it as a condemnation of Russia's youth, more as a 'lament' over the way in which their social context and the ideas they were exposed to led them astray. The end of the book did not disillusion Strakhov, either. Although he had hoped that it could have ended in more triumphant affirmation of life, the end of *Crime and Punishment* is by no means sentimental. Strakhov's review was appreciated by Dostoyevsky, who wrote that Strakhov alone had understood him.

In the end Raskolnikov's conversion is understated. He and Sonya face the prison sentence together, for she follows him to Siberia. In the last scene, Raskolnikov is still unsure and asks himself, 'Can her convictions not be mine now?' Dostoyevsky leaves the reader guessing: 'But that is the beginning of a new story – the story of the gradual renewal of a man, the story of his gradual regeneration, of him passing from one world into another, of his initiation into a new unknown life.'[7] Raskolnikov is punished, and he must reconcile himself to his crime and face the consequences of living on as a redeemed criminal.

However, while some reviewers condemned the novel as poorly written, others were so squeamish that they had had to give up reading the book precisely because it was so well written; yet others defended the reputation of the young people of St Petersburg and the serial (the manner in which it was first published), sold by the thousands. Among the much-debated young people as a class, Raskolnikov became the James Dean figure of the 1860s, a rebel with an axe. Several young men were so influenced by Raskolnikov that they actually planned similar murders; an identical double murder did take place just before publication. This event, though uninfluenced by the novel, focused public attention on it and helped its sales.

Crime and Punishment was important not only as a description of social conditions and political ideas but as an indication of the place Christianity was beginning to have in Dostoyevsky's work. Although Raskolnikov was a murderer, he was not unredeemed, and the religious content did not please everybody. The publisher was nervous about hearing Christian words from a prostitute, and these scenes were not sent to the printer until considerable revision had been done under the eye of the editor, Katkov, of *The Russian Messenger*. 'I wrote it in a positive inspiration', wrote Dostoyevsky to his friend Milyukov of the dispute he was having over the scenes and then, expressing a true writer's sensitivity, he went on:

> But it may be that it's really bad; however, with them it's not a question of the literary value, but of nervousness about the morality of it. In this respect I am in the right: the chapter contains nothing immoral, quite the contrary indeed; but they're of another opinion, and moreover see traces of Nihilism therein.[8]

The best portrayal of the character of a nihilist up to that time had been credited to Turgenev for his character Bazarov in *Fathers and Sons*. Now that same compliment was applied to Raskolnikov. Dostoyevsky accepted the accolade, but he had wanted to expose nihilism by redeeming Raskolnikov from it, and it was the manner of this redemption that brought him into conflict with his editors. Raskolnikov's redemption is as important to the character as his nihilism. At his trial, Raskolnikov is defended by friends who testify to his good character, his acts of charity and his heroism in rescuing some children from a fire. The death of the old drunk Marmaledov, Sonya's father, portrays a priest as he chants a useless ritual, while Raskolnikov gives the family money for the funeral. Thus the futility of heaven is juxtaposed against a positive, down-to-earth act. Raskolnikov is not without his saving graces and the church is not without its futility; Dostoyevsky does not entirely forsake the idealism of his youth in favour of mindless concessions to a heartless orthodoxy.

Raskolnikov's positive side and Dostoyevsky's hope to convert and so redeem him worried his editors. They felt that the demarcation between good and evil should be clearer: to them it was unbelievable that a character so unsympathetic should convert to Christianity and be willing to serve his penance. It also denied the reader that sense of justice, for it meant that, despite his sentence to Siberia, Raskolnikov got away with the crime, at least spiritually. There would be no eternal consequences to his act of murder. They did not understand the concept that Dostoyevsky was trying to embed, the idea that had begun to form as he sat at his dying wife's bedside, when he read the commandment 'Love thy neighbour as thyself'. The idea that actions are less important than a faithful cast of mind is encapsulated in the figure of Sonya, who though a prostitute could also be a holy person due to her simple Christian humility; this essentially religious attitude is more important to her salvation than being able to live a good life. Raskolnikov could be forgiven because he changed his attitudes and lost the pride that had persuaded him to take another human life. However, despite the publisher's and the reviewers' doubts, *Crime and Punishment* was a success and Raskolnikov entered the annals of literary history worldwide. The haunted dreamer of the St Petersburg landscape became an archetype for a modern anti-hero, and the formula of the book itself became the basis of a modern phenomenon:

Our template for *Columbo* was Petrovitch, the detective-inspector in *Crime and Punishment*, Dostoevsky's great novel;

Dick [Richard Levinson] and I read it in college ... And Peter Falk, you know, gave it a whole new spin, because the cop in the book was not humorous at all ... In this one man, you have both Sherlock Holmes and Watson. There's the intellectual, the very clever, great detective and Sherlock Holmes and then you have the everyman Watson ... He's a regular working-class guy – who's got a brilliant mind ...[9]

No discussion of Dostoyevsky's *Crime and Punishment* is complete without a discussion of Porfiry Petrovich, the magistrate in charge of the investigation into the murder of the two women. The way in which Porfiry pursues Raskolnikov is the template for the TV detective *Columbo,* played by Peter Falk. First and foremost, anyone familiar with the series will know that the audience always recognises who the murderer is, if not why or how they actually did the deed. The task for Columbo is to establish motive and opportunity, followed by the proof he needs. The audience always has the sense that Columbo knows from the start that the protagonist has committed the crime: Columbo plays with his perpetrator a little like a cat does with a mouse, and so it was with Porfiry.

The first meeting Raskolnikov has with Porfiry Petrovich finds Porfiry in battered slippers and a dressing gown, unabashed by the way he presents himself and only concerned to make the acquaintance of his prey. When he suggests to Raskolnikov that he simply submit his claim for his goods by writing it down on an ordinary piece of paper, Porfiry appears to screw up his eyes and maybe even winks at Raskolnikov: 'Raskolnikov could have sworn he winked at him, goodness knows why.'[10] Like Columbo, Porfiry lures his culprit into an ostensibly irrelevant conversation. It is Porfiry who engages Raskolnikov in conversation about the nature of a human being's right to kill another person, for like Columbo he has done his research, and he has discovered an article entitled 'On Crime' published by Raskolnikov in a university journal: 'My article? In the Periodical Review?' Raskolnikov asked in astonishment.'[11] The information makes Raskolnikov uneasy. Porfiry uses the article as a means to discuss the nature of crime as well as Raskonikov's theory that there are some who have a right to 'wade through blood' in order to destroy the present and make the future better. The magistrate interrogates the young radical: 'There is, if you recollect, a suggestion that there are certain persons who can … that is, not precisely are able to, but have a perfect right to commit breaches of morality and crimes, and that the law is not for them.'[12]

Like Columbo, Porfiry appears to take the side of Raskolnikov, only wanting him to clarify his opinion on crime, to enjoy a discussion as it were between one criminologist and another, and to reassure himself that Raskolnikov has been rigorous with his theory. Porfiry's conversation is full of phrases that suggest to Raskolnikov that he, Porfiry, is the fool and simply wants to clarify certain minor details. He comments that his mind has been set at rest by Raskonlnikov's explanations. He flatters him; his conversation is designed to suggest to Raskolnikov that he has great wisdom even if his ideas are radical. Even so, Raskolnikov is unnerved. The familiarity and the good humour, even the winking, worries Raskolnikov: '"He knows," flashed through his mind like lightning.'[13]

Just as Raskolnikov is about to leave the room, Porfiry then moves the conversation to just some little details about Raskolnikov's whereabouts and when; Raskolnikov begins to feel threatened while Razumihin, who is listening, appears to offer credence to Raskolnikov's version. The response is classic *Columbo*:

'Foo! I have muddled it!' Porfiry slapped himself on the forehead. 'Deuce take it! This business is turning my brain!' he addressed Raskolnikov somewhat apologetically. 'It would be such a great thing for us to find out whether anyone had seen them between seven and eight at the flat, so I fancied you could perhaps have told us something … I quite muddled it.'[14]

Porfiry pursues his culprit effectively, and the reader soon understands that Raskolnikov will not get away with his crime. Each clue is dropped into the conversation and Raskolnikov begins to understand that Porfiry really does know the full extent of his crime, not least because Raskolnikov makes the rookie mistake of not coming forward to claim the things he pawned from the sisters:

> 'But we know all who had pledges, and you are the only one who hasn't come forward,' Porfiry answered with hardly perceptible irony.
>
> 'I haven't been quite well.'
>
> 'I heard that too. I heard, indeed, that you were in great distress about something. You look pale still.'
>
> 'I am not pale at all ... No, I am quite well,' Raskolnikov snapped out rudely and angrily, completely changing his tone. His anger was mounting, he could not repress it. 'And in my anger I shall betray myself,' flashed through his mind again. 'Why are they torturing me?'[15]

Gradually Razumihin perceives the truth and Raskolnikov confesses, first to Sonya and then to Porfiry. The climax of the book is reached and Porfiry's part in it fades into the history of the story – although not into the history of literature or modern media.

16

THE GAMBLER

> Do you know that I am absolutely aware that if
> I could have spent two or three years at that book – as
> Turgenev, Gontscharov and Tolstoy can – I could have
> produced a work of which men would still be talking in
> a hundred years from now.
>
> Dostoyevsky.[1]

Columbo notwithstanding, *Crime and Punishment* has been reimagined and dramatised many times. It is perhaps the most famous of Dostoyevsky's works and is, indeed, talked about over one hundred and fifty years after its initial publication. It is as relevant today as it was then and is frequently used as a shorthand for establishing intellectual credentials – even Gromit in *The Wrong Trousers* is seen reading *Crime and Punishment* by Fido Dogstoevsky! However, the success of *Crime and Punishment* did little to alleviate Dostoyevsky's financial problems. The situation was so bad that Anna sold her dowry in order to pay off some of the more urgent debts. After their marriage ceremony, the couple moved in with Dostoyevsky's remaining family for three months but, like Maria Isayeva before her, Anna found that her welcome into the family was neither warm nor willing. Dostoyevsky's sister-in-law, Mikhail's widow, and her family feared that this new wife would divert not only Fyodor's attention but his money from the pressing debts he had agreed to take on after Mikhail's death.

Dostoyevsky's stepson Pasha, Maria's son, was already exhibiting many of the faults of his natural father. He was dissolute, selfish and lazy, and he drank too much. Until Dostoyevsky married Anna, Pasha had set his sights on inheriting the copyright to Dostoyevsky's books. Anna's arrival on the scene made inheriting the copyright very unlikely, and so Pasha was all the more keen to get what he could from his new parents as quickly as possible. His requests for money became all the more pressing.

Everyone who knew Dostoyevsky must have viewed his second marriage with trepidation. His first marriage had been a failure from the start, and now he had married a young woman more than twenty years his junior. Her inexperience and immaturity alone might have been expected to cause the couple problems. Thus Anna had an uphill struggle before her to convince her critics that she could make a success of her marriage to Dostoyevsky and provide some much-needed emotional and physical stability. She had to fight hard to win the support of her new relatives and friends, and it was a struggle in which, at first, she failed.

The family hardly acknowledged her presence, and they ignored her on the pretext of assuming that she would prefer to be with people her own age, not with her new family. Her new relatives found fault with her in every detail, particularly her housekeeping. When upset, she looked to Dostoyevsky to defend her; he abandoned her to the censures of her new relatives. His failure in this respect was not so much because he agreed with the criticism of her housekeeping, but rather because it did not matter to him whether it was done well or not. The circumstances he now inhabited were all considerably better than a Siberian barracks; inadequate housekeeping was not one of his preoccupations.

Anna, however, felt let down. Pasha ate them out of house and home, and often sent the maid on false errands in order to raid the larder while she was gone. After three months Anna collapsed in tears and begged Dostoyevsky to take her away from the household. She felt that they must have some time on their own together to get used to being married. Dostoyevsky agreed; it was ignorance not heartlessness that had made him inconsiderate. Thus with the proceeds of her dowry they paid off their most immediate debts. They then packed up a few belongings and left their remaining chattels in the care of the family and left Russia for Europe, intending to stay there only three months. They stayed almost four years, despite the fact that their first weeks together were fraught with difficulties and disappointment.

Anna is often criticised for keeping diaries that dealt with the petty day-to-day existence of their life together rather than with her observations of the genius at work. She largely confined her discussions to money problems, housekeeping difficulties and small arguments with Dostoyevsky. Biographers and enthusiasts may have wanted to read of Dostoyevsky's struggle to write, of the ideas he may have discussed with her, of the agonies of creating a great work and the anecdotes associated with the artist. Anna, however, was a practical woman and was extremely proud that she, 'a girl of the sixties', had been given a chance to earn her own living. Her training as a stenographer had brought her to Fyodor, and it had also brought her the knowledge that she could be independent; and whatever the quality of her housekeeping, now that she was married to Fyodor, she had to keep constant track of the money. His work, however important it was to other people, was the least of her worries, and she did confess in her diaries that although she admired her husband's talents and knew very well how exceptional he was as a writer, she admitted that she could not really understand his work: 'Fiodor thought highly of me, and attributed to me a much deeper understanding of his works than, I think, was actually the case. He was convinced, for instance, that I understood the philosophical side of his novels.'[2] Understanding his thought processes was far less important to Anna than trying to provide an amenable environment in which Fyodor could work – and that meant keeping track of every penny or louis.

His gambling, in fact, dominated their tour of Europe. Anna wrote, 'I was not so much annoyed by his loss, as by the fact that he simply couldn't rid his mind of the idea that he was going to become rich through playing roulette. It is this idea that makes me wild, for it has done us so much harm.'[3]

Dostoyevsky was quite sure that if he only remained calm and kept to one system he would inevitably win at roulette. However, even if his theory was workable, he could never keep cool enough to carry it out and he could never quit while he was ahead. He watched more than one fortune pass through his fingers, making him first a rich man and then a pauper in the same night. Anna paid much of the price for this devastating habit:

> I felt very uneasy. When I returned, Fedya, too, came in a few minutes, and, with a pale face, said that he had lost, and asked me to give him the last four thalers. I gave them to him; but I was sure that he was bound to lose, that it could not be otherwise. Over half an hour passed; he returned home, having of course lost, and began imploring me to give him five louis.[4]

In Dresden she went each day for consecutive five days to the station to greet her husband on his return from Hamburg, where he had gone to gamble. Each day, after finding that he was not on the train, she went to the post office, only to receive letters begging her to send more money so that he could pay his way out of the hotel or pay for the fare to come back. Each time, he received the money with the best of intentions but lost it in one more attempt to win.

Anna pawned almost everything she had: 'I got out my earrings and brooch, and looked at them for a long, long time. It seemed to me I was seeing them for the last time.'[5] She became so shabbily dressed that she did not want to go out and meet people. She often remained in their flat crying. In one town they stayed in, when she wanted to listen to the band in the park, she climbed a hill near the park and listened from there. Only occasionally did he exercise enough discipline to come out ahead, and only then were the couple able to redeem the jewellery, shoes, coats and shawls that they had pawned.

All this led to inevitable quarrels about money and sessions of repentance on Dostoyevsky's part. He was not unaware of the folly of his habit or of its effect on Anna. He wrote to Apollon Maikov from Geneva, after watching four thousand roubles he had just won slip through his fingers: 'The worst thing of all is that my nature is ignoble and too passionate: everywhere and in everything I go to extremes; all my life I have always overstepped the mark.'⁶ Although the remorse was genuine enough, the repentance was short-lived. Even when Anna's mother came to stay with them, Dostoyevsky left for a gambling destination, using a pretext in order to hide the real reason from his mother-in-law. Anna connived in this conspiracy. When Dostoyevsky wrote to her for more money, he advised her to tell her mother that he needed the money to replace a mattress he had spoiled during a fit. The long-suffering Anna supported him on this occasion, and others, because she felt that he needed to get gambling out of his system or else he could not write.

What Anna feared more than debts were Dostoyevsky's seizures. The begging letters she received from him when he was on one of his gambling jaunts indicated, at least, that he was well. Each time he returned later than expected she feared for his life. She pictured him lying alone somewhere after a convulsion, perhaps even dead from choking on his false teeth or his tongue. Dostoyevsky was also afraid of that kind of death. His fits became frequent and violent. In the summer of 1867 he wrote to Apollon Maikov of one particularly bad patch he had gone through: 'My fits had begun to recur every week, and to feel and clearly recognise this nervous and cerebral disturbance was insupportable. My reason was really becoming disturbed – that is the truth. I could feel this; and the disturbance of my nerves sometimes drove me to moments of frenzy.'⁷

The fits often wiped his memory clean and for days left him depressed and confused, unable to recall people he had met, some of whom he knew quite well. The seizures also left him bad-tempered. Strakhov, Dostoyevsky's one-time friend and biographer, describes one such example: 'In Switzerland in my presence he so harassed a waiter that the latter took offence and spoke out, "But surely I am a man!"'[8]

Living abroad did little to improve Dostoyevsky's opinion of foreigners. He was already beginning to nurture the xenophobia that was later to colour his attitudes to almost everything that was not Russian. Fyodor possessed an almost paranoid mistrust of foreigners, once telling Anna that he lost at gambling because the Englishman standing next to him had used such a heavy scent that it put him off. The Swiss, he claimed, were petty and argumentative:

> The bourgeois life is developed in this abject little republic to the ne plus ultra in the government and in the whole of Switzerland – factions and ceaseless squabbling, pauperism, terrible mediocrity in everything; the workman here is not worth our worker's little finger … What drunkenness, what robbery, what petty dishonesty raised to legality in trade. They have, however, a few good traits, which place them immeasurably above the Germans.[9]

The Italians were noisy, and wherever he went he could never get any decent tea. But the people whom he most venomously despised were Russian expatriates living abroad.

These were the westernisers, the people who felt that Russia had so little to offer them that it was no longer worth living there. They criticised Russia for being industrially backward. They abhorred its agriculture because it was old-fashioned, and thought its people were forced to live under a near-feudal system. Moreover, Russia's religion, they believed, was now held in contempt by most of its people. Amongst these unashamed expatriates was Dostoyevsky's long-time nemesis, Ivan Turgenev, who had now set up home in Baden-Baden.

Since Dostoyevsky was in Baden-Baden, it seemed only good manners to visit Turgenev. Besides, Dostoyevsky owed Turgenev money, which he could not yet afford to pay back, so he needed to keep the irascible writer sweet. The visit, however, was not a success. Turgenev's view of Russia could hardly have been more opposed to Dostoyevsky's: 'If Russia were destroyed by an earthquake and vanished from the globe it would mean no less to humanity – it would not even be noticed,' he declared to Dostoyevsky.[10] He went on to say that the Russians were bound to crawl in the dust before the Germans, a comment surely calculated to enrage the patriotic and xenophobic Fyodor. Dostoyevsky could not resist the argument, but Turgenev was undeterred and told Fyodor that he intended to write an article against the Russophiles and Slavophiles. Dostoyevsky retorted that he had better get himself a telescope and direct it on Russia in order to see more clearly what he was writing about. Scenting victory, Fyodor went in for the kill with a particularly patronising comment about Turgenev's latest novel, which was drawing bad reviews: 'Really I should never have supposed that all the articles derogatory to your novel could have discomposed you to this extent; by God, the thing's not worth getting so angry about. Come spit upon it all.'[11]

The conversation degenerated into a row. Dostoyevsky insulted the German people; Turgenev defended them by saying that any insult to them was an insult to him, as he had now become one. Dostoyevsky realised that, once again, he had overstepped the mark. He apologised and asked Turgenev for forgiveness. The next day, Turgenev returned Dostoyevsky's visit, as manners required, but he came at ten in the morning when he knew full well that Dostoyevsky would not be awake. He left his calling card, instead; the manner of the visit clearly stated that all conversation between them was over. Once again they were not on speaking terms.

Dostoyevsky's ever-growing prejudice did not extend to all aspects of foreign culture. He was impressed with Europe's art and architecture. He and Anna made a special trip to Basel in order to view a painting by Holbein the Younger, *The Dead Christ in the Tomb*. Dostoyevsky, fascinated by the painting, climbed on a chair to get a closer look at it. He became so intensely absorbed in it that Anna, afraid he was going to have a fit, had to pull him away. Anna found the picture repulsive, for it portrays Christ as a corpse, blue at the lips and grey with the onset of decay.

In Dostoyevsky's next novel, *The Idiot*, he referred to the painting as a picture that could make a man lose his faith, as it seemed to deny all possibility of resurrection:

> But, strange to say, as one looks at the dead body of this tortured man, one cannot help asking oneself the peculiar and interesting question: if such a corpse (and it must have been just like that) was seen by all His disciples, by His future chief apostles, by the women who followed Him and stood by the cross, by all who believed in Him and worshipped Him, then how could they possibly have believed, as they looked at the corpse, that that martyr would rise again? ... And if, on the eve of crucifixion, the Master could have seen what He would look like when taken from the cross, would He have mounted the cross and died as He did?[12]

In this painting Dostoyevsky saw the embodiment of doubt. It portrayed in visual form much of what he addressed through his novels – the sense in which the Christian story was almost impossible to believe.

Dostoyevsky went on from Basel to Geneva, where he attended an international peace congress. This gathering was addressed by the Italian hero Garibaldi as well as by Bakunin, a Russian radical who had escaped from Siberia to join fellow exiles in the West. Dostoyevsky was not impressed: the meeting reminded him of the utopianist preaching of the Petrashevsky Circle. He came away feeling that such humanism offered no solutions.

Amid the gambling, the travelling and the writing, Anna became pregnant. In her diaries she confesses to episodes of crying when Dostoyevsky left her in this state for yet another gambling trip. Their first child, Sonya, was born in Geneva in March 1868. Dostoyevsky was utterly delighted; it seemed at last he had found something that could eclipse the pleasure of winning at roulette. Sonya's birth changed his whole attitude to life. Parenthood, he claimed, is three-quarters of what life is about; nothing else matters beside it.

However, this new and uniting joy was short-lived. When Sonya was barely three months old, she caught pneumonia and died. In despair, he wrote to Apollon Maikov:

> She was beginning to know me and love me, and smiled when I went near. When I sang to her in my ridiculous voice, she liked to listen. She did not cry or frown when I kissed her; she stopped crying when I went to her. And now people say to comfort me that I shall have other children. But where is Sonya? Where is that little person for whom, I am bold enough to say, I would accept crucifixion if it meant she would live?[13]

The couple were devastated. They cried night after night for their little Sonya, so much so that their unsympathetic neighbours banged on the wall to shut them up.

They could no longer bear to stay in Geneva, so they moved to Vevey on the other side of the lake. Downhearted though they were, their daily routine continued much as before. Anna went to bed early and Dostoyevsky went to bed late. When he got up, he would light the fire and drink a strong cup of coffee. After breakfast, he would work until four in the afternoon; then he would go out for a cheap meal somewhere. Anna would dine at home, perhaps feeling that her clothes were not smart enough for public show, as much of her good-quality clothing had been pawned. After his meal, Dostoyevsky would read the *Moscow News* from cover to cover, walk for half an hour and then return home. Once home, he relit the fire, had another cup of coffee and started to work again, while Anna went to bed. Dostoyevsky buried the tragedy in his words on the page. The novel he had commenced writing was the second of his most celebrated novels, *The Idiot*.

17

A SUPERFLUOUS MAN

1869 was a landmark year for Russian literature. Leo Tolstoy published *War and Peace* in book form, having already serialised it in *The Russian Messenger*, and Dostoyevsky began serialising *The Idiot*, also in *The Russian Messenger*. *The Idiot* is perhaps the most personal of Dostoyevsky's works, despite the fact that he had recounted his time in gaol in *The House of the Dead*, approached some of his own failings in *The Gambler*, and almost always set his characters against the background of St Petersburg. The eponymous idiot, Prince Myshkin, is an epileptic, and it is through this character that Dostoyevsky refers to his own experience of facing the firing squad.

Dostoyevsky's initial wish in writing *The Idiot* was to depict a thoroughly good man, a Christ-like figure, and to explore how this figure might act as a catalyst in the lives of contemporary Russians. He wrote to his favourite niece, Sofia:

> The main idea of the novel is to present a positively beautiful man. This is the most difficult subject in the world, especially as it is now. All writers, not just ours, but European writers, too, have always failed whenever they attempted a portrait of the positively beautiful. Because the task is so infinite. The beautiful is an ideal, but both our ideal and that of civilized Europe are still far from being shaped. There is only

one positively beautiful person in the world, Christ, and the phenomenon of this limitlessly, infinitely beautiful person is an infinite miracle in itself.[1]

Dostoyevsky went on to say that he believed that Don Quixote was the most perfect figure of Christian literature to date.

Don Quixote, by Miguel de Cervantes, presented its audience with the ultimate philanthropist, a man who wanted to impart the values of chivalry to a society that had already moved on from such an archaic ideal. Don Quixote, then as now, is an anachronism, and as such he was often made to look a fool. He frequently failed in his projects, and yet his goodness did, indeed, at the same time seem to ennoble him. Dostoyevsky was also enamoured of characters such as Jean Valjean in Victor Hugo's *Les Miserables*, and, since his time in prison, Mr Pickwick in Charles Dickens' *Pickwick Papers*. Dostoyevsky wanted to do the same for Russian literature as these authors had done for the canon of their own countries: he wanted to create an equivalent character for Russians, a Russian Christ figure, which by example and true goodness was therefore a holy fool.

It turned out to be a far easier aim to declare than it was to achieve. His notes on the development of *The Idiot* show that he started out with a plot and characterisation very different from the final novel. The main character, Prince Leo Nikolayevich Myshkin, was originally a far cry from the 'perfectly beautiful man' that he finally became. He began as much more of a dual personality, a double, resembling his successor Stavrogin of *The Devils*, generally thought to represent 'the great sinner' that Dostoyevsky also wanted to portray. The original Myshkin suffered from spiritual pride and used self-abasement and humiliation as a way of overcoming his baser instincts. In January 1868, Fyodor wrote to Maikov that he had just ripped the whole lot up and started again. After eight versions in note form and several different characterisations, he settled on the book he published. After publication, he wrote to Sofia that he had not said even a tenth of what he had intended to say.

In the final version Myshkin is naturally humble. He is so self-abasing that he does, indeed, appear to be an idiot; like Don Quixote he either offends or is mocked. Myshkin is uninhibited and lacks social graces, and he is quite happy to turn up to various social events uninvited. The story starts with his return from Switzerland, where he was being treated for epilepsy; he has only his 'bundle' of goods and an address. On the journey he makes friends with the character who might be considered his diametric opposite, Nikolay Rogozhin, who has just inherited a fortune. From then on, their fates are entwined.

Physically Myshkin resembles the many portrayals of Christ in Russian icons: 'The owner of the cloak with the hood was also a young man of about twenty-six or twenty-seven, slightly above medium height, with very thick, fair hair, hollow cheeks, and a thin pointed and almost white little beard.'[2]

Myshkin is also a virgin, although he is not dedicated to celibacy. He lacks social perception and often fails to see the joke. His fellow travellers are much amused by his bundle of possessions, and when he arrives at the Yepanchin house in order to introduce himself to his distant relative, Lizaveta, his only contact in St Petersburg, he engages the servant of the house in conversation, a social faux pas – it was not appropriate for a prince to address a servant as an equal. But Myshkin sees no class, no inferiority, merely someone to confide in, and he tells the servant of how he witnessed an execution. Later his indiscretion is discovered and he must tell his story again:

'No, the thing is, I was telling all about the execution a little while ago, and–'

'Whom did you tell about it?'

'The man-servant, while I was waiting to see the general.'

'Our man-servant?' exclaimed several voices at once.

'Yes, the one who waits in the entrance hall, a greyish, red-faced man–'

'The prince is clearly a democrat,' remarked Aglaya.

'Well, if you could tell Aleksey about it, surely you can tell us too.'[3]

Myshkin obliges, speculating as he does so as to how it would be if suddenly someone in that situation was to be reprieved. Eventually his gruesome speculation considers whether or not someone remains conscious when their head flies off – hardly teatime conversation for the ladies he has come to see. The conversation then turns to a discussion of his relationship with a child called Marie, who was orphaned and suffered from tuberculosis, a disease that Dostoyevsky was well qualified to describe. Myshkin's treatment of Marie is redemptive: at first, she is ostracised by the children of the community; with his help, she is eventually rehabilitated in the village, but only in order that she can die accepted and happy. He saves her, if not physically at least spiritually, which to Dostoyevsky was becoming the more important element of salvation. Myshkin also wins the affection of the children of the community for both himself and Marie. His affinity with children echoes Jesus' words: 'Whoever does not receive the kingdom of God like a child shall not enter it.'⁴ While he is fascinating to the daughters of the Yepanchin house he is visiting, his 'democratic' tendencies and his choice of conversation does demonstrate both ignorance and innocence and thus makes him the fool, the subject of laughter and mockery. When he ascribes some of his own personal healing, while on his travels, to an encounter with a donkey, the mood collapses and the women resort to a fit of the giggles. He is a laughing stock but remains unabashed; where some would withdraw, he continues, such that when the conversation turns to the trivial and he is asked to discuss the beauty of the youngest daughter, he concedes that she is truly beautiful – almost too beautiful to look at. But he does qualify his compliment:

> 'Most wonderfully so,' said the latter, warmly, gazing at Aglaya with admiration. 'Almost as lovely as Nastasia Philipovna, but quite a different type.'
> All present exchanged looks of surprise.⁵

This introduces the Yepanchins to the character of Nastasya Filippovna. Nastasya Filippovna is a wild-spirited young woman who was seduced by her guardian, Totsky, while she was still very young. She vacillates between her guilt about the affair and her desire to become a new woman. Myshkin is attracted to her because she needs him, because he can do something for her. Rogozhin falls in love with her and she with him, although her affection may stem from her sense of damaged self-worth, and the relationship that she and Rogozhin undertake is mutually destructive. Totsky is keen to marry her off to another character, Ganya, for the price of 75,000 roubles. He has, in a sense, made an indecent proposal, largely in the hope that he might carry on his relationship with Nastasya as his concubine. Nastasya is torn between the choices she has, and much of the novel is preoccupied with the tension of her possible choices. Rogozhin, Ganya and finally Myshkin are all smitten by her charms. She taunts them by holding off on her decision until her birthday party. Ganya's family are appalled by the prospect of him marrying such a fallen woman; Rogozhin ups the price on the indecent proposal and offers to marry her for 100,000 roubles; at the party tempers are short and Nastasya succumbs to the self-destructive tendencies brought on by her lack of self-worth. She chooses Rogozhin, not for the money, which she flings into the fire, and in spite of Prince Myshkin proposing to her himself to save her from Rogozhin. Thus Nastasya flees to her fate, the only fate of which she considers herself worthy.

Ultimately Myshkin bears obvious similarities to Christ. He appears to save the soul of a child; as an outsider, he causes the kind of upset that might be expected of a visiting prophet. He insists on placing himself between potential harm and its victim, and as a consequence finds himself slapped by Ganya – an insult that should have caused him to challenge Ganya to a duel, but, Christ-like, Myshkin turns the other cheek. Throughout the book, the company he prefers is unreliable and dubious in its reputation: the publicans and sinners of their day. In his relationships, particularly with respect to the two women in his life, Myshkin, like Jesus, devotes himself to those who need healing; but his love is not completely redemptive. He is unable to save all those he encounters: 'From the beginning of Part II, the Prince is cast in a tragic (or at least self-sacrificial) role; and the inner logic of his character now requires that the absolute of Christian love should conflict irreconcilably with the inescapable demands of normal human life.'[6]

Doubt and failure enter the novel. The central conceit for this is a discussion of Holbein's *Dead Christ*, the painting that depicts the evident decomposition of the body of Christ and visualises doubts as to the possibility of the resurrection, the same painting that Anna and Fyodor visited in Basel. The discussion of the painting signifies the failure of Myshkin's project and establishes him as the fool. In addition, his capacity to love becomes confused between the various types of love expressed in the book. Myshkin is smitten by Nastasya but becomes engaged to Aglaya, who is infatuated by his impulse to sacrifice himself for others. The two women act as binary opposites: Aglaya, the respectable innocent, who can marry for choice, has no self-loathing and perhaps no concept of the depths of depravity that others can achieve; Nastasya, by contrast, is only too aware of how low human beings can sink – Totsky's use of her as concubine since she was sixteen has made that all too clear. Rogozhin's sado-masochistic attraction to her is also dangerous and she remains torn between the two opposites of Myshkin and Rogozhin, to the extent that for a while she and Myshkin are engaged, thus destroying the Prince's chances of marriage with Aglaya:

> As a characteristic addition to the above, it was currently reported that the young prince really loved the lady to whom he was engaged, and had thrown her over out of purely Nihilistic motives, with the intention of giving himself the satisfaction of marrying a fallen woman in the face of all the world, thereby publishing his opinion that there is no distinction between virtuous and disreputable women, but that all women are alike, free; and a 'fallen' woman, indeed, somewhat superior to a virtuous one.[7]

Thus Myshkin appears to all society to be an idiot. Even his definition of love and its power to be redemptive is challenged. Moreover, his relationship with Nastasya is doomed: Rogozhin is driven mad by the liaison and attempts to stab Myshkin, who is only saved from a fatal wounding by the onset of an epileptic fit. In addition, Nastasya cannot forgive herself and feels that she would destroy the good in Myshkin if she married him. Thus, she is unable to accept forgiveness from Myshkin and places herself beyond his redemptive love.

Myshkin's love is not sufficient for her, for she does not want to be loved merely so that he can look after her. His love, which is intended to save rather than to adore, lacks lust and passion; it is a holy love. It is not the kind of love that persuades a woman to marry; it is not like Sonya's love for Raskolnikov in *Crime and Punishment*, which is indeed redemptive, but also not universal, being focussed only on Raskolnikov, whereas Myshkin is enraptured by his love for all.

Myshkin has been called a Russian Hamlet: both men are taken for idiots, whether their idiocy is real, apparent or feigned. Myshkin is sabotaged by his humility, just as Hamlet is sabotaged by his good conscience: not wanting to take revenge for his father's murder without being sure it is the right thing to do, Hamlet is slow to act. Similarly Myshkin, not wanting to commit a selfish or proud act, decides to go to Nastasya, who is sick and needs him, and does not go to Aglaya, with whom he is in love. Like Christ, Myshkin is not successful in the way that society judges success. He does not save Nastasya from marriage to Roghozhin, who murders her, and he finishes up mad himself. In addition, his attempts to save Nastasya destroy Aglaya, who marries a Polish count and converts to Roman Catholicism – a fate worse than death as far as Dostoyevsky was concerned. Once again a contradiction is revealed: Myshkin's selflessness does not heal or save, it hurts and divides.

Dostoyevsky took what he believed to be an ideal man and placed him in a normal environment. This man was humble and loving, able to subjugate himself to others, the living expression of the commandment: 'You shall love your neighbour as yourself.'[8] But, in a cruel irony, a person who lives by this commandment appears to be an idiot, a fool. Even his names, Leo (for lion) and Myshkin (mouse-like), indicate the tension between holiness and worldly success. Christ was crucified, hardly a successful ending; Myshkin goes mad. An ideal man, then, does not create an ideal world.

Myshkin is weaker and less effective than Sonya in *Crime and Punishment* as a representation of the Christian faith, but as the representation of the ideal man he exposes the world's standards. Myshkin is not in contact with the real world, and he is isolated from its Christian community. The first Orthodox Christian rite he attends is a funeral. Dostoyevsky was later to develop the idea that contact with the Christian community is essential to Christian survival; that the profession of faith cannot exist outside the structures of the Church. Myshkin is identified as a Christian only because he is called so by other characters, not because he practices the Orthodox faith. *The Idiot* was not a critical success, and Dostoyevsky did not think that it achieved what he had wanted as a writer, but it consolidated some of the ideas that he was to develop in his later works.

18

FAITH AND FASCISM

Dostoyevsky had hoped that *The Idiot* would be the novel to pull him out of debt and provide a chance for him and Anna to go back to Russia. However, because he had to ask for money in advance, much of what he earned from his books was spent well before publication, and his desperation meant a publisher could drive a hard bargain with him. His publishers informed him that the novel had its 'shortcomings'.[1] This too, made negotiations difficult: 'What most people regard as fantastic and lacking in universality, I hold to be the inmost essence of the truth,' he complained of his critics.[2] However, it was not only the critics but also the reading public who did not like *The Idiot*. Dostoyevsky was losing money on the book and on reprints of his existing works because he had no agent in Petersburg to defend his interests.

The situation got so bad at home that Pasha, who had spent all the money he had been sent and still wanted more, threatened to go to Katkov, Dostoyevsky's publisher, and ask that Dostoyevsky's advance be given directly to him. Dostoyevsky dreaded the effect that this might have, not only on his own financial prospects but also on Katkov's good will and therefore his chances of publishing with him again. When he heard of the threat, Dostoyevsky wrote to Katkov to ask him not to release the money to Pasha. He also wrote to Maikov, to see if he could find out whether Pasha had carried out his threat. In the end he did not; perhaps he was simply attempting to jolt his stepfather into sending more money back to Russia, but it was a ruse that did not work.

Dostoyevsky knew that Pasha was a parasite but the letters he wrote to him show great understanding – and perhaps too much tolerance:

> Remember that you can always count on me. So long as I live, I shall regard you as my dear son. I swore to your mother, the night before she died, that I would never forsake you. When you were still a little child, I used to call you my son. How could I, then, forsake you and forget you?[3]

Dostoyevsky never had been able to resist a hard-luck story.

By 1869 Anna was pregnant again. This time she was much more apprehensive about the confinement. They spent a hot summer in Florence, which to Dostoyevsky was a city that never slept. The noise from the market outside was so great and continuous that Dostoyevsky could not work and, to cap it all, a tarantula crept into their room. A search for it flushed it out, but then it disappeared into the mattress. Fyodor and Anna spent an anxious night wondering where it was, and Dostoyevsky balefully recalled the death of a man in Siberia from a tarantula's bite. The spider was found the next morning and was promptly executed.[4]

And then a sort of miracle happened: all of a sudden, Dostoyevsky stopped gambling.

In 1868 he claimed that he had had a dream in which his father appeared to him, and this provided sufficient motivation for him to overcome his addiction. No one quite knows how or why he managed to stop; some theories are more mundane than the dream. He may have had increasing difficulty gaining access to gambling casinos, for not everywhere in Europe allowed legal gambling. Anna's pregnancy, or perhaps a basic realisation that his finances never benefited from his habit, may have been contributing factors. Whatever the reason, though, this time Dostoyevsky wrote to Anna that he had finished with gambling. He had made these promises before, and she was probably sceptical for quite some time – but now he kept to them.

Thus, Dostoyevsky had overcome a personal flaw that was a major contributing factor to his financial problems, but he had not yet started to earn sufficient money from his writing to pay off his debts. He still had a lot of work to do before establishing any kind of secure lifestyle. Dostoyevsky was now writing a novel he called *Atheism*. The idea of this book was to track the progress of an atheist and sinner as the character explored various philosophies of religion. His journey would take him through some rather weird practices, including flagellation and mutilation, until finally he came to accept Orthodox Christianity.

Atheism was never completed in the original form that Dostoyevsky had planned. The central character, however, continued to grip his imagination. Dostoyevsky began to consolidate an idea he had referred to before, of portraying a man who lived with the knowledge of having committed a great sin. Thus, the proposed novel *Atheism* developed from a description of a search for faith to a description of the life of a great sinner. He wrote to Apollon Maikov: 'The fundamental idea, which will run through each of the parts [of the novel], is one that has tormented me, consciously and unconsciously, all my life long: it is the question of the existence of God.'[5] Neither *Atheism* nor *The Life of the Great Sinner* was to be published as books in their own right. The character Dostoyevsky created for these novels, however, would recur, most particularly in his next novel, *The Devils*, which he was to commence writing during the second half of his stay in Europe.

In 1869 he wrote to his niece Sofia: 'In three months, we shall have been exactly two years abroad. In my opinion it's worse than deportation to Siberia. I mean that quite seriously; I'm not exaggerating.'[6]

What Dostoyevsky saw of Europe not only compounded his xenophobia but brought into being a patriotism that went beyond a simple love of country. He became increasingly attracted to a school of thought that defended Russia and her people against Western European influence, proclaimed Russian nationalism and worked to give the empire a unique identity. This school of thought held that instead of submitting itself to the vagaries of Western Europe as the westernisers recommended, Russia should proclaim its own identity. It did not need to follow the rest of Europe into an inhuman industrial revolution; if it did so it would lose its national character in a mass of factories. Russia needed to go back to the roots of its culture and build a country, and by extension an empire, on traditional Russian values.

Russia, however, was such a huge and diverse country that it was difficult to identify one culture – or even one language – that was common to all its citizens and could identify Russia as a unit. One solution to this heterogeneity lay in identifying Russian heritage with the Slavic language and culture. In the Middle Ages, when Christianity came to Russia, the language of the Orthodox Church was Church Slavonic, just as the language of the Roman Church was Latin. This argot began life as a clerical language, but unlike Latin, Slavonic became the basis for the common form of Russian European speech. Thus when Russians looked for their cultural roots, they looked to the Church and to the Slavic people.

The Slavs were the indigenous inhabitants of the geographical areas of Bulgaria, Yugoslavia and Montenegro. Not all Slavs were under Russian rule; they were in fact small independent countries. Slavophiles believed that the Slavs should be under Russian administration because in the Slavic people pulsed the purest form of Russian blood, spirit and culture. Slavophiles therefore supported moves to defend the Slavs from outside enemies, such as the Turks, even advocating war against such oppressors in order to liberate the Slavs from foreign rule and bring them under Russian jurisdiction.

Russophiles based their political beliefs on a similarly patriotic philosophy. Rather than see their country's traditions diluted by Western values of materialism, science, industrialisation and gradual secularisation, Russophiles wanted a united Russia that encouraged the Russian peasant spirit, honoured the tsar and respected and practised the religion of Orthodoxy.

Both schools of thought were attractive to Dostoyevsky, for they were in line with much of what he already believed. One writer who Dostoyevsky read during his time abroad was Nikolai Danilevsky. Like Dostoyevsky, Danilevsky had been a member of the Petrashevsky Circle and a keen advocate of Fourierism; also like Dostoyevsky he had undergone a conservative conversion. His book *Russia and Europe* was serialised in 1869 in a journal called *Dawn*, which Dostoyevsky was sent while he was abroad. This journal, a successor to Dostoyevsky's own journals *Time* and *Epoch*, was edited by his friends Strakhov and Maikov. In Russia and in Europe, Danilevsky attempted to re-establish the doctrine of the Slavophiles. Danilevsky was trained as a natural scientist and his racial philosophy seemed to presage the later use of the theory of evolution to justify systemic racism. A dominant race, he thought, had a right to survive and flourish; a weaker race could justifiably be oppressed. These were the unpleasant beginnings of some of the more pernicious philosophies that would haunt the twentieth century.

Danilevsky stated that four different races, Jews, Greeks, Romans and Western Europeans, had dominated the world in different areas of human interaction: the Jews in religion, the Greeks in culture, the Romans in politics, and Western Europe in economics. The Slavs and the Russians, he claimed, grew from common racial roots and were irrevocably linked with each other. Europe was their natural enemy and it was now their turn, whether by military force or united spirit, to dominate the world in the areas of religion and culture. The Slavs were at the beginning of their most influential era. Danilevsky regarded their cause as so important that he was willing to tolerate the subordination of ordinary human rights, such as freedom and education, in order to achieve the Slavic ideal: none of these things would be worth anything until Slavdom had received its proper place in human history.

Dostoyevsky now began to be attracted to this political philosophy. He would develop it and link it to Christianity, not so much in his fiction as in his later political writings. In 1869 he wrote to Maikov and suggested that he, Maikov, write a national poem depicting Russia conquering Constantinople (now Istanbul) and restoring to it its status as the capital of the Christian world. Dostoyevsky, though not a poet, advised his friend on the metre and style of the poem. The latter indicates how firmly Dostoyevsky believed in the theory of Russia as a uniquely Christian nation, with the right even to invade Constantinople in order to drive out Islam and so resurrect it as the capital of Christendom.

Perhaps because he felt alienated abroad, Dostoyevsky had come to regard Russia in a very rosy light and Europe as its inferior. In his earlier travels, in 1862, Dostoyevsky had condemned London's Crystal Palace as a representation of the Tower of Babel. He now saw industrialisation and the advance of science as being closely linked to a loss of faith. European nations, he observed, were becoming secular: 'In Western Europe the peoples have lost Christ (Catholicism is to blame), and therefore Western Europe is tottering to its fall,' he said in a letter to Strakhov, in 1871, just before he returned home to Russia.[7] Even the brilliant architecture of the Piazza San Marco, which he admired, could not bring him to concede that Europe had anything superior to offer. He had come to believe that Russia was not only a great nation, but a holy nation; Russia had a better grasp of religious truth than did any other nation. Very soon Dostoyesky would state that it was Russia's duty to point the way to the rest of the world.

Not surprisingly, Dostoyevsky wanted to visit a Slavic country. In August 1869, just one month before their second baby was due, the couple made a visit to Prague in Czechoslovakia. They had hoped to have the baby there but they were able to stay only three days: none of the apartments in Prague were furnished and it would have cost too much for the couple to arrange furniture for themselves. They gave up and returned to Dresden where, in September, their second daughter was born. Lyubov was a fine, healthy child with whom Dostoyevsky fell in love immediately. This time he would not be bereaved. Lyubov would survive not only her childhood but also her father, and would write her own account of living in Europe as an expatriate Russian, as well as an interesting, if sometimes inaccurate, account of her father's life.[8]

The Dostoyevsky family had yet to remain in Europe, but Fyodor's long disturbed and turbulent life was beginning to settle and his reputation, although always controversial, was beginning to offer him that place in history he felt was always just beyond his reach.

19

POSSESSED

And when he had come out of the boat, there met him out
of the tombs a man with an unclean spirit, who had lived
among the tombs; and no one could bind him any more,
even with a chain; for he had often been bound with fetters
and chains, but the chains he wrenched apart, and the fetters
he broke in pieces; and no one had the strength to subdue
him. Night and day among the tombs and on the mountains
he was always crying out, and bruising himself with stones.
And when he saw Jesus from afar, he ran and worshipped
him; and crying out with a loud voice, he said, 'What have
you to do with me, Jesus, Son of the Most High God?
I adjure you by God, do not torment me.' For he had said to
him, 'Come out of the man, you unclean spirit!' And Jesus
asked him, 'What is your name?' He replied, 'My name is
Legion; for we are many.' And he begged him eagerly not
to send them out of the country. Now a great herd of swine
was feeding there on the hillside; and they begged him, 'Send
us to the swine, let us enter them.' So he gave them leave.
And the unclean spirits came out, and entered the swine; and
the herd, numbering about two thousand, rushed down the
steep bank into the sea, and were drowned in the sea.

Mark 5:2–23, RSV.[1]

In the darkness of a Moscow park, a young man by the name of Ivan Ivanov was lured by his fellow students to a meeting. He was taken by trickery or violence to a small grotto in the grounds of the Moscow Agricultural College where five men attacked him and held him down. He screamed for help but the park was deserted. He bit and kicked his attackers but only managed to inflict a small wound on the finger of one of them. There were too many of them for even a strong young man to overcome. They set a gun against the back of his neck and fired. The bullet came out through his eye. Once he was dead, they bound him and flung him into the park lake, where he was later found frozen solid in a block of ice.

A few weeks before, in the autumn of 1869, while the Dostoyevskys were still in Dresden, they had received a visit from Anna's brother, also Ivan, a friend of the doomed student Ivanov. Her brother told the couple of the student unrest in the college and of the spread of nihilistic ideas. He spoke of the large number of students fascinated with secret societies and revolution. It must have stirred Dostoyevsky's memory to hear of conspiracies, illicit gatherings and feverish discussions. He felt apprehensive, however, for he knew from personal experience that these conspiracies usually ended in disaster. He was horrified to read, a few weeks later, of the death of his brother-in-law's friend.

Dostoyevsky once wrote that if someone could give him the crime he would create the criminal. The murder of the young student gave him a plot into which he could weave his own characterisations. The event inspired his next novel, *The Devils*, sometimes called *The Possessed*. In it, Dostoyevsky combined a fictional retelling of the events surrounding the murder with his knowledge of conspiracy and revolution.

Ivanov's murder was an act of terrorism led by a dangerous student revolutionary, Sergei Nechayev. Nechayev had been trained by the well-seasoned revolutionary Mikhail Bakunin, a follower of Hegel's idealist philosophy who, like Dostoyevsky, had served time in Siberia. It was Bakunin who had known

Petrashevsky and who had commented of Nikolai Speshnev that he was 'quietly cold'. In the late 1860s Bakunin and Nechayev collaborated on writing a training manual for revolutionaries called *Revolutionary Catechism*. Armed with his catechism, Nechayev set up an organisation called 'The People's Justice': an axe was their mascot and revolution was their aim. The idea was to destabilise the country through terrorist cells of about five men. It was one of these cells that killed Ivanov – and Nechayev himself was its leader.

The group of five terrorists under Nechayev wanted to see the tsar brought down on the ninth anniversary of the end of serfdom; but Ivan Ivanov's death curtailed their plans. Just why Ivanov was murdered is not known. It is probable that his initial interest in the group was as an intellectual, keen on ideas about change but not so enthusiastic about direct action. Once he knew what the group was about, he wanted no part in their activities, but by then he was already too deeply involved. He knew too much. Whether he was killed as an example to others, as a punishment at the whim of the evil Nechayev, or as a method of ensuring the loyalty of the others is a matter for speculation. Whatever the reason, after the killing the gang was implicated and Nechayev had to leave the country. He was arrested in Zurich in 1872, nearly three years later, and handed back to Russia, where he stood trial. He died in the St Peter and Paul Fortress in 1882, having served less than half of his sentence.

The incident fired Dostoyevsky's imagination. He had told Maikov and others that he intended to write a novel both about an atheist who found faith and about a man who had committed a great sin. *The Devils* provided him with the opportunity to explore both possibilities. Dostoyevsky's great sinner, his atheist, was a man searching for God and an answer to the eternal questions. If there is a loving God, why does suffering exist in His world? In what way does humanity have free will and from where does mankind's moral perceptions originate? In the murderers' revolutionary philosophies Dostoyevsky saw a way of exploring evil, suffering and conflict, while at the same time exposing nihilistic atheism as fraud.

Unlike many of his previous novels, *The Devils* is not set in St Petersburg, although St Petersburg does feature, as Paris does in many of the works of Balzac, including *Eugenie Grandét* translated by Dostoyevsky so many years before. *The Devils* is set in a small town where the mystery of St Petersburg and its high society is discussed, and sometimes attended, but in the main is inaccessible to the Russian landowner in whose home the story begins. While the setting may not be the underground passages of the Petersburg dreamer, the *mechtatel*, the social setting is familiar and some of the characters have the essence of fact rather than fiction.

Whereas Dostoyevsky probably never met a Raskolnikov or Golyadkin (*The Double*) or the Underground Man, the concept of this secret cell of subversive individuals may well have its roots in the activist 1840s when Dostoyevsky was part, first of the Petrashevsky Circle and then of the more secretive Palm-Durov Circle, and where he had met Nikolai Speshnev. Speshnev was the cool and handsome aristocrat, who was then the keenest proponent of direct action. It was Speshnev who leant money to Dostoyevsky to help clear a debt and then refused to let him pay it back. It was Speshnev who persuaded the Palm-Durov group that they must construct a printing press. It was Speshnev who Dostoyevsky referred to as his personal Mephistopheles, and it was Speshnev who stood next to him in the line of execution and commented that life was all 'a handful of dust':

> I had expected to see a dirty ragamuffin, sodden with drink and debauchery. He was on the contrary, the most elegant gentleman I had ever met, extremely well dressed, with an air and manner only to be found in a man accustomed to culture and refinement. I was not the only person surprised.[2]

The novel is narrated in the first person, in the form of reportage. Again it evokes the atmosphere of many a recent novel or film wherein a narrator observes the wild goings on of other characters. The narrator of *The Devils* is Anton Lavrentyevich, a local civil servant and friend of Stepan Verkhovensky. Lavrentyevich observes the progress of Stepan and Stavrogin and their circle of characters as all of them tragically descend into murder, suicide and madness. The story starts with the entry of Nikolai Stavrogin, which excites the small provincial community in which the novel is set.

Like his real-life predecessor Speshnev, Stavrogin is young and handsome, and went to the same school, the Lyceum; like Speshnev he too is an atheist, which points to one of the main themes in the book. Though he appears to be one of the main characters in the novel, his appearances in the narrative are rare: it is his shadowy influence that dominates the action.

Dostoyevsky begins the book with the above passage quoted from the Bible, the story of the Gadarene swine, where the Devil is cast out of a human being by Jesus and then takes possession of a herd of pigs that launch themselves to their own destruction over a cliff. The metaphor is clear: the political cell is the Devil's work. Dostoyevsky then preoccupies his characters with the meaning of life in the context of belief, or lack thereof, in God, so that he can explore his themes of atheism and sin. In order to do this Dostoyevsky uses a binary narrative.

In *The Double*, Dostoyevsky used binary literally (long before it was formally proposed by the narrative theorist Claude Levi-Strauss as standard structure of almost all narratives – especially those that lend themselves for film).[3] Dostoyevsky represented the inner conflict of Golyadkin by presenting him with his own opposite, whereas in *The Devils* the binary is a more subtle figuring element. It is present both in the concepts discussed and the way in which the characters embody those concepts, as Joyce Carol Oates observes: 'Dostoyevsky's characters generally present mirror images of one another; it is perhaps too reductive to say they are "doubles", but they certainly echo one another, parody one another.'[4] Concepts are, then, opposed through characters. Oates in the same article posits that Stepan Verkhovensky, friend of Stavrogin's mother and also his tutor, is 'Old Russia', and Stavrogin in turn stands for 'New Russia'. It is Stepan who hears read to him on his deathbed the story of the Gadarene swine, told by Sofya Matveyevna in much the same way as Sonya reads the raising of Lazarus to Raskolnikov; Stepan's Old Russia is coming under threat from *The Devils* incarnate and their impulse to sedition, violence and atheism.

Stavrogin, the devilish villain of the piece, is flawed by his own self-knowledge. A womaniser and abuser, he cannot quite forgive himself for the way he behaves. In the darkest corners of the novel unhealthy relationships are referred to, and Dostoyevsky seems to suggest that Stepan, who was once Stavrogin's tutor, may have had too intimate a relationship with his tutee. Stepan is described as waking Stavrogin at night and, at the very least, confiding his darkest secrets to him, sometimes in tears: 'Stepan Trofimovitch succeeded in reaching the deepest chords in his pupil's heart, and had aroused in him a vague sensation of that eternal, sacred yearning which some elect souls can never give up for cheap gratification when once they have tasted and known it.'[5] The narrator, Anton, then goes on to say that teacher and pupil were separated and 'none to soon'. Dostoyevsky, the psychological profiler, was probably all too aware of the self-loathing that accompanied the violations of abuse in childhood. Stavrogin's cruelty is ultimately self-destructive, as he participates in a duel brought on by an insult involving the pulling of the nose of his challenger. He accepts the challenge, but mocks the ritual by deliberately missing or not even bothering to fire: 'Again they advanced, again Gaganov missed and Stavrogin fired into the air. There might have been a dispute as to his firing into the air. Nikolay Vsyevolodovitch {Stavrogin} might have flatly declared that he'd fired properly, if he had not admitted that he had missed intentionally.'[6] No one is killed, but Stavrogin's reputation as a dangerous but romantic rogue is enhanced. Perhaps here Dostoyevsky is recalling the death of his literary hero Pushkin, by mocking the futility of such challenges and the waste of lives, which in Pushkin's case was his doom. Stavrogin has a death wish and also the luck of the Devil. He is enigmatic; indeed, the physical description of him at his introduction hints at the devilish – he is somehow too perfect, described both as a 'paragon of beauty' and as somehow repellent. In Stavrogin something of the dual nature of *The Double* persists, although in this case it is as if the better half is merely a mask, a cover for the evil antagonist beneath. Nevertheless Stavrogin is adored by his followers and by his women, despite the fact that he is often cruel to all those around him:

> You married from a passion for martyrdom, from a craving for remorse, through moral sensuality. It was a laceration of the nerves ... Defiance of common sense was too tempting. Stavrogin and a wretched, half-witted, crippled beggar! When you bit the governor's ear did you feel sensual pleasure? Did you? You idle, loafing, little snob. Did you?[7]

Stavrogin's reply to Shatov is to suggest that Shatov is a psychologist, and Shatov to his shame replies that, despite himself, he cannot but love Stavrogin and kiss the ground he walks on – 'I cannot tear you out of my heart!' – and Stavrogin can only reply that he can feel no affection for Shatov.

Stavrogin's self-loathing and guilt is compounded by his apathy or his failure to challenge. The marriage that Shatov refers to appears to be some kind of a joke: initially Stavrogin denies it to his mother, and the wife, Marya, who appears in the town and is viewed as insane. In fact she is being driven mad, just as many of the characters are in *The Devils*; they descend into a possessed madness. Marya is a problem that needs solving, and the arrival of the convict Fedka, the former serf to Stepan Verkhovensky, who has form and is willing to execute her, may be the solution for Stavrogin. However, Stavrogin does not directly commission Fedka to do the deed. He ignores Fedka's persistent suggestions until Stavrogin is forced to turn on him and threatens him. But he also throws money at him, which Stavrogin later concedes might have been seen as a commission. Never once does he actually tell Fedka to murder his wife, but Fedka goes ahead with it, and murders her brother into the bargain. The question is who is really responsible?

While Stavrogin is the enigmatic aristocrat with the hint of the Prince about him, Peter Verkhovensky is a much more traditional agitator. He is a manipulator: it is Peter that hints to Fedka that Stavrogin may need assistance; and Fedka, the convict and murderer, identifies Peter as 'hard hearted', citing his atheism as the cause of his lack of compassion. He is further reputed by the narrator to have connections with the Internationale, otherwise known as The Internationale Working Man's Association, co-founded by Karl Marx in 1864. If Stavrogin is Speshnev then Peter Verkhovensky is Nechayev, the founder of the group that murdered Ivan Ivanov. Peter is a nihilist and activist, and is glad to pronounce himself as such; for him, the destruction of society by any means necessary is the only path to a renewed Russia. Peter is also fascinated and enthralled by the enigmatic, self-obsessed Stavrogin and he tries to recruit Stavrogin to his cell. He even calls Stavrogin a prince and compares him to the hero of a folk tale, appealing to him to act as Tsarevich, a character who competes with his brothers to take the throne – perhaps Peter recognises in Stavrogin a true leader. Being a leader is something that Peter Verkhovensky himself cannot quite achieve; something in his character is lacking, a certain charisma or enigma, both of which Stavrogin possesses. Peter's nihilism expresses itself in his discussions with Shigalov, who is forming an idea for the rule of society. It is a bleak and utilitarian vision: enlighten the few and rule the rest. Despotism, Dostoyevsky seems to be saying, is the natural consequence of nihilism. Shigalov's ideas became a neologism in Russian, and 'shigalyovism' entered the Russian language: it denotes 'a form of sociopolitical demagogy and posturing with a tendency to propose extreme measures and total solutions'.[8]

While Peter Verkhovensky sets out to agitate and form a group, another character, Kirilov, sets out on an individual mission, and while Stepan Verkhovensky reverts to faith, Kirilov's atheism denies it and he is driven to suicide. A suicide that proves significant and useful for Peter, incidentally, as he uses it to scapegoat Kirilov for the murder of Shatov. It is Shatov who cannot agree with the group and it is Shatov who becomes the informer; it is Shatov who the group murders, shooting him and weighing him down in the ice-cold water, like Ivan Ivanov before him. In contrast, Kirilov's suicide is a futile attempt to demonstrate man's power over life and death in a world where there is no God; he owns his death and manages it in order to prove his divinity.

While Kirilov might have been a minor character in this ensemble of *The Devils*, his philosophy as portrayed by Dostoyevsky is a philosophy that hinges on the absurdity of life and the existence of God, and this attracted the attention of French philosopher and twentieth-century icon, Albert Camus.[9] Camus contributed towards the philosophy of existentialism, developing the theme of essential angst that attends the sentience of humankind. The awareness of existence combined with the knowledge of death brings on a kind of permanent dissonance about life, and forces human beings to re-examine their existence constantly in a kind of agony. Camus was so interested by *The Devils* that he dramatised it as a play. He felt that Dostoyevsky's rendition of nihilism was something he held in common with the Russian; perhaps what he did not have in common with Dostoyevsky was a big budget for his production, which cost 30 million francs (around $330,000, perhaps £220,000) – a lot to stage a play in 1959. There were thirty-three actors, twenty-six set changes and the performance was over three hours long. Camus felt that this adaptation was important. The murder of Ivan Ivanov as a real-life crime was a precursor to modern terrorism; Camus described it as the 'first crime of its kind'. Camus saw Dostoyevsky as prophetic, the latter's preoccupation with nihilism also being a contemporary preoccupation for Camus; he felt the characters 'were much closer to us than you would expect':[10]

All of Dostoevsky's heroes question themselves as to the meaning of life. In this they are modern: they do not fear ridicule. What distinguishes modern sensibility from classical sensibility is that the latter thrives on moral problems and the former on metaphysical promise. In Dostoevsky's novels the question is propounded with such intensity that it can only invite extreme solutions.[11]

However, of all the characters, Kirilov fascinated Camus precisely because his logical conclusion was one of those 'extreme solutions'. Camus conducted a brief study of Kirilov in his essay *The Myth of Sisyphus*, an essay focussing on the existential problem – and contradiction – of suicide. Kirilov is an engineer and might be considered therefore to have a logical temperament; he has spent some time abroad, in America, where he has explored what in modern parlance might be considered the search for the meaning life. He has concluded that fear of pain and suffering is what prevents people committing suicide, which appears to him to be the logical conclusion of human existence if God does not exist. In fact, even if he does, either way it seems logical to Kirilov to commit suicide. As Erwin Brody summarises:

> There is a fatal paradox in Kirilov's thought. The engineer holds that God, the benevolent ruler of the universe, is indispensable for man's happiness and therefore such a God must exist. Yet, with his mind trained in exact sciences, Kirilov also knows that such a benevolent God does not exist, and what people think to be a meaningful universe is, in reality, a shameful illusion. As a result of this paradox, the longing of his heart and the rigid truth of his scientific mind clash in a spectacular moral dilemma and he finds it impossible to go on living with such contradictory ideas.[12]

The question for the reader and specifically for Camus's argument with Dostoyevsky is: was Kirilov sane or insane? In many ways Kirilov is like Myshkin: his impulse as a human being is for the good of humankind and his march towards suicide is as much about self-sacrifice for the sake of enlightenment as it is the act of a mad man. While Dostoyevsky appears sympathetic with Kirilov's dilemma, the final act of Kirilov's suicide is much more akin to the act of a madman than it is the demonstration of perfect logic. In the final confrontation between Kirilov and Peter Stepanovitch, Stepanovitch has more or less given up on the idea that Kirilov might commit suicide, leaving behind the confession that will clear them all of killing Shatov. Instead, Stepanovitch is considering how to shoot him first and lay him out so that he is framed for the murder and appeared to commit suicide. In the last analysis Kirilov does the deed himself, but not before he has bitten off most of Stepanovitch's little finger – a reference to the only injury that Ivan Ivanov inflicted on his murderers. Thus Stepanovitch is forced to flee, hearing only the repeated screams of 'Directly' over and over again until the final shot. Camus glosses over the madness of Kirilov's final moments and focusses on the unforgiving logic that Dostoyevsky attributes to Kirilov: 'The reasoning is classic in its clarity. If God does not exist, Kirilov is god. If God does not exist, Kirilov must kill himself. Kirilov must therefore kill himself to become god.'[13]

This thinking is absurd as Camus rightly points out, but the absurdist nature of thought is not the same as sanity or insanity; the contradictory logic, to Camus, is sane. Kirilov's act of suicide is an act of independence, of free will, that in itself affirms his divinity: he takes control of death by killing himself. This is the ultimate paradox of life, for it is an expression both of radical faith and of radical doubt. He goes on to suggest that Kirilov is a character as important in Dostoyevsky's philosophy as the great sinner Stavrogin and the nihilist Ivan Karamazov in the later novel *The Brothers Karamazov*. Stavrogin is an ironic character, and his actions and words lead to tragedy; he is hated by almost everybody, and yet in the last analysis, Stavrogin admits that he, himself, hates no one. Camus was a little general in ascribing the words 'All is well' to Kirilov, which Dostoyevsky does not appear to have written for him, and Camus also points to the Dostoyevskian idea that 'If God does not exist, then everything is permitted', often attributed to Dostoyevsky in *The Brothers Karamazov* but never actually written as directly as it has been quoted. Albert Camus's treatise on Kirilov's suicide might be the source of this much quoted misquotation!

In this novel more than in any other of his novels, the innocent are damaged and destroyed by the actions and philosophies of the sleeper cell. Shatov, like many of the characters in the novel, is a victim; an innocent woman and her brother are murdered by fire, another innocent woman by the mob; others are driven mad, others mocked; and children are abused and destroyed by the adults in their lives. Like so much of Dostoyevsky's work, it explores the failings of human nature. Camus sensed that Dostoyevsky was struggling with his own internal conflict between faith and doubt. His representations of doubt and the contradictions that it engendered are potent – more potent often than the declarations of faith that populate his novels, particularly *Crime and Punishment*. This imbalance led Camus to speculate that Dostoyevsky's later conversion back to Christianity may not have been as genuine as the author implies: in Kirilov both doubt and faith are terrible things, but in *The Devils* the fate of the atheist and the nihilist is akin to judgement. Dostoyevsky may doubt the effectiveness of Christian faith in the face of the fallen nature of humanity, but despite this he continues to represent redemption, even if only through the medium of self-sacrifice and suicide.

Historians have complained that the mix of fact and fiction makes it difficult to separate Dostoyevsky's myth from the truth. But the truth Dostoyevsky sought to expose had only a tenuous link with the murder of Ivan Ivanov: 'I have never known and still do not know anything about either Nechayev or Ivanov, or the circumstances of the murder, except from the newspapers,' he wrote to his publisher, 'And even if I had, I should not have copied them. I use only the accomplished fact. My fancy may be altogether different from what actually happened, and my Peter Verkhovensky completely unlike Nechayev; but I think that … my imagination has created the character, the type, that corresponds to this crime.'[14]

While *The Devils* is rooted in reality, it is probably the most symbolic of his major works, a novel raised almost to the level of allegory. As he did in *Crime and Punishment*, Dostoyevsky used deterministic names: Stavrogin, the great sinner of *The Devils*, derives from both *stavros* or 'cross' and *rog* or 'horn'. Peter Verkhovensky, the leader of the terrorist group, was snake-like in appearance: 'His head was elongated at the back and somewhat flattened at the sides, so that his face looked rather sharp. His forehead was high and narrow, but his features rather small; his eyes were sharp, his nose small and pointed, his lips long and thin.'[15] Even the novel's title suggests its themes: *The Devils*'s alternative title, *The Possessed*, is based on the story of the aforementioned tale of Gadarene swine. As one of the characters explains,

> But now an idea has occurred to me; *une comparaison*. An awful lot of ideas keep occurring to me now. You see, that's just like our Russia. These devils who go out of the sick man and enter the swine – those are all the sores, all the poisonous exhalations, all the impurities, all the big and little devils, that have accumulated in our great and beloved invalid, in our Russia, for centuries! ... They are we, we and them, and Peter – *et les autres avec lui*, and perhaps I at the head of them all, and we shall cast ourselves down, the raving and the possessed, from the cliff into the sea and shall all be drowned, and serve us right, for that is all we are good for.[16]

The five terrorists in *The Devils* were possessed with an idea that drove them mad, an idea that had infected Russia. They wished to break down society, to create anarchy and replace the old ways with an irreligious socialist utopia dependent on the West. Much of their plotting occurred in a place whose name, Fillipov, recalled a predecessor in revolution: the Russian heretic Danilo Fillipov who, as a monk, decided that Christianity could do away with authority and flung all the rule books into the river.

Exposing their ideas as mercilessly as he could, Dostoyevsky cast the demons into his characters. They became possessed by their objectives, but everything they attempted to achieve ended only in disaster, taking them ever farther from their goals. Peter Verkhovenksy's idea to murder the apparent informer Shatov was supposed to rid the group of a threat to their existence and bind them ever more closely together in a loyal conspiracy. It did nothing of the sort. In the course of the chaotic and brutal murder, the group fragmented. Their violent act became the catalyst for their own destruction.

Thus the task of *The Devils* is not just the reimagining of a true crime, but the construction of an allegory. It is a testament to Dostoyevsky's talent that he could construct the story with the realism of verisimilitude and mix its contents with the dimension of myth. However, this is consistent with the Dostoyevsky who at the beginning of his career wrote first the social realist novel *Poor Folk* and followed it up, a fortnight later, with the magical realism of *The Double*. In *The Devils*, then, the story of the Gadarene swine is not the only biblical allusion. Geir Kjetsaa, in his biography *Dostoyevsky: A Writer's Life*, suggests that the characters of Stavrogin and Peter Verkhovensky are based on the first and second beasts of the Apocalypse. Just as Prince Myshkin is a contemporary representation of Christ in human form, so these characters are human representations of beasts in Revelation. Kjetsaa points out that Stavrogin is beast-like: he bites someone's ear, and much of the imagery used to describe him is related to birds of prey. Peter, who is snake-like, first appears in a chapter called 'The Wise Serpent'. Like the second beast in Revelation 12, he prepares the way for the first beast, to whom he is devoted but who fails to fulfil his dreams. Stavrogin is infected by apathy, the mark of the church at Laodicea in Revelation 3: 'And to the angel of the church in Laodicea write: – "I know your works: you are neither cold nor hot. Would that you were cold or hot!"'[17] Knowing that his wife is going to be murdered, Stavrogin neither wants it to happen nor tries to stop it, and it is the same kind of bored, disinterested curiosity that led him to commit his great sin earlier in his life.

A final chapter, 'Stavrogin's Confession', is often added to current editions of *The Devils* as an appendix. In this chapter, left unpublished in Dostoyevsky's day until after the Russian Revolution, because Katkov, the publisher, felt it was too indecent to offer to his readers, Stavrogin goes to the priest, Tikhon, and confesses to the seduction of a little girl of twelve. The child suffers such shame that she hangs herself, but she reappears to Stavrogin in his dreams, shaking her little fist. It is not a pleasant story, and it is all the harder to accept in Stavrogin who, though he leads an entirely dishonourable life, is not as repulsive as his counterpart Peter Verkhovensky, who confines himself to straightforward murder and political conspiracy. In Stavrogin, the duality of human nature is evident; he attempts to live with the evil within himself. But after his great crime he cannot forgive himself, and so he goes to Tikhon with a written confession that he intends to publish as a form of expiation. However, Tikhon discourages this. Publication is, after all, a grand gesture, and an egotistical act; complete obscurity is preferable, but Stavrogin is too proud to allow that. In the end he hangs himself. In his dramatisation of *The Devils* in 1959, Albert Camus not only put the omitted chapter in but placed it in the novel, where Dostoyevsky had intended it to be placed, rather than as an appendix. Camus felt that doing this informed the character of Stavrogin more effectively – it is in effect a director's cut, with the deleted scene included.

Suicide, murder and futile death are the melodramatic climax of *The Devils*. Just as the Gadarene swine flung themselves into the sea, so the protagonists of the novel die as the result of their own actions. This is as true of Kirilov, the other major suicide in the novel, as it is of Stavrogin, even though the two men die for quite different reasons. Stavrogin cannot forgive himself and so cannot live with himself; Kirilov commits suicide for an idea. His suicide seems to be a utilitarian act: he offers it to the group of five, so that they can pin Shatov's murder on him. But this is not the death of a suicide bomber, even though Kirilov is offering his death to the party. Kirilov cares little for the cause, in fact, for he wonders what relevance any man's action can have in a meaningless world. Instead, this is an act of individual free will: because he is an atheist and does not believe in immortality, he believes that suicide is the ultimate assertion of his will:

> For three years I've been searching for the attribute of my divinity, and I've found it: the attribute of my divinity is Self-Will! That's all I can do to prove in the main point my defiance and my new terrible freedom. For it is terrible. I am killing myself to show my defiance and my new terrible freedom.[18]

The characters constantly ask themselves and each other if they believe in God. Are they atheists or believers, and what are the implications of their beliefs? To Stavrogin, Dostoyevsky attributes words similar to those he wrote to Natalya Fonvizina in 1854: 'But didn't you tell me,' Shatov accuses Stavrogin, 'that if it were mathematically proved to you that truth was outside Christ, you would rather remain with Christ than with truth?'[19] This identification with Stavrogin may have been the source of the accusation that Dostoyevsky shared not only Stavrogin's doubts but also his crime. In a letter from Nikolai Strakhov to Leo Tolstoy (published in 1913 after the deaths of both Strakhov and Dostoyevsky), Strakhov, Dostoyevsky's one-time friend and biographer, makes this same accusation. Dostoyevsky's wife roundly rebutted the charges. She rightly pointed out that if Dostoyevsky had had to commit all the crimes he portrayed, he would have been not only a rapist but a murderer – and unlikely to have got away with it. In the end, little credence has been given to these accusations.

The discussion of God in *The Devils* reveals the conflict in Dostoyevsky's own faith. He could believe in Christ but found it hard to believe in God. Shatov, the victim, is sometimes thought to be the character that most reflects Dostoyevsky's essential uncertainty. Shatov's name means 'shaky' or 'loose minded', and the character bears some other similarities to Dostoyevsky: he was a revolutionary who went away for four years, during which time he was converted to some sort of faith, which makes him a danger to the group. And, like Dostoyevsky, he wants to believe: when asked whether he believes in God, he says, 'I shall believe in God.'[20]

In *The Devils* Dostoyevsky takes revolutionary beliefs and works them out in the characters to logical extremes. Just as Raskolnikov's personal philosophy led him to justify murder as a utilitarian act, so the beliefs of the characters in *The Devils* lead them inexorably to the tragic, albeit all too logical, consequences. Unlike *Crime and Punishment, The Devils* offers no salvation to the protagonists; it is a portrait of evil, of darkness without redemption. Even the wife and newly born child of Shatov are not allowed to live to carry a torch of hope to the end of the novel.

The only indication of Christian influence in *The Devils* is the setting, a church-going community. Nevertheless, this background has little influence in the situation: the authorities are weak. Western liberalism, of the sort that Dostoyevsky himself once embraced, is the dominant philosophical force, and it is the consequences of liberalism that Dostoyevsky examines. The father, Stepan Verkhovensky, holds to the kind of liberalism that Dostoyevsky himself had embraced in the 1840s. Peter, his son, as well as being his physical offspring is also the extension of Stepan's beliefs ranging from liberalism to nihilism. Thus the 'devils' flee or destroy themselves at the end of the novel and Dostoyevsky himself exorcises a dark ghost. A catharsis occurs in Dostoyevsky's writing at this point, an insight which prepared him to examine not just the nature of life but to go home to Russia.

20

DEBTS AND CREDIT

Anna Dostoyevsky sat at a table opposite an angry man, a creditor of her husband's. Her welcome back to Russia in 1871 was to deal with the queue of creditors who besieged their apartment. Most creditors had been owed their money for the full four years that the Dostoyevskys had been abroad. Other debts went back to the time of Mikhail's death, if not before that, to the collapse of their first journal *Time*.

This creditor proved particularly difficult to shift. Almost past negotiating with, he demanded cash on the table immediately. He told Anna that the debtors' prison was where he intended to put Fyodor Dostoyevsky if the debt was not repaid forthwith. The Dostoyevskys had no money, as Anna well knew, so she brazened out the situation. She told the creditor that if he went to the trouble of throwing Dostoyevsky into prison, she would find an apartment near the prison, visit her husband regularly and provide him with food and the means to work. In short, she would make his time in prison so comfortable that the creditor would have only the meagre satisfaction of seeing a man flung in a gaol where he could rest comfortably and thus delay even further the possibility of repaying the debt. The creditor saw that she was serious. There would indeed be no profit for him in immobilising Dostoyevsky in a debtors' gaol. He backed down and they renegotiated the debt.

Thus began Anna's lifelong career as manager of Dostoyevsky's estate and business affairs. Her ambition to earn her own living may not have been fulfilled in quite the way she had intended, but her contribution to her husband's career, and in particular the work of building up his reputation that she continued after his death, should never be underestimated.

However, in St Petersburg in 1871 there seemed to be a thousand creditors outside the door and thousands of roubles yet to pay. On their return Anna had hoped to clear the debts by selling her small house in Peski, part of her inheritance that she had let during their absence, but the tenant had been unreliable. He had failed to pay his taxes and so the house had been sold from under her at much less than its value, which did not leave nearly enough to pay their debts. Not only that, when they returned they discovered that many of their personal possessions left in the care of the family had also been sold in order to cover debts and shortfalls in what Dostoyevsky had sent from abroad. Much of the furniture and many treasures now had to be replaced. Worst of all, Dostoyevsky's library, including valuable signed first editions, had been broken up and sold by his errant stepson Pasha. Anna commented in her own diary that this was a great loss to them and, although she managed to buy back some of the books, she could never fully replace the rare books that Dostoyevsky had so carefully collected.

Their four years of travel had included many significant events: watching her husband gamble away fortunes and pawn her most valued possessions; the birth and death of their first child, and the strain and fear of a second pregnancy and birth; the coming to terms with her husband's worsening epilepsy and hacking cough. They arrived home just a week before their third child, Fyodor, or Fedya, was born. After such an eventful time it is small wonder that she was told she had aged: 'My women friends assured me that I had aged terribly during those four years, and reproached me for paying no attention to my appearance, and for not dressing fashionably.'[1]

Life abroad may have been hard on Anna but she felt that it had benefitted Dostoyevsky, although perhaps that was partly due to her influence. She said with some satisfaction on their return:

> There is no doubt that during his retirement from Russia, in his new situation, and as a result of long and quiet reflection, there occurred that particular unfolding of the Christian spirit that had always lived in him. That essential change was evident to all his friends, when Dostoyevsky returned from abroad. He continuously turned the conversation to religious themes.[2]

Despite a new, easygoing manner with his friends and his increasing interest in Christianity, Dostoyevsky was still easily upset by financial matters. He was, perhaps understandably, enraged when rich Aunt Kumanina died and left forty thousand roubles to a monastery instead of the family; his new-found faith was stretched to its limits.

The strain of carrying not only his own debts but also Mikhail's must have made his aunt's action seem a bitter blow. He respected the Church, but he knew it was rich and he was poor. Just as he had badgered his relatives for money from his father's will, he contested his aunt's decision. The ensuing argument was to split the family apart. His sister Vera and his favourite niece, Sofia, stood firm against him. Unlike the other beneficiaries, he had received an advance against his inheritance, and by contesting the will he prevented anyone from benefitting at all. Sofia had received many of his letters and he had dedicated the first edition of *The Idiot* to her, but in later editions her name was redacted. The feud was to carry on until the day of his death.

Dostoyevsky could not master his disappointment. His debts were still pressing and a life of toil and constant financial juggling stretched before him and his family. Anna decided that she should try to get a job as a stenographer. The children were settled at home with the maid, so Anna now had the time to work, but

Dostoyevsky, overwhelmed by jealousy, could not tolerate the idea. Despite the fact that Anna even dressed in a dowdy fashion to try to allay his fears, he could not trust her or other men, and she had to give up the idea of going out to work. However, the need to make money was so urgent that Anna decided that the only solution remaining for the Dostoyevskys was self-publishing.

Most major novels in Russia at that time were published first in serial form, in one of the many literary journals, and then in a book edition, issued by a printer. Anna saw that the more middlemen there were involved in the process, the less money the Dostoyevskys received from the profits of their books. Anna decided that they must publish *The Devils* themselves. *The Devils* had already been serialised by Katkov in *The Russian Messenger*, but Anna saw to it that they kept the rights to publish it in book form. By avoiding a middleman they received less money up front, but once they started selling the books to the booksellers they received payment immediately and much more directly. Anna even sold the books from their apartment – queues of booksellers stood at the door and Anna served each one of them personally. The domestic upheaval worried the maid. Hearing people come to the door and ask for *The Devils*, she became convinced that some sort of witchcraft was going on and complained that since Satan had come into the house the poor boy Fedya had not been able to sleep.

Writing *The Devils* temporarily exhausted Dostoyevsky of ideas. He too decided that he must get a job, and by the end of 1872 he was offered a post editing a weekly newspaper published by Prince Meshchersky, a well-intentioned man who was very conservative politically. An upshot of the prince's respectable conservatism was that the authorities were persuaded to restore to Dostoyevsky another of his civil rights denied to him by his crimes: the right to edit a publication. Over the years many of Dostoyevsky's ideas had become more conservative, and this enabled Prince Meshchersky to plead successfully on his behalf. Dostoyevsky remained, however, under surveillance by the Third Department, or secret police.

Fyodor accepted the editorship of *The Citizen* and began to work for Prince Meshchersky. The task was not easy. He found the censors awkward and interfering. They altered his work constantly and sometimes actually prevented him from publishing some parts of the newspaper. The censors, however, were not the only people to make life as an editor difficult for Dostoyevsky: he was hired on the understanding that Prince Meshchersky would contribute frequently to the newspaper. This left Dostoyevsky with the delicate job of editing his own employer, who according to Dostoyevsky was 'illiterate to the point of incomprehensibility and with howlers that would have made him a laughing stock – for ten years'.[3] Dostoyevsky himself was so demanding an editor that his colleagues nicknamed him 'spitfire'.

Although Dostoyevsky had become more conservative himself, he still did not find all the prince's opinions either to his taste or professionally acceptable. They argued often over what the censors might or might not allow and over what Dostoyevsky thought was permissible. He was infuriated by one of Meshchersky's articles that advocated rounding up radical students and putting them in one place so that they could be watched more easily by the secret police. In the end, Dostoyevsky went to gaol once again because of his employer. The good prince had neglected to ask permission to quote the tsar in one of his articles. The error was, of course, ultimately the editor's responsibility, and Dostoyevsky's punishment was two days in gaol, which the authorities allowed him to serve at his own convenience.

Editing the newspaper also took him away from his family. St Petersburg in the summer was no place for young children to be cooped up in a four-roomed apartment, so the Dostoyevskys rented a small wooden house in Staraya Russa, about a hundred and thirty miles from St Petersburg, for the summer months. Because of his commitment to *The Citizen*, Dostoyevsky could not always join them. Like his father before him, he hated being separated from his children and was constantly worried about their welfare. If he did not receive regular correspondence from Anna reassuring him, he became convinced that something dreadful had happened to them. He wrote,

> Once more I beg and implore you: Write about once every five days, if it is only twelve lines, like a telegram, about the children's health and your own. You cannot believe how much I worry about the children and what I suffer on this account. Now, not having received any letters, I can only think of them. If I don't hear something by Tuesday i.e. by the day after tomorrow, I shall send a telegram.[4]

Despite the numerous disadvantages of editing *The Citizen*, the family needed the money and the newspaper gave Dostoyevsky an opportunity that he had not had so far in his career. Unable, as yet, to write another novel, Fyodor concluded that some sort of journal or diary would be the next step in his writing career. *The Citizen* offered him the opportunity to write what became known as the *Diary of a Writer*, which at first appeared as a newspaper column. When he finally left the paper, after one row too many with the prince had taken its toll on his health, the column was well established and he and Anna were able to continue publishing it independently.

Demand for his novels continued. Both *Crime and Punishment* and *The Idiot* were reprinted, while Nekrasov, impressed by *The Devils*, made Dostoyevsky an offer for a new novel. By the time Dostoyevsky was ready to leave *The Citizen* he had been sufficiently reinvigorated to offer the publisher a new plot, and Nekrasov published *A Raw Youth* in *Notes of the Fatherland* in 1875.

Nekrasov's offer came as a surprise as, after *Poor Folk*, there had been little love lost between the two men. Nekrasov, however, was willing to recognise talent when he saw it, and he was wise enough to go back on some of the things he had said when Dostoyevsky had disappointed him with his second novel, *The Double*. Nekrasov, always the astute businessman, offered Fyodor more than Dostoyevsky's usual publisher, Katkov, could. Katkov had just bought *Anna Karenina* from Tolstoy and did not have enough cash to top Nekrasov's offer, probably feeling he could rely on Dostoyevsky because the author had already sent him the first half of the novel. Nekrasov was delighted with his triumph, although the novel is not counted today among Dostoyevsky's greatest works. When he died in 1878 he was reconciled with Dostoyevsky and seemed convinced, as he was at the beginning of both their careers, that Dostoyevsky was a genius.

Dostoyevsky had not left *The Citizen* only to write *A Raw Youth*, or because he saw it was possible to publish the *Diary of a Writer* on his own. He left because the pressures of editing a weekly newspaper were aggravating his already failing health. Now in his early fifties, he was living with the results of years of late nights, hard labour, violent fits and – perhaps most of all – constant chain-smoking of strong cigarettes. His general health was breaking down and he was developing the first signs of emphysema. Unable to carry on working in this way, with a hacking cough and breathing difficulties, Dostoyevsky left his post at *The Citizen*. He did not, however, forget to serve the brief prison sentence imposed for his publisher's oversight in quoting the tsar.

In addition, Anna had also suffered some difficulties during this time. Her sister had died of typhoid, and her own life had been threatened by the development of a large boil on her neck.

The fact that Dostoyevsky left *The Citizen* did not automatically give the family more time together, and in the summer of 1875 Dostoyevsky had to suffer separation from his family once again, this time going to the spa at Bad Ems in Germany where he could get medical treatment for his condition. He went alone.

21

THE DREAM

Dostoyevsky's *Diary of a Writer* was published between 1873 and 1877, with a further special issue in 1881. It is not one of his better-known works in the popular market because much of it is opinion and contemporary comment. However, it contains several famous short stories, and it explains much of what is known about Dostoyevsky's early life. *Diary of a Writer* is the temperature gauge of the development of Dostoyevsky's religious thought at that time. In it, he was working out the themes that he was to encapsulate in his last great novel, *The Brothers Karamazov*.

Diary of a Writer gave Dostoyevsky an opportunity to make money from his writing without putting pressure on him to write fiction, which required not only time but also the strength of a good idea and a strong plot. At last he could afford to give adequate time to his fiction, and perhaps it is no coincidence that *The Brothers Karamazov*, conceived and written not long after the publication of the *Diary*, has been critically acclaimed throughout the world as the pinnacle of Dostoyevsky's achievement. The Dostoyevsky finances were by no means secure, but the *Diary* provided sufficient leeway to give him some choice about what he did next.

The *Diary* was any writer's dream: a forum for the writer's opinion about anything that took his fancy, not unlike a modern day blog. He was his own editor as well as the only contributor. The *Diary* was, as ever, limited by the censors, but Dostoyevsky was so loyal a citizen now that he rarely transgressed in the eyes of the authorities. In fact, it was a good chance for him to expiate his early revolutionary sins. He was able to explain to his readers, one of whom was the tsar, his present beliefs by exposing and criticising his previous political and non-Christian philosophies.

In the *Diary* he recounts much of what is known about his relationship with Belinsky. He retells the story of that first night when he met the great critic, and relates how for years he had admired Belinsky from afar and then found himself face to face with the great man's own praise for him and his novel *Poor Folk*: '"But do you, yourself, understand," he repeated to me several times, screaming, as was his habit, "what you have written!" He always screamed when he spoke in a state of great agitation.'[1] Now many years removed from that sudden fame, followed just as quickly by the sudden split with this man, Dostoyevsky was able to reminisce with humour.

Dostoyevsky also used the *Diary* to criticise his own past, to denounce his former beliefs and to outline his own manifesto for the future. Even while reorganising his political beliefs, however, he never lost his love or sympathy for the people of Russia, the peasants. When some critics suggested that peasants may also have had character defects, Dostoyevsky turned on them with the passion of one who has experienced more than any of them could know:

> So, don't tell me that I do not know the people! I know them: it was because of them that I again received into my soul Christ, Who had been revealed to me in my parents' home and Whom I was about to lose when, on my part, I transformed myself into a 'European liberal'![2]

Dostoyevsky credited the people with his salvation: their expression of the Christian faith had opened his eyes and they were crucial to his theories of Russian Christianity that he expanded upon later in the *Diary*.

Despite this, he was not blind to man's inhumanity to man, of whatever class. Over the years Dostoyevsky had taken an active interest in crime, not so much for fictional purposes, although his knowledge informed his novels, but because he had a keen sense of justice and was able to see that justice was not easy to dispense.

In the first few pages of the *Diary* he describes in harrowing detail the treatment of a young woman peasant by her husband:

> At length she grows quiet; she shrieks no longer; now she merely groans wildly; her breath comes in gasps every minute; but right then the blows come down more frequently, more violently ... Suddenly he throws away the strap; like a madman, he seizes a stick, a bough, anything, and breaks it over her back with three last, terrific, blows. – No more! He quits, plants himself by the table, sighs, and sets himself to his Kvass.[3]

The young woman finally gathered the courage to go to the police and report her husband's treatment of her. They replied that they could do nothing and suggested that she should learn to live 'amicably' with her husband. Driven to despair she committed suicide, but her suicide solved nothing. Since the husband had not been charged or convicted, the little daughter who watched the maltreatment of her mother would soon become the next victim of his violence. Thus the violence would be perpetuated down the generations.

Though Dostoyevsky was moved to pity for the woman, he was not unaware of what might today be called 'contributing factors'. He knew only too well what conditions such peasants had to endure: small one-roomed cottages, mud- or perhaps wood-walled, were their only accommodation and their lives were a constant struggle against starvation and ill treatment. Since their so-called liberation the serfs' situation had grown substantially worse, not better; small wonder, then, that men were driven to violence. But,

Dostoyevsky points out, if the conditions cause the violence, why does not every peasant beat his wife?

The young, idealistic Fyodor had hoped that a perfect environment would create a perfect man. In prison he learned that human nature is much more complex than he had first suspected. On one hand, among his fellow prisoners were murderers 'who were so gay and so carefree that one might have made a bet that their consciences never for a moment reproached them'.[4] On the other hand, men whom he had come to regard as wild beasts 'would manifest such a wealth of fine feeling, so keen a comprehension of the sufferings of others, seen in the light of the consciousness of their own, that one could almost fancy that scales had fallen from one's eyes'.[5]

This apparently contradictory view of the common people is evident in his comments in the *Diary*. Millions of peasants, he points out, live perfectly decent and honest lives despite the fact that they are ground down by the ever-present threat of starvation. Others, however, succumb to temptation. Why? How much does environment contribute to crime? How much are the individuals themselves to blame for their crimes, and how much is society to blame? It was these questions that Dostoyevsky debated openly in the *Diary*. Through the *Diary* he even became actively involved in a case by virtue of the opinion he expressed and published.

The case featured a young woman, Yekaterina Kornilova, who threw her six-year-old stepdaughter out a fourth-floor window. Kornilova, pregnant at the time, had just had a row with her husband and wanted to get at him, so she flung his little girl out of the window and then went straight to the police to confess. Extraordinarily enough, the child survived with only a mild concussion, but since Kornilova had confessed to the child's murder the police charged her with attempted murder. She was convicted of that crime, although the first conviction was rescinded on a technicality, and Dostoyevsky became publicly interested in the retrial.

Dostoyevsky protested against the initial conviction. In his article he argued that her pregnancy might have affected her mind. Paranoia during pregnancy and post-natal depression are conditions well known to the medical profession now. (However, even today some experts will deny the relevance of these conditions to women's actions.) Dostoyevsky felt that Kornilova's pregnant state at the time of committing the crime was an important mitigating factor. In many ways he was ahead of his time – and his article caused a great deal of public controversy. At the retrial expert evidence was called in and Kornilova was acquitted, despite the fact that the judge warned the jury not to be too influenced by the open debate that Dostoyevsky had provoked.

Dostoyevsky's understanding of the criminal mind, evident in *Crime and Punishment* and in *The Devils*, had won him great respect. He was always concerned to understand the motivation and circumstances behind evil acts. He was always seeking for the just solution, although he was the first to agree that justice did not always mean acquittal; an unpunished crime was unfair to both the perpetrator and victim. He protested this principle in an article he wrote when a woman who slashed her husband's lover was acquitted on the grounds that it was a crime of passion. The defence lawyer pleaded that she would have been less than a woman if she had not slashed her unfaithful husband's lover, and the judge agreed with him. Dostoyevsky said that by letting her off they were condoning the crime and therefore encouraging the woman to be less than human, for part of being human was the ability to control oneself and to take responsibility for one's actions. Dostoyevsky held the conviction that criminals must be held responsible for their crimes, although each case merited an individual approach.

Although much of the *Diary* was comment on contemporary events, occasionally Dostoyevsky included a short imaginative piece, such as the story of a man who lies down on a gravestone just after a funeral and listens to the voices of the dead talking in their graves beneath him ('Bobok'). In his waking dream the listener hears the newly dead talk to one another until, after a few months in their limbo world, they fall silent again. The story faces Dostoyevsky's own fear of being buried alive; in his youth he had feared this so much that he left instructions that, in case of his death, everyone must wait a week before burying him, in order to be sure that he was dead.

Regular readers of the *Diary* must have found the short stories a pleasant relief after much intense and insightful comment on current affairs. At least two of the stories, 'The Dream of a Ridiculous Man' and 'At Christ's Christmas Tree', indicate the state of Dostoyevsky's faith. The latter, a Russian equivalent to 'The Little Match Girl' by Hans Christian Andersen, tells the story of a little boy who runs out in the city streets after his mother dies. It is Christmas, and outside it is bitterly cold and snowing. The little boy has never been in the city before, and the window displays, the mechanical puppets and the tantalising smells of food delight him. At last, tired and cold, he settles down behind a pile of wood in a yard and goes to sleep. All at once his mother comes to get him and takes him to Christ's Christmas tree. The other children who are gathered at the tree tell the little boy that Jesus always has a Christmas party for little boys and girls who have no tree of their own. In the morning, of course, a cold, stiff little body is found amid a pile of wood. The story moistened the eye of every Russian who read it, and although it is not as well known outside of Russian, as many similar stories are, it is indeed a children's classic.

However, Dostoyevsky's adult short story *The Dream of a Ridiculous Man* has a far more sinister atmosphere:

> I resolved to kill myself that night. I had firmly resolved on it two months earlier, and, poor as I was, had bought an excellent revolver and loaded it that same day. But two months had passed and it was still lying in the drawer; but it made so little difference to me that I wished finally to seize a moment when it was less so – why, I didn't know.[6]

Thus Dostoyevsky returns to a favourite theme: the contradiction between the understanding of life and its inevitable, concomitant knowledge of death. The man describes himself as ridiculous because his life is futile; he is educated, he went to school to university, but the purpose of all that, it seems, was merely to explain to him just how he is a Ridiculous Man. He progresses through his life but he cannot shake the feeling that he is ridiculous and, like Kirilov before him in *The Devils*, he decides that suicide is the only sensible solution. Once again the powerless man seeks to take power over life and death; and since the example of Rasknolnikov the nature of this power has been much more to do with self-slaughter than about the slaughter of others. Nevertheless, the futility of life juxtaposed against the inevitability of death makes suicide appear an appropriate solution. However, before the Ridiculous Man reaches his inevitable conclusion he meets a little girl. There is no clear clue given to geography, but the streets are urban, dull and gloomy:

> Rain had poured down all day, and it was the coldest and gloomiest rain, even some sort of menacing rain, I remember that, with an obvious hostility to people, and now, between ten and eleven, it suddenly stopped, and a terrible dampness set in, damper and colder than when it was raining, and a sort of steam rose from everything, from every stone in the street and from every alleyway, if you looked far into its depths from the street.[7]

The man returns to his fifth-floor room. Dostoyevsky thus establishes him as not entirely successful – in St Petersburg society, the higher the room, the less it is respectable. The man is interrupted in his designs by a little girl who seeks his help, but the man rejects her, on the basis that he is already a 'zero' and therefore she can be nothing to him. He is distracted by his response to her, and while thinking through his response he falls asleep and he dreams.

The Ridiculous Man, who is contemplating suicide, dreams that he commits the act and that in death he flies far beyond the earth to another planet. On this planet he finds that the inhabitants have not yet sinned. They live an ideal and decent life, in harmony with each other and with him for centuries, but inevitably this does not last. They do not survive the visit of their sinful friend unscathed, says the dreamer:

In the end I corrupted the lot of them! How I managed to do it, I can't say; I don't remember too clearly. My dream flashed through eons, leaving in me only a general impression of the whole. All I know is that I caused their fall from grace. Like a sinister trichina, like a plague germ contaminating whole kingdoms ... They learned how to lie, they came to love it, and they grew to appreciate the beauty of untruth.[8]

If the Ridiculous Man were Kirilov or Stavrogin this might be the end of the story, but Dostoyevsky develops this theme of corruption. There is no doubt that this Ridiculous Man is not unlike Underground Man, in that he is unredeemed and futile, sees his potential suicide as his cure and, now that he has corrupted a whole new idyllic planet, thinks he should deserve to be a 'zero'. He even muses sometimes that perhaps these events are real – that he has actually travelled beyond the stars to another earth where sin does not exist. All is not lost for the planet, however, for despite their descent into corruption, they choose to rebuild, to adapt and evolve into an understanding of themselves as no longer innocent, as prone to suffering, but also able to learn and achieve. The Ridiculous Man wanders among them appalled by what he has done, but they tell him that they cannot remember a time when they did not sin, when there was no suffering. Although the Ridiculous Man offers himself as a sacrifice to them, and even shows them how to crucify him, they send him away. His sacrifice is unnecessary: they will continue in their changed state without him. When the dreamer awakes he is a changed man, and he resolves to love others as he loves himself: 'And that's all there is to it. Nothing else is required. That would settle everything ... And I shall fight it. And if everyone wanted it, everything could be arranged immediately.'[9] The dreamer has now become a preacher of a fundamentally Christian message, and his first task is to find the little girl and offer her help.

The story has parallels with Charles Dickens *A Christmas Carol*. However, as perhaps would be expected of Dostoyevsky, it is not an outside force or ghost that confronts the protagonist with his own inadequacy, but the force of his own guilt, the angst of his own self-knowledge. 'The Dream of a Ridiculous Man' is redemptive, just like the redemption of Scrooge, although this redemption is less selfish. Scrooge wakes on Christmas Day, delighted that he has another chance, a chance to do good – and Scrooge can be given the benefit of the doubt on his motivation – but much of what he must do from the night after his Christmas visitations is done in order to save himself from Marley's fate, rather than to perpetuate goodness for others. The Ridiculous Man, by contrast, offers himself as a sacrifice; he thinks of himself only as a zero. His motivation for doing good is only that it is possible so to do – whether that brings him the reward of eternal life in God is not as clear.

The Ridiculous Man is redeemed in his state and does see hope in belief, but a question mark still hangs over his ideas of futility. Dostoyevsky still approached ideas of faith by exploring some of the less orthodox aspects of Russian Christianity. Much religious practice in Russia at his time was superstitious. Christianity was a blend of the old folk religion, with its ancient legends, and the modern stories of the coming of Christ and the activity of the saints. Most of the population lived on a knife-edge, and so many turned to superstition and folk religion to help solve their problems. Dostoyevsky found comfort in some of these solutions, at least at first. After his first wife, Maria Isayeva, left Semipalatinsk with her husband, he had consulted a fortune teller, which had stirred an interest in spiritualism that fascinated him for some years after that.

During his four-year stay abroad with Anna, he read the works of Swedenborg, who after a spiritual experience claimed he had witnessed societies of spiritual beings functioning in civilisations much like those on earth. When Dostoyevsky returned from Europe, he began to investigate more thoroughly the possibility of contact with the dead. He attended séances, at the time the fashionable thing to do – St Petersburg was well-populated with mediums. There were so many séances, in fact, that a government inquiry was set up to investigate them. The inquiry concluded that the séances were a fraud. Dostoyevsky was not entirely convinced, for he had even held a séance with his wife and children that he claimed worked without the help of deception. However, he could not ignore the Bible's explicit condemnation of spiritualism. His desire to contact another dimension, however possible, was condemned by the Christian faith he now espoused. In the *Diary* he finally renounced spiritualism, using the government's report as the occasion for his own comments:

> Briefly, spiritism is undoubtedly a great, extraordinary and most foolish fallacy, a lecherous doctrine and ignorance; but the trouble is that all this, perhaps does not transpire around the table as the Committee order us to believe, and, indeed, it is also impossible to call all spiritists humbugs and fools … The mystical meaning of spiritism - this most harmful thing – should have been taken into particular consideration. Yet the Committee has not given thought to this particular significance. Of course, under no circumstance, would it have been in a position to crush the evil; but at least, by different – not so naive and haughty – methods the Committee could have inculcated in spiritists even a respect for its findings, while it could have exercised a strong influence on the wavering followers of spiritism.[10]

In his last novel, *The Brothers Karamazov*, Dostoyevsky has a humorous dig at the spiritists: when the Devil appears to Ivan, he remarks how fond he is of spiritists. The presence of an immortal soul in each human being has a more serious side: immortality implies responsibility. In *The Brothers Karamazov* and in the *Diary* Dostoyevsky is not afraid to suggest that some things are immoral and dangerous because of their possible effect on the immortal soul.

22

EXPANSION

In April 1876 the Bulgarians rebelled against the Turkish Empire. The Ottomans crushed the uprising quickly and with cruelty. The atrocities they committed on Bulgarian civilians enraged Russia and shocked Europe. Thenceforth, Turkey had no allies in Western Europe and so was vulnerable to Russian action. In Serbia a similar uprising took place, and in Moscow prayers were said on behalf of the Serbs. However, despite some help from Russian volunteers, this uprising was also suppressed.

The Pan-Slavic movement in Russia, which received the support of the Orthodox Church, felt it was a Christian's duty to show solidarity with their persecuted brethren under Turkish rule. In England and other Western European countries fears grew that, should the Turkish Empire collapse, Russia would sweep in and invade so much of the fallen empire, and that would mean Russia would become too powerful in Europe. Initially Russia tried to get promises from the Ottomans that the rights of Christians would be respected and that they could consider themselves under the authority of the Metropolitan of Moscow in religious matters. European diplomats attempted to get both countries to agree to a treaty, but the Turks wanted no interference, and on 24 April 1877 Russia declared war on Turkey. By January 1878 the Russians looked set to invade Constantinople. However, an armistice was agreed that prevented this, and a treaty was signed that set up an independent state of Bulgaria and ceded the Caucasus to Russia. This agreement did not go far enough for many Pan-Slavists, including Dostoyevsky. Dostoyevsky believed that Russia's political ambitions were inextricably linked with its Christian mission.

When its Emperor converted to Christianity in AD 321, Constantinople had been the capital of the Roman Empire. The Emperor Constantine's conversion meant that Constantinople became the capital of all Christendom. The form of Christian faith that emanated from this source was therefore purer and more orthodox than the later forms of Christianity to develop in Rome and throughout the European Reformation. It was this tradition that the Russian Orthodox Church adhered to. Therefore the invasion by Russia of Constantinople would restore to Christianity the original capital of Christendom, all in the name of Russian power and glory; this was now Dostoyevsky's dream.

As early as June 1876 Dostoyevsky was so excited by the success of the military campaign against the Turks that he predicted Russia would take Constantinople. He anticipated that a new faith would evolve, which would be Christianity in its purest form: 'This would be a genuine exaltation of Christ's truth preserved in the East, a new exaltation of Christ's cross and the final word of Orthodoxy, which is headed by Russia.'[1] Nine months later, Dostoyevsky had to concede that Russia would not soon take Constantinople, but this did not distract him from what had come to be his creed: that it was Russia's mission to restore proper faith in the world. Both Roman Catholicism and Protestantism had failed to proclaim the true message of Christianity: 'Catholicism sold Christ when it blessed the Jesuits and sanctioned the righteousness "of every means for Christ's cause",' he wrote.[2] Catholicism had chosen to perpetuate Christianity by earthly means, he continued: it used the methods of the Spanish Inquisition to convert people to its creed, and the Pope considered himself an earthly ruler and wanted political, not spiritual, power.

Dostoyevsky particularly abhorred the doctrine of papal infallibility, propounded in 1870. He wrote a satirical speech for the Pope that expressed what Dostoyevsky believed the Pope really wanted:

> So you thought that I was satisfied with the mere title of King of the Papal State? Know that I have ever considered myself potentate of the whole world and over all earthly kings … and sovereign over all sovereigns, and to me alone on earth belong the destinies, the ages and the bounds of time. And now I am proclaiming this in the dogma of my infallibility.[3]

Dostoyevsky feared an aggressive Catholicism. He believed socialism was an inevitable consequence of living in proximity to Catholicism. The Catholic Church at that time offered little earthly reward to its people. Millions suffered great injustice while the Catholic Church did nothing to alleviate their earthly suffering, on the grounds that they would be compensated in the life hereafter. The consequences of the evil of Catholicism were clear enough in France: first the revolution and then the Paris Commune.

Fyodor was little more impressed with Protestantism than with Catholicism, although he conceded that at least the Protestants had some educational value. However, industrialisation, science and secularisation were the inevitable consequences of Protestant thought, and they, too, led to atheism. The Protestant work ethic combined with a negating rationality resulted in modes of thinking that were guided by the scientific method, and it was this that led to secularisation. This was a process that Dostoyevsky felt he could already see taking place in Western Europe, particularly in Germany and England.

Dostoyevsky predicted that the two great representative nations of Catholicism and Protestantism, France and Germany, would go to war. Germany would defeat France and, once dominant, would collapse. It would be at this moment of crisis that Russia could convert and dominate both weakened nations. In view of events in the twentieth century, it could be argued that he was not far wrong, although the creed the Russians carried with them in the twentieth century owed more to Belinsky than it did to Russian Orthodoxy.

Meanwhile Dostoyevsky wrote in favour of the Bulgarians and against the Turks. The treatment of the Bulgarians by the Turks was barbaric, and Dostoyevsky retold the stories of torture in graphic detail. Women were raped and pregnant women disembowelled; babies were gored on Turkish bayonets while their doomed mothers watched. It was a matter of honour that Russia, an Eastern Orthodox state, saw to it that these people were protected and rescued.

Dostoyevsky asserted that the war against Islam proved that the Russian people possessed the purest form of Christianity that could exist. He cited the celebrated case of the peasant Foma Danilov, martyred by the Turks because he would not renounce Christ. Danilov was offered pardon by the Khan himself if he would accept Islam and serve in the Turkish army. He refused to betray his faith and his country, and was tortured to death. Danilov's act was entirely selfless: he could not have known that his cruel martyrdom would become public knowledge, that his death would make him a hero and a martyr. If he had renounced Christ and saved his life, who would have known? Here was a true Russian Christian able to sacrifice himself to a cruel fate for the sake of Christ and the honour of his country. The Russian people and the Slavs were inextricably linked both religiously and racially, and the Russians were therefore obliged to defend their brothers. For Dostoyevsky, defence of the Slavs was the only honourable course for an Orthodox Christian nation.

'Undeniably, there lives in the people the firm belief that Russia exists for the sole purpose of serving Christ and protecting ecumenic Orthodoxy as a whole,' wrote Dostoyevsky.[4] If Russia lost its integrity in this matter, it would be severely weakened if not destroyed: 'To abandon the Slavic idea and to leave without a solution to the problem entailing the fate of Eastern Christianity

(N. B. which is the substance of the Eastern problem) – would be equivalent to smashing Russia into pieces, and to inventing in her place something new, but not Russia at all.'[5]

Ultimately Russia did not invade Turkey or take Constantinople, and Dostoyevsky had to revise some of his opinions. Neither France nor Germany looked substantially weakened or likely to go to war with each other again. The Catholic community's loyalty to the Pope was as strong as ever.

The settlement of the 'Eastern Question' was not to be as simple as Dostoyevsky had envisaged, but he had now established a creed from which he would not depart. The Russian community of peasant Christians, linked to God through their affinity with the simple life of the soil, could redeem Christianity for Russia and thence for the world. Dostoyevsky wanted the Christianity that he had come to acknowledge as part of his artistic development to contribute to a better society, rather than to point only to a distant Kingdom of Heaven, achieved by not complaining on earth. He may have criticised the Pope for coveting earthly power, but he saw no contradiction in urging Russia to take that very power to facilitate the spread of Orthodoxy. This, in fact, was Russia's mission:

Let at the same time our faith grow still firmer that precisely herein lies Russia's genuine mission, her strength and truth, and that the self-sacrifice for the oppressed and forsaken by everybody in Europe, in the interests of civilisation, is a real service to its actual and true interests. Nay, it is necessary that in political organisms the same Christ's truth must be preserved; some nation at least must radiate. Otherwise what would happen? Everything would be dimmed, distorted and would be drowned in cynicism. Otherwise you would be unable to restrain the morality of individual citizens, too, and in this event how is the entire organism of the people going to live? Authority is needed. It is necessary that the sun shine. The sun appeared in the East, and it is from the East that the new day begins for mankind.[6]

23

THE DARK OPINIONS

You write about yourself, about your state of mind at the
present moment. I know you are an artist, a painter. Let me
give you a piece of advice straight from the heart. Do not
give up your area but devote yourself more than ever to it.

Dostoyevsky.[1]

This was an answer to one of the steady stream of letters
Dostoyevsky was now receiving in response to the *Diary of a
Writer*. His correspondent complained of suffering from the
duality that Dostoyevsky so ably portrayed in his characters. She
was painfully aware of the division between the 'is' and the 'ought'
in her own life. Dostoyevsky pointed her to art and creativity as
a good cure for painful memories. She was the daughter of the
Vice-President of the Russian Academy of Art in St Petersburg,
and she was a great admirer of Dostoyevsky's work, especially *The
Brothers Karamazov*.

Dostoyevsky carried on a conscientious correspondence with
his readers, answering as many letters as he could. To one woman,
at a loss as to how to educate her daughter in good literature
and ideas, he sent a reading list including his old favourites –
Dickens, Walter Scott and Pushkin (he also recommended
Turgenev, although not until the daughter was a little bit older).

To another mother he suggested that she teach the gospel to her son through her own example and goodness. Not all the letters Dostoyevsky received were complimentary. One woman accused him of squandering his talent on the *Diary* instead of focusing it on his novels; Dostoyevsky replied that he was always observing life and that he was using the *Diary* to recount it and order it. While Fyodor could be charming and diligent in his replies to the many letters he got, particularly from women, his approach to what was then known as the 'Women's Question' was less charming. In fact, the position of women in Russian society at the time was better than in other parts of Europe: Russian women were able to possess property, had a right to education and civil rights, and even certain professions, such as medicine, were opening up to them in the latter part of the nineteenth century. However the role of women and their position in society was still at issue, although Dostoyevsky did not appreciate discussing it in public. The publisher of *The Citizen*, Prince Meshchersky, recalls hosting a party where Dostoyevsky was approached by a lady who wished to press her point on the rights of women. So keen was she to express her opinion to Fyodor, that she ignored some of the warning signs. Meshchersky recalls:

> Several times, I was present at such meetings. A contemporary woman entered the room. She failed to notice the forbidding expression on Dostoevsky's face. She did not hear his cold tone of voice or his formal question, 'What do you want?' This lady, filled with her own motives, began to tell her story, with animated and shining eyes and flushed cheeks.[2]

The ladies were so enamoured of their meeting with the writer, and, perhaps convinced by his writing and their knowledge of his life that he would agree with them, they did not spot the hostility with which the ungracious Fyodor greeted them. His reply was more in the manner of a rant than a polite debate. Meshchersky observed that he looked as if he had a 'volcano burning within', a sign the woman with 'short hair' failed to notice. (Short hair and sometimes gender neutral clothing, even bright colours, were worn by some women in the feminist movement to emphasise their bid for equality.) Dostoyevsky informed his admirer in this case that 'there is no, there was no, and there will not be any other "social purpose" of a woman. This is all stupidity, senseless talk, and gibberish. All that you have told me here is nonsense, do you hear me? It was nonsense, and I am not going to say anything else to you.'[3]

Despite the fact that Dostoyevsky was frequently harsh on this subject, his treatment of the women in his own life was at least that of someone who was dependent on them, and perhaps defensively he understood that without the business acumen of Anna, his project as novelist would probably have failed. His rejection of women's rights is perhaps another oversensitive overreaction.

The 'Women's Question', however, was not the only area of politics where his more unpleasant opinions could be expressed. A more serious charge was levelled by a correspondent who took him to task for his anti-Semitic statements, comments which were particularly vitriolic in the *Diary*:

> I should like to know why are you protesting against the Yiddisher, and not the exploiter in general? ... Is it possible that you are unable to lift yourself to the comprehension of the fundamental law of any social life to the effect that all citizens of a state, without any exception, if they are paying all taxes required for the existence of the state must enjoy all rights and advantages of its existence?[4]

Dostoyevsky believed in Jewish conspiracy theories, which were prevalent in his day, and, sadly, he uncritically accepted every evil story about Jewish people that ever came to his attention. In America, he said, they corrupted the liberated slaves, and in Lithuania they blackmailed the locals. He assured the Jewish community that he did not hate them on religious grounds: his prejudice, he said, did not stem from the fact that Judas sold Christ. He insisted that it was the Jews' behaviour that made him despise them so, and he cited these pernicious stories as the proof: 'Ask the native population in our border regions: What is propelling the Jew – has been propelling him for centuries? You will receive a unanimous answer: mercilessness.'5

His attitude was by no means a minority view or a socially unacceptable one. It was common all over Europe to believe that the Jews were a threat to social stability, that they were cruel, godless and money grabbing. Anti-Semitism, built on centuries of prejudice, was almost a mark of respectability; no Christian would dream of espousing a view to the contrary. A Jewish man who wrote to Dostoyevsky admired his work and believed that his genius could extend to examining the Jewish question with the perspicacity that he applied to the more general human condition. It seemed surprising to the letter writer that Dostoyevsky could portray a murderer's psychology so accurately and yet cling to his damaging prejudices about the Jews.

He hoped that Dostoyevsky might one day be able to break out of his conditioning and reveal anti-Jewish prejudice as a fraud. But for all Dostoyevsky's understanding of human psychological motivations, in this instance he was blinded by his love of Russia, his devotion to the Orthodox Church, and his own prejudice. That being said, in spite of the anti-Semitism in the *Diary*, Dostoyevsky did not make Jews the villains in his novels. On the contrary, the novels are famous for exposing bigotry, small-mindedness and fanaticism. For example, in *The Devils* one of the conspirators, the Jew Lyamshin, is no more evil that the rest of them. When the gang comes to commit the murder, it is Lyamshin who loses control and is unable to do it. It would not be true to say that none of Dostoyevsky's prejudice is present in his novels, but in the novels' polemic thrust it is not his main concern. Some characters do express anti-Semitic views, but Dostoyevsky's fundamental concern is human psychology and the existence of God. This was the project, and not his contemporary prejudices, that was to occupy his final novel.

The truth of the time was that Dostoyevsky's *Diary* proved a success; his writings were popular and his opinions considered appropriate – so appropriate, in fact, that this ex-convict who had once been sentenced to execution by Tsar Nicholas I was now introduced to his descendants. Admiral Arseniev, tutor to Tsar Alexander II's children, introduced Dostoyevsky to the family in 1878, because he thought that Dostoyevsky could be a good influence on them. The once-ostracised radical now entered the sphere of influence of the most reactionary.

24

THE BROTHERS

Everything in Dostoevsky's novels tends toward dialogue,
toward a dialogic opposition, as if tending toward its center.
All else is the means; dialogue is the end. A single voice ends
nothing and resolves nothing. Two voices is the minimum
for life, the minimum for existence.

Mikhail Bakhtin,
Problems of Dostoevsky's Poetics.[1]

Now in his late fifties, Dostoyevsky prefaced every letter he wrote
with an apology for the delay, explaining that he was hampered
by ill health. In 1877 he had set himself a programme of projects
to be completed before his death: to write a book about Jesus
Christ, release a Russian *Candide*, write a classic poem and
pen his memoirs. By 1880 Dostoyevsky had realised none of
these ambitions, but he was writing his last great novel, *The
Brothers Karamazov*, where he represented most scrupulously the
mechanisms of human psychology, studied the matter of belief and
examined the debates of faith versus doubt.

Sigmund Freud wrote that *The Brothers Karamazov* was the
most 'magnificent novel ever written', a book that could hardly
be over-praised.[2] His admiration, though, was generally limited
to Dostoyevsky's immensely complex and authentic psychological

studies of the characters. Here was an author who understood the psychology that motivated the disenfranchised and depressed, and evidently could explore this in depth. What Dostoyevsky had to say about God, Freud dismissed as a part of the author's neuroticism. Nevertheless, Dostoyevsky wanted to say a great deal about God and the nature of faith in this novel; he wanted it to be a definitive answer to the then opposing movements of the time.

One such movement, nihilism, had been well examined by Dostoyevsky in his portrait of the young murderer Raskolnikov, who imposes his superiority by permitting himself to commit murder. His quasi-divine decision-making over the life and death of others thus makes God irrelevant to his man-god status. Like Raskolnikov, Kirilov in the *The Devils* sees power over death as the last remaining instantiation of the divine, only this time it is his own death that bestows that divinity on him. Dostoyevsky's novels draw on the experience of his youth and the doubt of the nation as a whole. Russia struggled with meaning while science and evolution increasingly evoked an empty universe divested of divinity.

The Brothers Karamazov was to be his response, a reply to Russia and a reply to his younger self. The terrifying implications of the emptiness of nihilism had preoccupied Dostoyevsky throughout his life. Where Vissarion Belinsky, the first mentor of his youth, had proclaimed the innate ability of humankind to rise to the task of moral responsibility, Dostoyevsky countered with Underground Man, Raskolnikov and his 'great sinner' Stavrogin. These characters, like many others, failed to live up to the call of a higher moral existence; without God they collapsed into a vindictive anarchy and an impotent nihilism. *The Brothers Karamazov*, written in two volumes, is the culmination of Dostoyevsky's attempt to resolve the contradictions between faith and doubt, action and consequence, and to attempt to put the case for, or apologise for, Christianity.

The novel, an almost thousand-page-long family saga, is set in a small rural community in Russia. It centres on the fortunes of three brothers, sons of the debauched and lecherous Fyodor Karamazov.

The Karamazov brothers all have a zest for life but they are tainted by the family wickedness, exemplified in its worst excesses by their father. The first volume details the inadequacies of the father, Fyodor Pavlovitch, and his lack of care for the three brothers; Ivan calls their father a 'pig'. Among Fyodor Pavlovitch's many past transgressions was the joy at the death of his wife, although it was reputed that she beat him, which is why he ran out into the street proclaiming her death. Dostoyevsky describes him as a 'vicious profligate' when he seeks to marry for a second time, to a very young and innocent girl. He drinks and he offers little affection to his three sons, Dmitry, Ivan and Alyosha. Despite the uncertainty of their early life, Ivan can see the rationale in his brutal and realistic upbringing. Ivan here is the nihilist, the middle sibling. He sees no validity to any action except in how it relates to him alone. He is not responsible, he says, for other people; but he is challenged in this thesis by the events of the novel itself. Thereafter much of the novel is focussed on the debate between Ivan and his existential angst, and Alyosha's – the youngest brother's – appeal to faith and his attempt to persuade Ivan of its necessity. Ivan's nihilism brings him to despair and he grows angry with a God he cannot believe in, whilst Alyosha is his antithesis, joyful, healthy and religious. He has spent some years in a local monastery as a novice and, as the story begins, he is about to go back out into the world. Between them Ivan and Alyosha oppose each other in the binary that binds so much of Dostoyevsky's work: faith versus doubt. They are the central focus of the dialogue on faith and reason, forming the 'dialogic opposition' identified by Bakhtin which reaches towards Hegelian synthesis. Thus the novel, in part, explores whether there is ever any possibility of a resolution of contradictory ideas – where belief in God can combine with the concept of reason.

Finally, there is Dmitry, the oldest son and the one who is most like his father: sensual, impetuous, lustful and violent. He is an ultimate human, perhaps less cerebral in character and more prone to instinct and impulse; he is greedy and profligate and far too quick to spend his inheritance. Ivan and Alyosha are Dmitry's half-brothers, the sons of a different mother; it is Dmitry's mother who may have beaten Fyodor Pavlovitch, the same woman whose death his father celebrates. However, there is one further possible brother lurking in the character of Smerdyakov, whose name literally means 'reeking one' – an appropriate epithet. Smerdyakov works on the family estate and is rumoured to be the illegitimate son of Fyodor Karamazov, and he too may have a claim on the dwindling inheritance. The structure of the novel is an exploration of a familiar theme: children with a claim, broken familial relationships and a murder that culminates in a long court case, represented in true courtroom style with long presentations of evidence and lengthy appeals to the jury, ultimately all for the wrong result.

Each of the brothers has a literary prototype in Dostoyevsky's earlier work or experience. Alyosha is a more successful version of the 'idiot', Prince Myshkin. He brings positive Christian values into the story but, unlike the prince, he is not afraid of action, nor is his presence divisive – at the end of the story he brings about a reconciliation between Dmitry and Katerina, whose relationship is stormy and detrimental to each of them.

Ivan Karamazov is a different matter. He wants his father dead. He believes that in a godless world everything is permitted or lawful – as in the often misquoted line, 'If God does not exist then everything is permitted.' Alyosha and Ivan discuss in detail the nature of responsibility in a world without God. Ivan also makes the mistake of discussing this with Smerdyakov, echoing Prince Myshkin's too-democratic conversations with the Yepanchin's manservant in *The Idiot*. Alyosha quizzes Ivan on the subject:

'What did he say?' Alyosha took it up quickly.

'I said to him, "Then everything is lawful, if it is so?" He frowned. "Fyodor Pavlovitch, our papa," he said, "was a pig, but his ideas were right enough." That was what he dropped. That was all he said. That was going one better than Rakitin.'[3]

Smerdyakov decides that the fact Ivan wants his father dead and that he considers all things lawful must mean that Ivan wants his father not just dead, but murdered. He gives enough warning to persuade him to leave town on the day he has chosen for the murder. The fact that Ivan leaves town seems to Smerdyakov to be the permission he is looking for: 'As you went away, it meant you assured me that you wouldn't dare to inform against me at the trial, and that you'd overlook my having the three thousand.'[4]

Ivan's silence on the subject and his subsequent agreement to leave, after a convoluted discussion of how he could be contacted in the event of an emergency, is enough for Smerdyakov. Once again Dostoyevsky returns to the theme of consent by omission: neither Ivan nor Stavrogin explicity instructs their henchman not to commit murder, and, whether through misunderstanding or wishful thinking, their surrogates commit the crime. Ivan has not prevented Smerdyakov in the same way that Stavrogin appeared to give permission to the convict Fedka to murder his wife.

Smerdyakov then fakes an epileptic fit to give himself an alibi and murders Fyodor Pavlovitch, although he does not attack the old servant Grigory. Dmitry does that in a separate act and thus puts himself at the time and place of the murder, with a motive, opportunity and a witness. Ivan, however, was not fully cognisant of what is going on; it is only in conversation with Smerdyakov that he realises his actions and words have been construed as orders. Once he realises what has happened, he takes the guilt upon himself; like Stavrogin in *The Devils*, Ivan comes to believe that he has somehow instigated his father's murder by not acting to prevent it. Moreover, in contrast to his earlier belief, he now realises that not everything can be permitted, even if God does not exist, and he goes mad trying to exonerate his brother, Dmitry.

Ivan is a more realistic version of that earliest of Dostoyevsky's anti-heroes, such as the 'double' Golyadkin. Ivan is divided in his conscience. He does not believe in God, and yet he fights against him. He believes that any action is permitted because without God there are no moral constraints, and yet he acts as if there are such constraints. He does not believe in the supernatural, and yet, after his last conversation with Smerdyakov, he sees the Devil in his room – or is the Devil really the other side of himself? Like the 'double', Ivan is brought face-to-face with his dark alter ego:

> 'No, no, no!' Ivan cried suddenly. 'It was not a dream. He was here; he was sitting here, on that sofa. When you knocked at the window, I threw a glass at him ... this one. Wait a minute. I was asleep last time, but this dream was not a dream. It has happened before. I have dreams now, Alyosha ... yet they are not dreams, but reality. I walk about, talk and see ... though I am asleep. But he was sitting here, on that sofa there ... He is frightfully stupid, Alyosha, frightfully stupid.' Ivan laughed suddenly and began pacing about the room.
>
> 'Who is stupid? Of whom are you talking, brother?' Alyosha asked anxiously again.
>
> 'The Devil! He's taken to visiting me. He's been here twice, almost three times. He taunted me with being angry at his being a simple devil and not Satan, with scorched wings, in thunder and lightning. But he is not Satan: that's a lie. He is an impostor. He is simply a devil-a paltry, trivial devil. ...'[5]

In fact the Devil is an ordinary, slightly shabby character, who quotes French and refuses to establish for Ivan the existence of God, even though he ought to know. When Alyosha arrives, he tells Ivan that Smerdyakov has hung himself without leaving a confession. There is no hope for Dmitry.

The model for Dmitry's character is slightly different in its genesis. It appears to have been taken from real life. Dostoyevsky's daughter believed that the evil Fyodor Karamazov was modelled on her grandfather, Dostoyevsky's father, although that seems a harsh portrait and was not confirmed by Fyodor. Just who the old man was modelled on may not be certain. However, what is known is that Dostoyevsky's use of parricide in the novel had a far more direct connection with a convict he met while serving his sentence in Siberia, than his feelings for his own father. Prince Ilyinsky, Dostoyevsky's fellow prisoner in Siberia, had been falsely convicted of murdering his father and was only exonerated by another criminal's confession years into his sentence. Dostoyevsky bestowed a similar fate on Dmitry Karamazov. Dostoyevsky was fascinated by the miscarriage of justice: he carefully constructs the evidence to 'frame' Dmitry, and the culmination of the courtroom scenes include the prosecution's apparently open and shut case, while the defence tries desperately to exonerate Dmitry:

> Dostoevsky is the creator of the polyphonic novel. He created a fundamentally new novelistic genre. Therefore his work does not fit any of the preconceived frameworks or historico-literary schemes that we usually apply to various species of the European novel. In his works a hero appears whose voice is constructed exactly like the voice of the author himself in a novel of the usual type.[6]

Although the narrator of *The Brothers Karamazov* is never named and takes no part in the events, he is able to relate the story from several different perspectives, and it is in the trial by jury of Dmitry Karamazov that the polyphonic narrator is most prevalent. The narrator opens the section 'A Judicial Error' by setting time and place in the conventional way: 'At ten o'clock in the morning of the day following the events I have described, the trial of Dmitri Karamazov began in our district court.'[7]

Throughout the court case the reader then sits in court alongside the narrator while defence and prosecution battle for the fate of the oldest brother.

Despite the dismal fates of these characters and Dmitry's unjust conviction, *The Brothers Karamazov* is one of Dostoyevsky's more optimistic novels. This is because of the presence of Alyosha and his teacher, Father Zossima, an 'elder' at a nearby monastery. The antithesis to Ivan, Alyosha believes in God and therefore believes in an absolute morality – not everything can be permitted because

God would not permit it and people must act according to God's judgment. People need the authority of God to guide them to an appropriate moral conclusion. However, just as Ivan is presented with a challenge to his creed by the appearance of the Devil in his room, Alyosha's beliefs are also tested.

When Alyosha's spiritual mentor dies, his body begins to smell of decay within twenty-four hours of his death. This is not the miracle that people of simple faith looked for to affirm that the revered monk was indeed a saint. Confirmation of sainthood would be looked for in quite the opposite sign, a lack of decay. It was said that a saint's body should smell of a wild meadow, or maybe there could be a healing miracle at the coffin. Whatever the folklore, Alyosha has to come to terms with the fact that even though God exists he has permitted something those who follow him would not. Thus he kneels beside the stinking coffin and he prays for enlightenment, only to find himself transported to the scene of the wedding at Cana, where Jesus turns water into wine. There at the feast he sees Father Zossima. The old man rebukes him gently for being surprised that he is there. The smell from the coffin is not a sign of God's displeasure: Father Zossima is a part of God's kingdom. Father Zossima repeats his instruction to Alyosha to leave the monastery and take the new wine to the people in the world outside. Just as the wedding at Cana was a miracle in a secular world, so Alyosha's vocation is to be engaged with the secular environment rather than within the confines of the monastery. It is Alyosha who counters many of the doubts expressed by Ivan, whose literary function is to challenge belief in the existence of God.

In the *Diary of a Writer* Dostoyevsky was explicit about his religious beliefs; he is less explicit in the novels. He was not unaware of the detrimental effect didacticism could have on a story but, in his account of Father Zossima's life and the repetition of some of his sermons, much of Dostoyevsky's theology may be discerned. In 'The Dream of the Ridiculous Man', Dostoyevsky had brought his hero back to earth with the realisation that if only everyone loved one another then the earth could be paradise. Father Zossima also proclaims the necessity of love:

> Brothers, be not afraid of men's sins. Love man even in his sin, for that already bears the semblance of divine love and is the highest love on earth. Love all God's creation, the whole of it and every grain of sand. Love every leaf, every ray of God's light! Love the animals, love the plants, love everything. If you love everything you will perceive the divine mystery in things.[8]

Not only should love motivate man; so should responsibility, as men are responsible for each other. Cain should have been his brother's keeper:

> Remember particularly that you cannot be a judge of anyone. For there can be no judge of a felon on earth, until the judge himself recognizes that he is just such a felon as the man standing before him, and that perhaps he is more than anyone responsible for the crime of the man in the dock.[9]

Brotherhood, mutual responsibility and love are the recipe for an earthly and Christian utopia. In the *Diary of a Writer* Dostoyevsky pictured these qualities emanating from the unique faith of the Russian people. In his sermons Father Zossima echoes this. Nevertheless, Russian nationalist theology is not a major theme in *The Brothers Karamazov*. Dostoyevsky does not use the brothers to propound Russia's claim on Constantinople or his opposition to western liberalism.

The fundamental issue in the novel is the place of suffering and sin in a world created by God. Through Father Zossima, Dostoyevsky attempts to answer the theodical questions raised by the coexistence of God's love with human misery. Love makes the world into an earthly paradise by making people good to one another; but, paradoxically, suffering and sin also have a necessary

place in this world. Father Zossima reads Jesus' words in John
12:24: 'Verily, verily, I say unto you, Except a corn of wheat fall into
the ground and die, it abideth alone; but if it die, it bringeth forth
much fruit.' This verse, later placed on Dostoyevsky's tombstone,
is the key to his religious thinking. Dostoyevsky suggests that sin
is necessary because without suffering there can be no individuality
or true happiness. Happiness without knowledge is nothing more
than ignorance: that is the essence of 'The Dream of a Ridiculous
Man'. Dostoyevsky is aware of the difficulties that this theory
presents and he voices his own his sceptical doubt through Ivan.

In a discussion with Alyosha, Ivan cites the suffering of children
as the greatest stumbling block to faith. It is not so much that Ivan
does not believe in God as that he disagrees with his priorities:
'Listen: if all have to suffer so as to buy eternal harmony by their
suffering, what have the children to do with it – tell me, please? It
is entirely incomprehensible why they, too, should have to suffer
and why they should have to buy harmony by their sufferings.'[10]
Listening to Ivan, even Alyosha concedes that he cannot tolerate
the suffering of children. Ivan, in a philosophical reversal of
Pascal's Wager,[11] tells Alyosha:

> I would rather remain with my unavenged suffering and
> unsatisfied indignation, even if I were wrong. Besides, too
> high a price is asked for harmony; it's beyond our means to
> pay so much to enter on it. And so I hasten to give back my
> entrance ticket, and if I am an honest man I am bound to give
> it back as soon as possible.[12]

In fact, Ivan's arguments are so cogent that they almost eclipse the
novel's aim – to affirm, not challenge, the existence of God and the
truth of Christianity.

Dostoyevsky's ambition to write a defence of Christianity and
of God foundered a little on the excellent characterisation of
the argument through Ivan Karamazov. Dostoyevsky was aware
of this, and he wrote that in attempting to present the *pro* and

contra arguments relating to Christianity he had been rather more successful with the *contra* than with the *pro*, which was not his intention. Dostoyevsky reassured a friend in a letter written in May 1879: 'My hero's blasphemy will be triumphantly refuted in the next (June) number for which I am now working in fear and trembling and with reverence, since I think the task (the defeat of anarchism) I have set myself would be a feat of heroism.'[13]

Thus, Alyosha counters Ivan's claims by pointing to Christ. Christ was innocent and suffered terribly, and by so doing he has bought the right to forgive man his terrible sins. God's justice is forgiveness and this somehow compensates for, or even justifies, the suffering. It is in the forgiving spirit of children that Dostoyevsky finds hope at the end of *The Brothers Karamazov*, just as Maria in *The Idiot* dies happy, forgiving her tormentors. Similarly in *The Brothers Karamazov*, at the funeral of a small child, Ilyusha, who died of consumption and whose bitter response to poverty and injustice made him an outcast among his friends, the reconciliation of these friends takes place. The children have come to recognise the importance of forgiveness, of mutual responsibility and of love for one another, and they have found faith:

> 'Karamazov', cried Kolya, 'is it really true that, as our religion tells us, we shall all rise from the dead and come to life and see one another again, all, and Ilyusha?'
>
> 'Certainly we shall rise again, certainly we shall see one another, and shall tell one another gladly and joyfully all that has been.'[14]

However, despite that joyful apologetic, *The Brothers Karamazov* is probably better known and more compelling for its description of doubt than its attempt to establish the credentials of Christian faith. In Part 2, Dostoyevsky allows Ivan to introduce the chapter that has become one of contemporary literature's most famous fables, 'The Grand Inquisitor'. It is this passage, rather than the redemptive tone of Ilyusha's story, that defines *The Brothers*

Karamazov. The parable comes just after the chapter (Part II, Chapter IV) where Alyosha and Ivan Karamazov have been discussing the problem of suffering, particularly of children. The fictional author of the piece calls it his 'poem', and it sits just a little uncomfortably in the text because it addresses an issue not entirely relevant to the discussion on suffering. It is, in fact, more relevant to Dostoyevsky's own debates about Christ versus atheism that he had in the Belinsky Circle in the 1840s.

In 'The Grand Inquisitor' (Chapter V) Christ himself returns to sixteenth-century Seville, when the atrocities of the Spanish Inquisition are at their peak. Seville was on the front line of the battle with Islam, and heresy was not just a question of unbelief but of betrayal. During this time, belief and faithfulness to a religion were irrevocably linked with political power and cultural dominance. Thus Christ returns at a time when people are converted to Christianity not by choice or by faith, but under the threat of unspeakable torture and a fiery death. When the Christ figure appears on the steps of Seville Cathedral, he is there just as a the funeral of a child is about to take place: just as he does in the New Testament, when he raises Jairus's daughter (Mark 5:21–43), the Christ figure takes the child's hand and says 'arise maiden' and she is resurrected from the dead. The crowd sees this and is convinced immediately of his divinity. However the presence of the incarnate Christ, with his humility and appeal to faith and free will rather than certainty and coercion, is not popular with the authorities, and the Grand Inquisitor, the man whose job it was to ensure religious conformity by force and by fire, witnesses the event, arrests Christ and throws him into gaol. The Grand Inquisitor is then compelled to visit the stranger in gaol to discuss the differences between them.

The essence of the argument is the discussion of freedom to believe or the choice to be told to be certain. Ivan cites the suffering of children as the reason he finds it hard to believe in God; Dostoyevsky voices something of this in the Inquisitor, who asks the returned Christ why he does not offer miracles to provide the certainty of his existence and dispense with the need for faith. The

Inquisitor goes further and reproaches Christ, saying that what he started fifteen centuries before, the Catholic Church, has completed its mission by coercing faith and providing certainty through force:

> For fifteen centuries we have been wrestling with Thy freedom, but now it is ended and over for good. Dost Thou not believe that it's over for good? Thou lookest meekly at me and deignest not even to be wroth with me. But let me tell Thee that now, to-day, people are more persuaded than ever that they have perfect freedom, yet they have brought their freedom to us and laid it humbly at our feet.[15]

The paradox presented by the Grand Inquisitor is that the people who submit themselves completely to the Catholic Church gain perfect freedom; in their submission, they do not need to have faith, they just need to be told. The Grand Inquisitor reproaches Christ because he did not succumb to the Devil's three temptations in the wilderness (Matthew 4:1–11). He did not turn the stones into bread, take earthly power or perform miracles in order to win people's faith. The Roman Catholic Church, on the other hand, says the Grand Inquisitor, has done all those things and so has been a good deal more effective in subjugating people and winning their loyalty for the purposes of God: 'You promised them bread from heaven, but, I repeat again, can it compare with earthly bread in the eyes of the weak, always vicious and always ignoble race of man?'[16]

The Inquisitor is anxious and challenges his prisoner, asking if he is back to spoil everything, to return to humankind their choice to have faith. He wonders whether he has returned to prove to the world the potency of his power through miracles and thus undermine the authority of the Church. The Inquisitor harangues the prisoner, reminding him that for the sake of 'common worship' human beings have gone to war and have killed each other in the name of their own gods: this violence can be avoided if they are given no choice in their beliefs and must merely submit to the authority that that priests in the Roman Catholic Church wield:

'Didst Thou forget that man prefers peace, and even death, to freedom of choice in the knowledge of good and evil? Nothing is more seductive for man than his freedom of conscience, but nothing is a greater cause of suffering.'[17]

The Roman Catholic Church of the Inquisition was battling both for certainty and power. Dostoyevsky does not link the story of 'The Grand Inquisitor' with his historical context. Human beings could not be allowed to rebel against the Church, and Christ, who could offer the populace certainty, failed so to do. The Grand Inquisitor assures Christ that individuals are a good deal happier being ruled and so deprived of free will and the responsibility that comes with it: humankind, says this sinister figure, is fundamentally a weak creature, and the Church looks after the weak by telling them what to do. It is, of course, the Roman Catholic Church that Dostoyevsky accuses of this crime and not the Russian Orthodox Church. In reply to Ivan, all Alyosha can do is defend Orthodoxy and deny its part in such crimes as the Inquisition.

In the fable of 'The Grand Inquisitor' the Church no longer needs Christ or God, for it has the earthly power it needs to rule. The returned Christ is interfering with fifteen centuries of Church domination and, inevitably, he must be burned. He is effaced by human evil just as Belinsky had said he would be when he and Dostoyevsky had speculated as to how a contemporary Christ would function in modern Russia. Still, the image of Christ in 'The Grand Inquisitor' is not without power, and Alyosha suggests that Ivan has written a poem in praise of Christ, not a disparagement of him.

In the same way as *The Double* has found its reflection in modern art forms, in media and film – just as Porfiry was the model for TV's *Columbo* – so too has 'The Grand Inquisitor' found its place in the the annals of popular media interpretations:

It made sense for him to become the Grand Inquisitor – this kind of cynically heroic character. He's like Nietszche's Socrates – he's the rational man saving the masses from their own imagination. I can't take credit for Dostoevsky ... I can just take credit for having been educated well. If it drives people to read that, that'd be great. But just read that part. It's short. Don't read the whole Brothers K.[18]

'Talitha Cumi' (Season 3, Episode 24) is an episode of the X-Files, no less, that used the motif of 'The Grand Inquisitor', and the debate it generated to extend the discussion to a more populist audience.[19] The title phrase *'talitha cumi'* means 'maiden arise' in Hebrew – it is reported in the New Testament as the words Jesus said to raise Jairus's daughter. This particular *X-Files* episode starts with a random shooting at a burger bar that kills, or apparently kills, three people. The shooting takes place in the Brothers K, a fast-food restaurant. Present at the shooting, initially trying to dissuade the gunman, is a strange man, Jeremiah Smith, played by Roy Thinnes, who by the touch of his hand heals the wounded and dead, and disappears through the crowd, leaving the detectives Mulder and Scully to pursue him.

The *X-Files* wove a master narrative over their more episodic stories. This master narrative related to Fox Mulder's (David Duchovny) belief in aliens and Dana Scully's (Gillian Anderson) scepticism and more rational and scientific approach to their investigations. Much of the series involves a discussion on the conflicts of faith and reason, even if the objects of faith in this case are transposed to the twentieth-century figure of aliens. Much of the action of 'Talitha Cumi' however takes place away from Mulder and Scully, for the healer and Christ figure is arrested, placed in a cell and visited by 'Cigarette Smoking Man' (William B. Davis):

I [David Duchovny] told Chris [the *X-Files* screenwriter] I saw The Cigarette Smoking Man as a Grand Inquisitor figure, because he has seen the truth and he is damning himself in order to save people. In his own twisted way, he's a very moving figure to me: the man who will go to hell so that other people may live more freely.[20]

The Cigarette Smoking Man and the Grand Inquisitor are very similar physically, both being aged and thin: 'He is an old man, almost ninety, tall and erect, with a withered face and sunken eyes, in which there is still a gleam of light.'[21]

Cigarette Smoking Man challenges the stranger with the same argument: 'We give them happiness, and they give us authority.' The Grand Inquisitor similarly states, 'But let me tell Thee that now, to-day, people are more persuaded than ever that they have perfect freedom, yet they have brought their freedom to us and laid it humbly at our feet.'[22] Jeremiah Smith responds that government has taken the people's freedom away in the guise of 'democracy'. The response from the *X-Files'* version of the Inquisitor is, 'Men can never be free, because they're weak, corrupt, worthless and restless. The people believe in authority, they've grown tired of waiting for miracle or mystery. Science is their religion, no greater explanation exists for them. They must never believe any differently if the project is to go forward.' The discussion between The Grand Inquisitor and his captive is further elaborated in a discussion of miracles: just as Ivan's character challenges the Christ on the use of miracles to invoke faith and belief, so Cigarette Smoking Man worries at the relationship between, miracles and belief in God:

SMITH: What you're afraid of is … 'they'll' believe I'm God.
CIGARETTE-SMOKING MAN: It doesn't matter, most of them have ceased to believe in God.
SMITH: Why?
CIGARETTE-SMOKING MAN: Because God presents them with no miracles to earn their faith.
SMITH: You think when man ceases to believe in miracles, he rejects God?
CIGARETTE-SMOKING MAN: Of course.
SMITH: You rule over them in God's name.
CIGARETTE-SMOKING MAN: They don't believe in him but they still fear him. They're afraid not to because they're afraid of freedom.[23]

As The Grand Inquisitor says, 'Didst Thou forget that man prefers peace, and even death, to freedom of choice in the knowledge of good and evil?'[24]

Perhaps if nothing else, this demonstrates that great literature engenders archetypes and discussions that are universal and destined to be repeated and reflected in a variety of ways, dependent on new contexts and audiences.

As it was written for its time, the story of 'The Grand Inquisitor' suggests that there is a central dichotomy in human nature. Dostoyevsky would argue that in order to attain true happiness, individuals must exercise free will, and perhaps even sin, in order to appreciate the nature of faith and belief. However, the rationalist would argue that it does not matter how human beings come across peace and happiness as long as they discover it, even if that is in the context of giving up their free will: 'Nothing is more seductive for man than his freedom of conscience, but nothing is a greater cause of suffering.'[25]

25

A WRITER FOR OUR TIME

> You judge very rightly when you opine that I hold
> all evil to be grounded upon disbelief, and maintain
> that he who abjures nationalism, abjures faith also.
> That applies especially to Russia, for with us national
> consciousness is based on Christianity. 'A Christian
> peasant people', 'believing Russia': these are our
> fundamental conceptions. A Russian who abjures
> nationalism (and there are many such) is either an
> atheist or indifferent to religious questions.
>
> Dostoyevsky.[1]

In this letter to a Dr A. F. Blagonravov, Dostoyevsky encapsulates what he believed to be the relationship between Russia and Christianity. In one small paragraph he discounts the faith of all but the most patriotic Russians and credits only Russia with a pure faith. Now, almost at the end of his life, Dostoyevsky was to have a chance to express this view to a larger public. In one moment of glory, he was to offer the culmination of all his thinking to Mother Russia.

By the end of the 1870s Dostoyevsky was famous enough to merit six lines in the Russian version of *Who's Who*; Turgenev, however, received twenty-four lines. Dostoyevsky was included in the honorary committee of the *Association Littéraire* where, once again, Turgenev was included – but so also was Victor Hugo, one of Dostoyevsky's own favourites.

The sales of his books were increasing. *The Brothers Karamazov* was such a great success that Anna began to build up a mail order company. However, despite their success, money was still a problem for the Dostoyevskys. Fyodor never did get over his propensity to give money away to what he thought were deserving causes. This frustrated Anna and they argued frequently. Fyodor accused Anna of not looking after him properly; she accused him of being too free with their money, spending it on clothes and other people instead of his family and his debts. The relationship was strained – perhaps Dostoyevsky was not as unlike his father as he would have hoped.

In her turn, Anna was not above using deceit to make sure her husband's affection was secure. She once wrote him an anonymous letter suggesting that she was having an affair with somebody else. In the letter she said that he should look in the locket that she wore around her neck and there he would see the likeness of her lover. Dostoyevsky's reaction was almost too gratifying. Obviously agitated, he stormed into her room and broke the necklace from around her neck. In the locket he found only a picture of himself. Anna explained her prank and Dostoyevsky was enraged. He warned her that he might have done something much more irresponsible than simply snatch away the locket.

Towards the end of his life, the couple spent much more time apart. Anna spent time in Staraya Russa, which provided a better environment for the children, while Fyodor was often in Ems, from where he wrote anxious letters enquiring about the children's health. They were finally able to buy the small house in Staraya Russa that they had rented, and Dostoyevsky would join his family there when the demands of work did not keep him in St Petersburg or Moscow. In Staraya Russa he had time to write, to be with his children and to enjoy the life of a country gentleman. The local priest often visited, and the family became a part of the community.

Among the Russian literary community it was well known that Dostoyevsky greatly admired the poet Pushkin. He had voiced his admiration for Pushkin at the grave of his old editor and rival, Nekrasov, and had then compared the talents of the two poets. His opinion had not been greeted with unanimous approval, but his admiration for Pushkin never wavered. He often did public readings of Pushkin's work and his recitations were said to be hypnotic. He was the obvious choice, therefore, to unveil a memorial to Pushkin in Moscow in the spring of 1880. The occasion, a celebration of the writer's work, was also to be a gathering of Russia's literary giants. It was Dostoyevsky's chance to offer his views to a wider public; it was also a major honour.

He accepted the invitation to unveil the memorial and to address an audience at a dinner to be held during that week. His correspondence with his wife suggests that she might have liked to go with him, but Dostoyevsky preferred to be on his own.

Dostoyevsky arrived in Moscow on 24 May 1880 ready for the ceremony that was to follow several days later. The other writers were now gathered in Moscow waiting to hear if the ceremony would continue, as Tsarina Maria Alexandrovna, the Imperial Majesty, had died on 22 May. This had delayed the ceremony, so the celebration was moved to the 26 May; with time on their hands, the writers decided to occupy themselves by giving a dinner in Dostoyevsky's honour. There were six speeches, Dostoyevsky wrote to Anna, some of them very long, but at long last this once rebellious political youth, ex-convict and gambling addict, hampered all the while by his epilepsy, was having his special contribution to Russian literature recognised.

The honorary dinner delighted Dostoyevsky, but arrangements for the Pushkin celebrations did not run so smoothly because Fyodor was not the only author taking part in the Pushkin celebration: Turgenev had also been allocated a slot in the programme of events. Even after nearly forty years, none of their old enmity had abated. Dostoyevsky had been hurt by being excluded from a dinner arranged in Turgenev's honour; worse, he was not present at the meeting that finalised all the arrangements for the celebrations in Pushkin's honour. Dostoyevsky was allocated Pushkin's poem 'The Prophet' to read when he would have preferred another.

The night of 26 May was to be Dostoyevsky's triumph. That night he gave a speech, published in a special edition of the *Diary of a Writer*, lauding Pushkin as the greatest Russian poet because he affirmed the great Russian virtues of Christianity and its affinity with the Russian soil and loyalty.

Always gifted as an orator, Dostoyevsky swept the crowds off their feet with his proclamation of Pushkin's genius and his theory of Russia's Christian mission. He brought his wrath down on the heads of the westernisers. Russia, he stated, was not to be the lackey for European intellectualism. Any Russian who denies his affinity with the Russian soil betrays the Russian ideal. Only Russian beauty is pure, and Pushkin was its greatest exponent.

The audience who listened to Dostoyevsky that night heard their country deified. Western Europe had become a conglomeration of atheist states and so would fall devastated before Russia. In his notes on the speech in the *Diary*, Fyodor said,

> Indeed, in the West there is no longer Christianity, there is no church, notwithstanding the fact that there still are many Christians who will never disappear, Catholicism, in truth, is no longer Christianity; gradually it is transforming itself into idolatry, while Protestantism with gigantic strides is being converted into atheism and into vacillating, fluent, variable (and not eternal) ethics.[2]

Dostoyevsky's delivery was the best it had ever been. The power of his oratory alone won over his audience. He described for Anna the effect of his speech on two listeners: 'Two old men, strangers to me, stopped me: "We have been enemies for twenty years, we have not spoken to one another, and now we have embraced and made peace. It is you who have reconciled us. You are our saint, you are our prophet!"'[3]

Even Turgenev embraced him in tears. The reception was so rapturous that the crowd shouted, 'You are the prophet!' Dostoyevsky had to be taken from the podium by his fellow writers. Women fainted at his feet and he was escorted through the wild crowds, whose behaviour was more suited to a twentieth-century pop concert than a nineteenth-century literary gathering.

But Dostoyevsky's triumph was, as ever, to be short-lived. It was one thing to hear the speech delivered by a great orator with fire and passion to a large and enthusiastic crowd; it was quite another to read it in the cold light of day. Almost immediately, Turgenev and other contemporary critics denounced the speech as romantic rubbish. Once again Dostoyevsky went from fame to ridicule in a matter of days, just as he had at the beginning of his career.

Nothing, however, could mar the triumph of *The Brothers Karamazov*. It sold out almost immediately, and the Dostoyevskys began arranging a second edition as well as further editions of his other novels. Business was booming: Anna had now grasped the fundamentals of publishing and was to continue to build up Dostoyevsky's reputation for the rest of her life. Dostoyevsky was an established literary figure, but he would not be able to fulfil his every literary dream, for he was never to write another novel. He had, though, produced several masterpieces, of which the world would be talking for the next hundred years and beyond. Dostoyevsky knew now that his own time was running out. His emphysema was untreatable and the walls of his arteries and veins were like paper; his zest for life was fading.

Even so, Fyodor's political reputation was to haunt him until almost his final moments. On the 25 January 1881, the tsar's secret police were sent to search his apartment. They came to the Dostoyevsky's apartment because, once again, the political circles of Russia's dreamers were planning direct action. This time a radical faction called the People's Will had formed out of a less zealous group, known as Land and Freedom. Like *The Devils*, the members of People's Will were dissatisfied with education and agitation alone; the politics of Land and Freedom was not enough, and they wanted revolution. Despite Dostoyevsky's now close relationship with the tsar, or perhaps because of it, his apartment was targeted as a possible source of radical activity. The People's Will went on to assassinate Tsar Alexander II a few months later, in March 1881. Whether it was because of the search or because of an accident at home in which Dostoyevsky dropped a pen and tried to lift a cupboard to get at it, is not known, but the writer suffered a minor haemorrhage.

The next day Dostoyevsky's sister, Vera, came to plead with him about their Aunt Kumamina's will, which they still disputed. Dostoyevsky was still short of money, and he knew he would soon be gone and that his inheritance was all he had to leave to his wife and children. Perhaps it was as they talked about the issue, perhaps in heated debate, perhaps what happened would have happened in any case, but Dostoyevsky began to haemorrhage more seriously; his hands grew wet with blood. Over the next few days his condition stabilised, hovering between improvement and relapse, until Fyodor said to Anna, 'Today I am going to die.' She comforted him and told him he would not die, but Dostoyevky was certain his time had come.

He asked for a priest and for Anna to get the New Testament that the wives of the Decembrists had given to him all those years ago – like him, it had survived Siberia, misfortune and fame. She opened it and read from where it fell open the story of Christ's baptism by John (Matthew 3:13–17). In the passage, John tries to protest against the baptism because he feels unworthy, but Jesus insists that it go ahead: 'Let it be so now; for thus it is fitting for us to fulfil all righteousness.'[4]

Dostoyevsky, who often allowed himself to be guided by reading from the Bible at random, saw great significance in this passage. He told Anna that the verse indicated that he was indeed going to die. Anna wrote, 'I could not restrain my tears. Fiodor began comforting me, saying kind and loving words and thanking me for the happy life he had enjoyed with me.'[5]

Not long after the reading he fell into a coma, and soon after that he died.

Throughout his life he had struggled with the knowledge of good and evil. He had tried to come to terms with the meaning of human free will in a world where God was the ultimate arbiter. He had advocated justice on earth for the poor and looked forward to the affirmation of eternal life. In his novels his characters wrestled with eternal questions, and he portrayed the mechanism of doubt with genius. None of his characters possessed simple answers; neither did his own journey in life.

Over the years, Dostoyevsky grew more courageous in proclaiming his own faith in God to his public, but in his novels he could never shake off the darker side of human evil and doubt. Perhaps there was always a part of him that, like Shatov in *The Devils*, believed in Christ but in the end could only say that he wanted to believe, that one day 'I shall believe in God'.[6]

END NOTES

1. Prelims quotation: Letter to Sofia Alexandrovna, August 1870, *The Letters of Fyodor Michailovich Dostoyevsky to His Family and Friends*, p.205.

1 – The Poorhouse
1. Dostoyevsky, F., 'One of the Contemporary Falsehoods', *Diary of a Writer*, p. 152.
2. Dostoyevsky, F., 'Peasant Marei', *Diary of a Writer*, p. 205–10.
3. Dostoyevsky, M., cited in Frank, J., *Dostoevsky: A Writer in His Time*, p. 21.

2 – The Cycle of Violence
1. Dostoyevsky, F., *Crime and Punishment*, p. 58.
2. Dostoyevsky, F., 'Russian Society for Protection of Animals', *Diary of a Writer*, p. 186
3. Dostoyevsky, F., 'Letter to Dr Dostoyevsky, February 1838', *Dostoyevsky: A Self Portrait*, p. 8.
4. Dostoyevsky, F., 'To his father 10 May1838', *Letters of Fyodor Michailovitch Dostoevsky to his Family and Friends*, PDF, p. 7.
5. Dostoyevsky, F., 'Letter to Mikhail, January 1840', *Dostoyevsky: A Self Portrait*, p. 14.

3 – The Glimmer of Hope
1. Fanger, D., *Dostoyevsky and Romantic Realism*, p. 33.
2. Dostoyevsky, F., 'To Mikhail (Michael) 30 September 1844', *Letters of Fyodor Michailovitch Dostoevsky to his Family and Friends*, PDF, p. 14.

3. Zweig, S., *Three Masters: Balzac, Dickens, Dostoevsky*, Kindle loc. 2030.

4. Dostoyevsky, F., *Poor Folk*, p. 126.

5. Zweig, S., *Three Masters: Balzac, Dickens, Dostoevsky*, Kindle, loc. 1518.

6. Grigorovich, D., 'Reminiscences of Dmitry Grigorovich, 1837 to 1846', *The Letters of Fyodor Michailovitch Dostoyevsky to His Family and Friends*, PDF, p. 132.

7. Dostoyevsky, F., 'Letter to Mikhail, October 1845', *Dostoyevsky: A Self Portrait*, p. 32.

8. Ibid.

9. Dostoyevsky, F., 'Old People', *Diary of a Writer*, p. 6–7.

10. Ibid., p. 7.

11. Dostoyevsky, F., 'Letter to Mikhail, October 1845', *Dostoyevsky: A Self Portrait*, p. 34.

4 – Doppelgängers And Dreamers

1. Dostoyevsky, F., *The Double*, p. 24.

2. Excerpts from BFI Q&A at the screening of *The Double*, dir. Richard Ayoade.

3. Dostoyevsky, F., *The Double*, p. 29.

4. Excerpts from BFI Q&A at the screening of *The Double*, dir. Richard Ayoade.

5. Dostoyevsky, F., 'Bad Health 33', *Letters of Fyodor Michailovitch Dostoevsky to his Family and Friends*, PDF, p. 22.

6. Dostoyevsky, F., *The Double*, p. 38.

7. Belinsky, V., cited by Fanger, D., 'Dostoevsky and Romantic Realism', p. 159.

8. Dostoyevsky, F., *The Double*, p. 58.

9. Dostoyevsky, F., '30 Dostoevsky's Letters', *Letters of Fyodor Michailovitch Dostoevsky to his Family and Friends*, PDF, p. 21.

10. Ibid., p. 133. (Quoting Belinsky)

11. Fanger, D., *Dostoyevsky and Romantic Realism*, p. 137.

12. Morson, G. S., *The Boundaries of Genre: Dostoevsky's Diary of a Writer and the Traditions of Literary Utopia*, p. 17.

13. Fanger, D., *Dostoyevsky and Romantic Realism*, p. 139.

14. Ibid.

15. Dostoyevsky, F., 'White Knights', *The Best Short Stories of Dostoyevsky*, p. 17.

16. Ibid., p. 18.

17. Fanger, D., *Dostoyevsky and Romantic Realism*, p. 146.

18. Dostoyevsky, F., cited by Frank, J., '*Dostoevsky: A Writer in His Time*', Kindle, loc. 3173, citation no. 1 1873. *Diary of a Writer*, p. 9.

5 – *The Arrest*
  1. Kjetsaa, G., *Dostoyevsky: A Writer's Life*, p. 56.
  2. Dostoyevsky, F., *Dostoevsky as Reformer: The Petrashevsky Case*, p. 46.
  3. Frank, J., *Dostoyevsky: A Writer in His Time*, Kindle, loc. 3670.
  4. Mochulsky, K., *Dostoevsky: His Life and Work*, p. 122.
  5. Belinsky, V. G., 'Letter to N. V. Gogol', www.marxist.org.
  6. Gogol, N. V., 'Selected Passages from Correspondence with Friends', Zeldin, J., p. xv.
  7. Belinsky, V. G., 'Letter to N. V. Gogol' www.marxist.org.
  8. Ibid.
  9. Mochulsky, K., *Dostoevsky: His Life and Work*, p. 128.
 10. Ibid., p. 129.
 11. Grigorovich, D., 'Reminiscences of Dmitry Grigorovich, 1837 to 1846', *The Letters of Fyodor Michailovitch Dostoyevsky to His Family and Friends*, p. 265.

6 – *The Shadow of The Executioner*
  1. Dostoyevsky, F., *The Idiot*, p. 47–48.
  2. Dostoyevsky, F., 'Letter to Mikhail, December 1849', *Dostoevsky: Letters and Reminiscences*, p. 9.
  3. Dostoyevsky, F., 'Letter to Mikhail, September 1849', *Dostoevsky: A Self Portrait*, p. 54.
  4. Dostoyevsky, F., 'Letter to Mikhail, December 1849', *Dostoevsky: Letters and Reminiscences*, p. 8.
  5. Dostoyevsky, F., 'Letter to Andrei, June 1862', *Dostoevsky: A Self Portrait*, p. 109.
  6. Dostoyevsky, F., *Dostoevsky as Reformer: The Petrashevsky Case*, p. 36.
  7. Frank, J., *Dostoyevsky: A Writer in His Time*, Kindle, Loc. 4046.
  8. Dostoyevsky, F., 'Old People', *Diary of a Writer*, p. 9.
  9. Dostoyevsky, F., cited in Frank, J., *Dostoevsky: A Writer in His Time*, Kindle, loc. 4343.
 10. Dostoyevsky, F., 'Letter to Mikhail, December 1849', *Dostoevsky: A Self Portrait*, p. 56.
 11. Dostoyevsky, F., cited in Frank, J., *Dostoevsky: A Writer in His Time*, Kindle, loc. 4371.

7 – Reprieve

1. Dostoyevsky, F., *The Idiot*, iBooks, p. 136.
2. Dostoyevsky, F., *The Idiot*, iBooks, p. 138.
3. Dostoyevsky, F., 'Letter to Mikhail, December 1849', *Dostoevsky: A Self Portrait*, p. 58.
4. Dostoyevsky, F., 'Reminiscences of A. P. Milyukov, 1848 to 1849', *The Letters of Fyodor Michailovitch Dostoyevsky to his Family and Friends*, p. 280.
5. Dostoyevsky, F., 'Letter to Mikhail, February 1854', *Dostoevsky: A Self Portrait*, p. 61.
6. Ibid., p. 62.

8 – The Wives of Tobolsk

1. Dostoyevsky, F., 'Letter to Mikhail, February 1854', *Dostoevsky: A Self Portrait*, p. 62–63.
2. Ibid., p. 63.
3. Dostoyevsky, F., 'Dostoevki's Letters to M Fonvisin 1 March 1854', *Letters of Fyodor Michailovitch Dostoevsky to his Family and Friends*, PDF, p. 39.

9 – The Unfortunates

1. Dostoyevsky, F., 'Memoranda of P. K. Martyanov, 1 At The House of Dead', *The Letters of Fyodor Michailovitch Dostoyevsky to his Family and Friends*, p. 142.
2. Ibid., p. 285.
3. Dostoyevsky, F., *The House of the Dead*, p. 164.
4. Ibid., p. 9.
5. Ibid., p. 121–122.
6. Dostoyevsky, F., 'Letter to Mikhail, 22 February 1854', *The Letters of Fyodor Michailovitch Dostoyevsky to His Family and Friends*, p. 59.
7. Dostoyevsky, F., 'The *House of the Dead*', p. 93.
8. Dostoyevsky, F., 'The *House of the Dead*', p. 14.
9. Ibid., p. 80.
10. Ibid., p. 228.
11. Ibid., p. 227.
12. Ibid., p. 136.

10 – Freedom in Exile

1. Dostoyevsky, F., *The House of the Dead*, p. 252.
2. Ibid., p. 171.

3. Dostoyevsky, F., 'Letter to Natalya Fonvizina, March 1854', *The Letters of Fyodor Michailovitch Dostoyevsky to his Family and Friends*, p. 71.
4. Dostoyevsky, F., 'Reminiscences of Baron Alexander Wrangel', *The, Letters of Fyodor Michailovitch Dostoyevsky to his Family and Friends*, p. 291.
5. Ibid., p. 296–97.
6. Ibid., p. 304.
7. Ibid., p. 301.

11 – *Love and Marriage*

1. Dostoyevsky, F., *Crime and Punishment*, p. 15.
2. Dostoyevsky, F., 'Reminiscences of Baron Alexander Wrangel', *The, Letters of Fyodor Michailovitch Dostoyevsky to his Family and Friends*, p. 300.
3. Dostoyevsky, F., 'Letter to Natalya Fonvizina, March 1854', *The Letters of Fyodor Michailovitch Dostoyevsky to his Family and Friends*, p. 21.
4. Dostoyevsky, F., 'Letter to General E. I. Totleben, March 1856', *The, Letters of Fyodor Michailovitch Dostoyevsky to his Family and Friends*, p. 91.
5. Dostoyevsky, F., 'Reminiscences of Baron Alexander Wrangel', *The, Letters of Fyodor Michailovitch Dostoyevsky to his Family and Friends*, p. 313.
6. Dostoyevsky, A., *Reminiscences by Anna Dostoyevsky*, p. 79.
7. Dostoyevsky, F., *The Idiot*, p. 267–268.

12 – *The Tower of Babel*

1. Dostoyevsky, F., 'Essay I, Four Essays, April 13, 1847', *Dostoevsky's Occasional Writings*, p. 3.
2. Seton-Watson, H., *The Russian Empire 1801–1917*, p. 329.
3. Dostoyevsky, F, *Summer Impressions*, p. 59.

13 – *Underground Man*

1. Dostoyevsky, F., 'Letter to Mikhail, January 1864', *Dostoyevsky: A Self Portrait*, p. 125.
2. Dostoyevsky, F., *Notes from the Undergound*, p. 122.
3. Ibid., p. 96.
4. Ibid., p. 136.
5. Dickens, C., *Great Expectations*, iBooks, p. 202.
6. Dostoyevsky, F., 'Notes from the Undergound', *The Best Short Stories of Dostoevsky*, p. 97.
7. Freedland, J., 'Guardian Opinion: Charlie Hebdo's refugee cartoon isn't satirical', 15 January 2016.
8. Dostoyevsky, F., 'Notes from the Undergound', *The Best Short Stories of Dostoevsky*, p. 95.
9. Dostoyevsky, F., *Notes from the Undergound*, p. 176.

10. Scorsese, M., cited in 'Footnote 2' in *The anguish of God's lonely men: Dostoyevsky's Underground Man and Scorsese's Travis Bickle,* by Swenson, A. J., Source Kelly M. P., *Martin Scorsese: A Journey,* p. 90–91 http://chabrieres.pagesperso-orange.fr/texts/anguish.html.

11. Dostoyevsky, F., *Notes from the Undergound,* iBooks. p. 201.

12. Schrader, p., *Taxi Driver,* dir. Martin Scorsese, 1976.

13. Dostoyevsky, F., 'Notes from the Undergound', *The Best Short Stories of Dostoevsky,* p. 156.

14. Swenson, A. J., *The anguish of God's lonely men: Dostoyevsky's Underground Man and Scorsese's Travis Bickle,* http://chabrieres.pagesperso-orange.fr/texts/anguish.html.

15. Ibid.

16. Dostoyevsky, F., *The Brothers Karamazov,* p. 77.

17. Dostoyevsky, F., 'Letter to Mikhail, March 1864', *Dostoyevsky: A Self Portrait,* p. 124.

18. Dostoyevsky, F., 'Letter to Baron Wrangel, March 1865', *Dostoyevsky: A Self Portrait,* p. 131.

14 – Loss

1. Dostoyevsky, F., 'Letter to Baron Wrangel, March 1865', *Dostoyevsky: A Self Portrait,* p. 132.

2. Kovalesky, S., 'Reminiscences of Sophie Kovalesky', *The Letters of Fyodor Michailovitch Dostoyevsky to His Family and Friends,* p. 323.

3. Ibid., p. 326.

4. Dostoyevsky, F., 'Letter to A. G. Snitkina, January 1867', *Dostoyevsky: A Self Portrait,* p. 150.

5. Dostoyevsky, A., *Dostoevsky: Portrayed by His Wife - The Diary and Reminiscences of Mme. Dostoevsky,* p. 9.

6. Ibid., p. 18.

7. Ibid., p. 35–36.

8. Ibid., p. 39.

9. lbid., p. 46.

10. Ibid., p. 112–13.

15 – The Raising of Raskolnikov

1. Baring, M., *An Outline of Russian Literature,* eBook, Project Gutenberg, p. 260–261.

2. Dostoyevsky, F., 'Letter to N. L. Osmidov, February 1878', *The Letters of Fyodor Michailovitch Dostoyevsky to his Family and Friends,* p. 234.

3. Dostoyevsky, F., *Crime and Punishment,* iBooks. p. 131.

4. Ibid., p. 166.

5. Gibian, G., 'Traditional Symbolism in Crime and Punishment', PMLA, Vol. 70, No. 5 (Dec 1955), pp. 979–996 (p. 984).
6. Dostoyevsky, F., *Crime and Punishment*, iBooks. p. 965.
7. Dostoyevsky, F., *Crime and Punishment*, p. 493.
8. Dostoyevsky, F., 'Letter to A.P. Milyukov, June 1866', *The Letters of Fyodor Michailovitch Dostoyevsky to his Family and Friends*, p. 111–12.
9. Kabatchnik, A., 'Blood on the Stage, 1950–1975: Milestone Plays of Crime, Mystery, and Detection', citing Tom Nolan interviewing William Link for *Mystery Magazine*.
10. Dostoyevsky, F., *Crime and Punishment*, iBooks. p. 607.
11. Ibid., p. 623.
12. Ibid., p. 624.
13. Ibid., p. 607.
14. Ibid., p. 644.
15. Ibid., p. 611.

16 – The Gambler

1. Dostoyevsky, F., 'Letter to Sofia Alexandrovna, August 1870', *The Letters of Fyodor Michailovich Dostoyevsky to His Family and Friends*, p. 205.
2. Dostoyevksy, A., *Dostoevsky: Portrayed by His Wife – The Diary and Reminiscences of Mme. Dostoevsky*, p. 153.
3. Ibid., p. 118.
4. Ibid., p. 67.
5. Ibid., p. 90–91.
6. Dostoyevsky, F., 'Letter to Apollon Maikov, August 1867', *Dostoyevsky: A Self Portrait*, p. 163.
7. Ibid., p. 162.
8. Strakhov, N., 'Letter to Leo Tolstoy November 1883', *Dostoevsky: Portrayed by his Wife – The Diary and Reminiscences of Mme. Dostoevsky*, p. 232.
9. Dostoyevsky, F., 'Letter to Apollon Maikov, December/January 1867', *Dostoyevsky: A Self Portrait*, p. 168.
10. Dostoyevsky, F., 'Letter to Apollon Maikov, August 1867', *The Letters of Fyodor Michailovitch Dostoyevsky to His Family and Friends*, p.121.
11. Ibid., p. 123.
12. Dostoyevsky, F., *The Idiot*, p. 447.
13. Dostoyevsky, F., 'Letter to Apollon Maikov, May1868', *The Letters of Fyodor Michailovitch Dostoyevsky to His Family and Friends*, p. 177.

17 – A Superfluous Man

1. Dostoyevsky, F., 'Letter to Sofia Ivanovna, January 1868', *Dostoyevsky: A Self Portrait*, p. 169.

2. Dostoyevsky, F., *The Idiot*, p. 28.
3. Dostoyevsky, F., *The Idiot*, iBooks, p. 145.
4. The New Testament, Mark 10:15, Revised Standard Version.
5. Dostoyevsky, F., *The Idiot*, iBooks, p. 179.
6. Frank, J., *Dostoevsky: A Writer In HIs Time*, Kindle loc 13662.
7. Dostoyevsky, F., *The Idiot*, iBooks, p. 1360.
8. The New Testament, Mark 12:13, Revised Standard Version.

18 – Faith and Fascism

1. Dostoyevsky, F., 'Letter to Sofia Ivanovna, March 1869', *The Letters of Fyodor Michailovitch Dostoyevsky to His Family and Friends,* p. 170.
2. Dostoyevsky, F., 'Letter to N. N. Strakhov, February/March 1869', *The Letters of Fyodor Michailovitch Dostoyevsky to His Family and Friends,* p. 167.
3. Dostoyevsky, F., 'Letter to P. A. Isayev, February/March 1868', *The Letters of Fyodor Michailovitch Dostoyevsky to His Family and Friends,* p. 145.
4. Dostoyevsky, F., 'Piccola Bestia', *Diary of a Writer,* p. 428.
5. Dostoyevsky, F., 'Letter to Apollon Maikov, March/April 1870', *The Letters of Fyodor Michailovitch Dostoyevsky to His Family and Friends,* p. 190.
6. Dostoyevsky, F., 'Letter to Sofia Ivanovna, January/February, 1869', *The Letters of Fyodor Michailovitch Dostoyevsky to His Family and Friends,* p. 161.
7. Dostoyevsky, F., 'Letter to N. N. Strakhov, May 1871', *The Letters of Fyodor Michailovitch Dostoyevsky to His Family and Friends,* p. 219.
8. Dostoyevsky, L. F., *The Emigrant.*

19 – Possessed

1. The New Testament, Mark 5:2–23, Revised Standard Version.
2. Dostoyevsky, F., *The Devils*, iBooks, p. 99.
3. Levi-Strauss, C., *Structural Anthropology* (New York, Basic Books, 1963).
4. Carol Oates, J., 'Celestial Timepiece', *Tragic Rites in Dostoyevsky's The Devils,* http://celestialtimepiece.com.
5. Dostoyevsky, F., *The Devils*, iBooks. p. 93.
6. Ibid., p. 696.
7. Ibid., p. 613.
8. Morley, Bob, *The Theme of Demons* http://www.fyodordostoevsky.com/essays/pdf/Demons-BobMorley.pdf.
9. French philosopher and novelist of the mid-twentieth century – *The Plague* and *The Stranger*.
10. Camus, A., TV Interview 1959
    http://www.openculture.com/2012/10/albert_camus_talks_about_adapting_dostoyevsky_for_the_theatre_1959.html.

11. Camus, A., *The Myth Of Sisyphus And Other Essays*, p. 66.
12. Brody, Ervin, C. 'Dostoevsky's Kirilov in Camus' En Mythe De Sisyphe', *The Modern Language Review* 70,2 (1975), p. 291–305.
13. Camus, A., *The Myth Of Sisyphus And Other Essays*, p. 67.
14. Dostoyevsky, F., 'Letter to M. N. Katkov, October 1870', *Dostoyevsky: A Self Portrait*, p. 192–93.
15. Dostoyevsky, F., *The Devils*, p. 187.
16. Ibid., p. 647–48.
17. The New Testament, Revelation 3:14–15, Revised Standard Version.
18. Dostoyevsky, F., *The Devils*, p. 615.
19. Ibid., p. 255.
20. Ibid., p. 259.

20 – Debts and Credits

1. Dostoyevsky, A., *Dostoevsky: Portrayed by His Wife – The Diary and Reminiscences of Mme. Dostoevsky*, p. 140.
2. Ibid., p. 139.
3. Dostoyevsky, F., 'Letter to Anna Dostoyevsky, July 1873', *Dostoyevsky: A Self Portrait*, p. 204.
4. Dostoyevsky, F., 'Letter to A. G. Snitkina, June/July 1874', *Dostoyevsky: A Self Portrait*, p. 206.

21 – The Dream

1. Dostoyevsky, F., 'Russian Satire'; 'Virgin Soil'; 'Last Songs'; 'Old Reminiscences', *Diary of a Writer*, p. 587.
2. Dostoyevsky, F., 'Concerning One Most Important Matter', *Diary of a Writer*, p. 984.
3. Dostoyevsky, F., 'The Milieu', *Diary of a Writer*, p. 19.
4. Dostoyevsky, F., *House of the Dead*, p. 10.
5. Ibid., p. 258.
6. Dostoyevsky, F., 'The Dream of Ridiculous Man,' http://www.colorado.edu/studentgroups/shortfiction/RidiculousMan.pdf.
7. Ibid.
8. Dostoyevsky, F., *Notes from the Undergound, White Nights, The Dream of a Ridiculous Man and Selections from The House of the Dead*, p. 220.
9. Ibid., p. 225–26.
10. Dostoyevsky, F., 'Again But One Word About Spiritism', *Diary of a Writer*, p. 306.

22 – Expansion

1. Dostoyevsky, F., 'The Utopian Conception of History', *Diary of a Writer*, p. 365.

2. Dostoyevsky, F., 'It is Necessary to Seize the Moment', *Diary of a Writer*, p. 911.
3. Dostoyevsky, F., 'Dead Force and Future Forces', *Diary of a Writer*, p. 256.
4. Dostoyevsky, F., 'Where Does the Business Stand?', *Diary of a Writer*, p. 555.
5. Dostoyevsky, F., 'Mollusks Taken for Human Beings', *Diary of a Writer*, p. 842.
6. Dostoyevsky, F., 'The Metternichs and the Don Quixotes', *Diary of a Writer*, p. 609.

23 – The Dark Opinions
1. Dostoyevsky, F., 'Letter to Yekaterina Yunge, April 1880', *Dostoyevsky's Occasional Writings*, p. 308.
2. Kogan, S., *Dostoevsky of Feminism* http://www.thinkinghousewife.com/wp/2013/08/dostoevsky-on-feminism/.
3 Ibid.
4. Dostoyevsky, F., 'The Jewish Question', *Diary of a Writer*, p. 638.
5. Dostoyevsky, F., 'Status in Statu. Forty Centuries of Existence', *Diary of a Writer*, p. 648.

24 – The Brothers
1. Bakhtin, M., 'Vol. 8', *Problems of Dostoevsky's Poetics*, p. 252.
2. Freud, S., *Psychoanalytical Study of the Author M. Dostoevsky: Stavrogin's Confession,* tr. Virginia Woolf and S. S. Koteliansky, p. 87.
3. Dostoyevsky, F., *The Brothers Karamazov*, iBooks, p. 1478.
4. Ibid., p. 1821.
5. Ibid., p. 1895.
6. Bakhtin, M., 'Vol 8', *Problems of Dostoevsky's Poetics*, p. 8.
7. Dostoyevsky, F., *The Brothers Karamazov*, iBooks, p. 1908.
8. Dostoyevsky, F., *The Brothers Karamazov*, p. 375.
9. Ibid., p. 376.
10. Ibid., p. 286.
11. Seventeenth century French philosopher who posited that belief in God served an individual's best interest, viz. if God does exist then there is a welcome in heaven, if not then what's the difference?
12. Dostoyevsky, F., *The Brothers Karamazov*, iBooks, p. 687.
13. Dostoyevsky, F., 'Letter to N. A. Lyabimov, May 1879', *Dostoyevsky: A Self Portrait*, p. 220.
14. Dostoyevsky, F., *The Brothers Karamazov*, p. 912.
15. Dostoyevsky, F., *The Brothers Karamazov*, iBooks. p. 704.
16. Dostoyevsky, F., *The Brothers Karamazov*, p. 297.
17. Dostoyevsky, F., *The Brothers Karamazov*, iBooks. p. 714.

18. *Today's Cherished Episode,* 6 December 2006, http://cleigh6.tripod.com/CTP/CTP-talithacumi.html.
19. *X-Files,* Season 3, Episode 24: Talitha Cumi, Original Air Date: 17 May 1996; Written by: Chris Carter; Story by: Chris Carter and David Duchovny; Directed by: R. W. Goodwin.
20. 'The X-Files Talitha Cumi, Review', *posted by Darren,* 9 December 2014 http://themovieblog.com/2014/12/09/the-*X-Files*-talitha-cumi-review/.
21. Dostoyevsky, F., *The Brothers Karamazov,* iBooks, p. 699.
22. Ibid.
23. *X-Files* Season 3, Episode 24: Talitha Cumi Original Air Date: 17 May 1996; Written by: Chris Carter; Story by: Chris Carter and David Duchovny; Directed by: R. W. Goodwin.
24. Dostoyevsky, F., *The Brothers Karamazov,* iBooks, p. 7.
25. Ibid.

25 – A Writer for Our Time
1. Dostoyevsky, F., 'Letter to Dr. A. F. Blagonravov, December 1880', *The Letters of Fyodor Michailovitch Dostoyevsky to his Family and Friends,* p. 258.
2. Dostoyevsky, F., 'Concerning One Most Important Matter', *Diary of a Writer,* p. 984.
3. Dostoyevsky, F., 'Letter to his wife, June 1880', *Dostoyevsky: Letters and Reminiscences,* p. 232–233.
4. The New Testament, Matthew 3:15, Revised Standard Version.
5. Dostoyevsky, A., *Dostoevsky: Portrayed by his Wife – The Diary and Reminiscences of Mme. Dostoevsky,* p. 187.
6. Dostoyevsky, F., *The Devils,* p. 259.

BIBLIOGRAPHY

Works by F. M. Dostoyevsky

Poor Folk and The Gambler, tr. Hogarth, C. J. (London: Everyman Classics, J. M. Dent & Sons Ltd, 1987)

Notes from the Undergound, The Double, tr. Coulson, J. (London: Penguin Classics, Penguin Books Ltd, 1988)

Notes from the Undergound, White Nights, The Dream of a Ridiculous Man and Selections from The House of the Dead, tr. MacAndrew, A. R. (London: Signet Classics, New English Library Limited, 1961)

The House of the Dead, tr. Sutherland Edwards, H. (London: Everyman Library, J. M. Dent & Sons Ltd, 1979)

The Eternal Husband, tr. Garnett, C. (London: William Heinemann, 1983)

The Village of Stepanchikovo, tr. Avsey, I. (London: Classics, London 1983)

The Insulted and Injured, tr. Garnett, C. (London: William Heinemann, 1915)

Crime and Punishment, tr. Garnett, C. (London: Pan Classics (in association with William Heinemann), 1979)

The Idiot, tr. Magarshack, D. (London: Penguin Classics 1955) Quoted by permission of Penguin Books Ltd *The Devils (The Possessed)*, tr. Magarshack, D. (London: Penguin Classics, 1971)

Quoted by permission of Penguin Books Ltd *A Raw Youth,* tr. Garnett, C. (London: William Heinemann Ltd, 1950)

The Brothers Karamazov (2 volumes), tr. Magarshack, D. (London: Penguin Classics 1958)

Quoted by permission of Penguin Books Ltd *The Crocodile,* tr. Cioran, S. C., (Ann Arbor, Michigan: Ardis, 1988)

The Best Short Stories of Fyodor Dostoevsky, tr. Magashack, D. (New York: Modern Library, 1992)

eBooks

The Idiot, tr. Martin, E., Project Gutenberg, 2015

The House of the Dead, ed. Rhys, E., Project Gutenberg, 2011

The Possessed (The Devils) tr. Garnett, C., Project Gutenberg, 2010

Crime and Punishment, tr. Garnett, C., Project Gutenberg, 2012

The Brothers Karamazov, tr. Garnett, C., Project Gutenberg, 2009

Pages from the journal of an author, Fyodor Dostoevsky, Project Gutenberg, 2016

Notes from the Underground, prod. Judith Boss, Project Gutenberg

The Double, tr. Garnett, C., Manybooks.net

The Dream of the Ridiculous Man, tr. Unknown, http://www.colorado.edu/studentgroups/shortfiction/RidiculousMan.pdf

Full Text of the Letters of Fyodor Michailovitch Dostoyevsky to his Family and Friends, tr. Coburn Mayne, E., Archive.org

Dostoevsky: A Writer in His Time (Abridged), Frank, J., Princeton: A Princeton University Press E-Book, 2010

Letters and Journals of F. M. Dostoyevsky

The Letters of Fyodor Michailovitch Dostoyevsky to his Family and Friends, tr. Mayne, E. C. (London: Peter Owen Publishers, 1962) Quoted by permission

Dostoevsky: Letters and Reminiscences, tr. Koteliansky S. S. and Middleton Murray, J. (London: Chatto & Windus, 1923)

Letters of Dostoevsky to His Wife, tr. Hill, E and Mudie, D. (London: Constable & Co. Ltd, 1930)

Dostoevsky: A Self Portrait, tr. Coulson, J. (Oxford: Oxford University Press, 1962) Quoted by permission of Oxford University Press *Dostoevsky's Occasional Writings*, tr. Magarshack, D. (New York: Random House Inc., 1963)

Summer Impressions, Fitzlyon, K., tr. Calder, J. (New York: Calder Publishing, 1955)

Notebooks for The Idiot, tr. Shelsky, K. (Chicago: The University of Chicago Press 1967)

Diary of a Writer (2 volumes), tr. Brasol, B. (New York: MacMillan Publishing Company, 1949) Quotations from the Diary are reprinted by permission of Charles Scribner's Sons, an imprint of MacMillan Publishing Company, New York. Copyright 1949 Charles Scribner's Sons.

Works by A. G. Dostoyevsky

Dostoevsky: Portrayed by His Wife: The Diary and Reminiscences of Mme. Dostoevsky, tr. Koteliansky, S. S. (London: George Routledge & Sons, Ltd, 1926)

Dostoevsky, Reminiscences, Dostoevsky, A., tr. Stillman, B. (London: Wildwood House, 1976)

Bibliography

Biographies

Dostoevsky, Grossman, L., tr. Mary (London: Mackler. Penguin Books Ltd, 1974)
Fyodor Dostoyevsky: A Writer's Life, Kjetsaa, G., tr. Hustvedt, S. and McDuff, D. (London: Macmillan, 1988)
Dostoevsky: Volume 1, The Seeds of Revolt, 1821–1849, Frank, J. (Princeton, New Jersey, Princeton University Press, 1976)
Dostoevsky: Volume 2, The Years of Ordeal, 1850–1859, Frank, J. (Princeton, New Jersey, Princeton University Press, 1983)
Dostoevsky: Volume 3, The Stir of Liberation, 1860–1865, Frank, J. (Princeton, New Jersey, Princeton University Press, 1986)
Dostoyevsky: His Life and Work, Ronald, H., tr. Elek, P. (London. 1978)
Dostoevsky, Magarshack, D. (London: Secker & Warburg, 1962)
Dostoevsky: His Life and Work, Mochulsky, K., tr. Minihan, M. A. (Princeton: Princeton University Press, 1971)

Others

The Religion of Dostoyevsky, Boyce Gibson, A. (London: SCM Press Ltd, 1973)
Dostoevsky and Christ: A Study of Dostoyevsky's Rebellion Against Belinsky, Dolenc, I. (York: York Publishing & Printing Co., 1978)
Dostoevsky, Jones, J. (Oxford: Oxford University Press, 1985)
Dostoevsky: Stavrogin's Confession, tr. Woolf, V., and Koteliansky, S. S., with a *Psychoanalytical Study of the Author by Sigmund Freud* (New York: Lear Publishers, 1947)
Dostoevsky: Myths of Duality, Anderson, R. (Florida: University of Florida Press, 1986)
Character Names in Dostoevsky's Fiction, Passage, C. E. (Ann Arbor, Michigan: Ardis, 1982)
Dostoevsky as Reformer: The Petrashevsky Case, ed. and tr. Knapp, L. (Ann Arbor, Michigan: Ardis, 1987)
The Orthodox Church, Meyendorff, J. (New York: St. Vladimir's Seminar Press, 1981)
Russia Under the Old Regime, Pipes, R. (London: Penguin Books, 1987)
The Russian Empire 1801–1917, Seton-Watson, H. (Oxford: Oxford University Press, 1988)
A History of the Russian Secret Service, Deacon, R. (London: Grafton Books, Collins, London, 1987)
Dostoevsky and Roamantic Realism: A Study of Dostoevsky in Relation to Balzac, Dickens and Gogol, Fanger, D. (Evanston, Illinois: Northewestern University Press, 1998)
Nikolai Gogol: Selected Passages from Correspondence with Friends, tr. Veldin, J. (Nashville: Vanderbilt University Press, 1969)

Problems of Dostoevsky's Poetics, Bakhtin, M., tr. Emerson, C. (Minnesota, University of Minnesota Press, 1993)

An Outline of Russian Literature, Baring, M. (USA: Sheba Blake Publishing, 2015)

Blood on the Stage, 1950–1975: Milestone Plays of Crime, Mystery, and Detection, Kabatchnik, A. (Plymouth: The Scarecrow Press, 2012)

Webography

The anguish of God's lonely men: Dostoyevsky's Underground Man and Scorsese's Travis Bickle, Swenson, A. J. (New York: Thunder Mouth Press, 1991) http://chabrieres.pagesperso-orange.fr/texts/anguish.html

Traditional Symbolism in Crime and Punishment, Gibian, G., *PMLA*, Vol. 70, No. 5 (Dec., 1955), pp. 979–996. Modern Language Association: http://www.jstor.org/stable/459881

Selected Philosophical Works, Belinsky, V. G. (Moscow: Foreign Languages Publishing House, 1948) tr. Fluss, H. www.marxists.org (Accessed February 2008)

Ayoade, R., BFI Screening transcribed by Zarina http://dutchgirlinlondon.com/2014/04/06/richard-ayoade-the-double/

http://player.bfi.org.uk/film/watch-the-double-qa-2013/

www.openculture.com

www.projectgutenburg.org

* * *

INDEX

Index